9/07

BUST

wm

An Imprint of HarperCollins*Publishers*

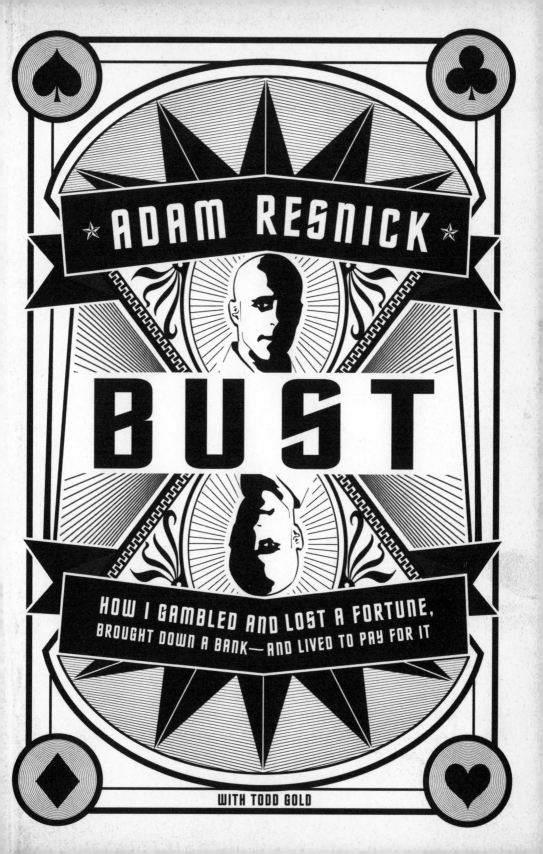

ADAM RESNICK

BUST

HOW I GAMBLED AND LOST A FORTUNE,
BROUGHT DOWN A BANK—AND LIVED TO PAY FOR IT

WITH TODD GOLD

HarperCollins books may be purchased for educational, business, or sales promotional use. For information please write: Special Markets Department, HarperCollins Publishers, 10 East 53rd Street, New York, NY 10022.

FIRST EDITION

Designed by Kris Tobiassen

Library of Congress Cataloging-in-Publication Data has been applied for.

ISBN 10: 0-06-134136-3
ISBN 13: 978-0-06-134136-6

07 08 09 10 11 WBC/RRD 10 9 8 7 6 5 4 3 2 1

Everything in Bust is pathetically true.
Only a few names and very minor details have been changed
to shield the identities of certain private individuals—
and to give aid and comfort to certain attorneys.
You wouldn't be reading this book
if I hadn't made believers out of my publishers.
Income I receive from this book will be subject
to the restitution order mandated by the court.

TO MY WIFE, MEREDITH, AND CHILDREN, ARIEL AND SAM

TO MY OTHER CHILD, HARLEY (WHO'S REALLY A DOG
BUT WE HAVEN'T TOLD HIM YET)

AND TO EVERY ADDICT AND PERSON WHO KNOWS AN ADDICT.
IT'S A CHOICE. CHOOSE TO BREAK THE PATTERN.

CONTENTS

1. IS THERE A PROBLEM? 1

2. ACCOUNTABILITY AND CHOICE 10

3. CHASING LEAVES 13

4. A CHIP OFF THE OLD BLOCK 18

5. THEY THOUGHT I WAS EIGHTEEN 26

6. BIG LOSSES 34

7. SO WASSA MATTER, SWEETHEART? 40

8. FINANCIAL AID 53

9. BOOKS, BOOKIES, AND BLACKJACK 62

10. THIS ISN'T NORMAL 75

11. A GOOD GUY 85

12. THE HEART OF THE MATTER 86

13. THE BIRTH OF MR. R 93

14. WHAT'S GOING ON UP THERE? 101

15. BANKRUPTCY: JUST WHAT
    THE DOCTOR ORDERED 115

16. THE BOAT 123

17. I DON'T PLAN ON GOING DOWN 129

18. THE HONEYMOON'S OVER 139

19. BOYS ONLY AT THE BELLAGIO 151

20. UNUSUAL ACTIVITY 162

21. NOT FOR NOTHING 173

22. SO MANY ISSUES 184

23. NO LIMITS FOR MR. R 193

24. THE WHALE 204

25. CASH COUNTING MACHINE 216

26. BUST 226

27. I'M A DEGENERATE,
    PATHOLOGICAL GAMBLER 234

28. BREAKING THE PATTERN 245

29. TRUTH AND CONSEQUENCES 255

LETTERS 263

ACKNOWLEDGMENTS 277

IS THERE A PROBLEM?

You always drown alone, and there I was.

Binion's Horseshoe Casino. A three-story riverboat transformed into a gambling mecca on the Indiana–Illinois border. The highway leading there from downtown Chicago, after the two-dollar tollbooth, was wide open and fast this morning, allowing me to step on the gas. Driving against the traffic, I flew by the morning commuters heading to their jobs in the city. Aerosmith and Run DMC's version of "Walk This Way" came on and I cranked the radio.

I could feel the buzz start to build. A few phone calls to friends and my bookie and suddenly I was exiting I-90 at Indianapolis Boulevard. Seven minutes later I pulled my Mercedes in front of the casino and tossed the key to the valet, the first person of the day to greet me as Mr. R, as in "How ya doin', Mr. R?"

How was I doing?

It was 10 AM, and I'd kissed my two small children good-bye, told my wife that I was headed to work, and then sped to the Horseshoe. I had a $1 million check wadded up in my pocket and I didn't know it. For the past seven months I'd written checks, illegally, off an internal account at Universal Federal Savings and Loan, during which time I'd cycled more than $200 million in and out of the local bank to fuel my gambling. I was on the binge of all binges. I had no idea that in a week I'd be walking into the same casino, at nearly the same time, needing to win at least $3 million to keep the bank from collapsing and my world from falling apart.

I was thirty years old, arguably the biggest gambling addict on the planet, and I was headed for a crash of epic proportions.

How was I doing?

I was phe-fucking-nominal.

I walked through the casino and nodded at a half dozen employees who greeted me. I went straight to the back room, the one reserved for the high rollers, where a dealer stood behind a green-felt blackjack table. She was in her early thirties, looked in her mid-forties, and wore her dirty brown hair in a feathered style she'd probably had since the mid-eighties. I'd played with her umpteen times before, and she was solid. She understood when to talk and—more important—when not to utter a word, not to make a sound, not to scratch her face if it meant interrupting the rhythm.

I didn't have the patience to play with other people at the table, so I sat by myself. I wanted the hands hypersonic, and I didn't want to wait between cards.

The casino knew that and everything else about me. They knew I played fast, bet the highest available limits, and pushed to get them higher. They knew I indulged a germ phobia by cleaning my hands with antibacterial wipes and patting my bald head compulsively with Stridex pads. They knew I pushed down on the top chip of each stack in front of me. They also knew I had no self-control as a gambler.

I started out slow, making small talk with the dealer until I got warmed up and started to feel the cards. It was like finding my way through a maze in the dark; eventually I found the pathway, then sped up confidently. Whether that confidence was deserved, that was another issue. But I stopped talking at that point and entered a zone—or *the zone*, as I called it—where the thoughts in my head washed away and nothing existed other than the dealer, the cards, and my wagers. The dealer picked up on it too; a good dealer feels the same thing as the player.

I didn't win every hand, but I won more than I lost, and the winnings piled up in front of me until I was up a couple hundred thousand dollars.

Then the game shifted subtly or, more accurately, the gamesmanship began. The casino's top chef came to the table and asked if I felt like something special. He interrupted the deal and broke my concentration. I glanced at the pit boss. He knew I wasn't there to eat lobster, prime rib, caviar, or anything else.

The pit boss looked away.

"No, thanks," I said.

I shook my head at the dealer.

"You hungry?" I asked.

"No," she said.

"Me neither. It's laughable."

We resumed the game. I sat forward. I wore a dull blue long-sleeved T-shirt and jeans. My leather shoulder bag was slung over the back of my chair. I breathed deeply several times, like a yogi reentering a meditative state. Despite the chef's intent to throw me off, the vibe continued, within an hour I was up five hundred thousand dollars.

I leaned back and stretched my arms above my head. I felt the leather strap of my shoulder bag slip off the back of my chair. When I turned to rehook it, I saw that security had let a handful of people gather about six feet behind me. I didn't like that. Worse, out of the corner of my eye, I saw a new dealer moving toward the table.

I was aghast. I motioned for the pit boss. He hurried to the table.

"Yes, Mr. R?"

"If you bring him in"—I glanced toward the new dealer—"I'm never coming back here."

"Is there a problem?" the pit boss asked.

"You know what's going on," I said. "There's going to be a problem if you bring him in."

I glanced at the new dealer to make sure he knew I meant nothing personal against him. I saw he was on my side. Likely a gambler himself, he had a look that appeared to say, *Sorry, Mr. R. I know this is bullshit. They're sending me in to fuck up your game.*

"I understand," the pit boss said. He nodded to the dealer, who appeared relieved to be let go. "Is there anything I can get you?"

"Nope," I said.

I wanted to get back to business. The dealer looked down at the floor. She was thinking about something. She was bothered. Then she looked up.

"Just go, Adam," she said under her breath. "Great win. Go have some fun for once."

"This *is my pleasure*," I said in a tone that left no doubt as to the lack of bliss and joy. "You know that."

"You just made five hundred thousand dollars. All the dealers on this floor combined don't make that much in a year."

"It's not about the money," I said.

Both of us knew that. If it were about money, I would've deposited millions in a Swiss bank when I first got access to Universal's money and lived an anonymous life of lazy decadence on the Mediterranean. I'd made a relative fortune legitimately by the time I was twenty-three and could've added to it significantly if I'd been motivated by money. A friend once said I could sell oil to OPEC. But I gambled whether I won or lost, whether I had money or had to borrow it. The only time it was about the money was when I needed to come up with some.

I went to the bathroom and washed my hands. I heard quiet chatter about me as I made the trip, though whenever I looked to see who was talking the people stopped. After sitting back down at the table, the dealer started up without a word as if we'd never stopped. I liked the synchronicity.

I was playing two hands simultaneously, betting thirty thousand dollars per hand, and the dealer, she had an ace. She asked if I wanted insurance even though she knew my response. We'd already danced this routine several times before. That was why she was trying not to smile.

"Screw you," I said facetiously. "Go outside and look at the Prudential Tower. They don't build those because insurance companies lose money."

"Gotcha."

"Just flip it and drip it."

She laughed.

"You like that?"

"It's the way you say it."

I knew she thought I was flirting with her. I'd seen it before, with women and even gay male dealers who'd misinterpreted my personal manner as intimate. They didn't understand my relationship to the cards. Yes, I was flirting, but my flirtation was directed at the kings, queens, and jacks in the deck, not at the dealers.

"Just flip it and drip it, baby."

The first of my hands was a six and a four. I doubled down on the ten against her soft six. She gave me a five. I had sixty thousand dollars on that hand. I had two aces on the second hand. I split them. That gave me two hands at thirty thousand dollars. I got another ace and split them. Next I pulled a three, a four, and a six. I had fourteen, fifteen, and seventeen. I had four hands on the table, bets of one hundred fifty thousand dollars, and a total of bullshit across the board.

I heard a muffled comment from one of the onlookers behind me. I turned and made a face.

"I hate the eyes," I complained.

"Sorry, Mr. R," she said.

"They don't let 'em watch when I lose."

I felt my heart pounding. I was breathing hard and biting on my lower lip. I had to remind myself not to bite through it. Once before I'd drawn blood and not known it until someone delicately pointed out that it was dripping down my chin.

"Come on already," I said.

The dealer had nothing but opportunity to make her hand. If she pulled an ace, I pushed on one and lost three. If she pulled a two . . . the possibilities zipped through my head like data in a supercomputer. I looked at her, then at the shoe, which is comprised of six decks. Sometimes, when I was in the zone, I felt as if I had a telepathic power to control the cards. I concentrated, focusing my eyes on the shoe. I never consciously counted cards, but after playing for countless hours over so many years I had an innate sense.

The dealer pulled a nine. Then an ace. She had to draw one more—a six. That added up to twenty-two. She busted.

It was a three hundred thousand dollar swing. That put me up

$1.2 million, an astounding mark even for me. A few people cheered. I didn't want to acknowledge them, but I couldn't help it. I turned in time to see a woman gasp, "Jesus Christ." JC? I muttered to myself, what the hell did JC have to do with this?

Then, unfortunately, I made eye contact with a tall, slender man. His eyes were unusually dark and intense. The second we locked eyes, I knew I'd made a mistake. He lurched forward and reached for me before security stopped him.

I shook my head. That guy had destroyed whatever vibe had fueled my run of good fortune. I felt it as clearly as I did the top of my head.

"Now I'm mushed," I told the dealer. "It's over."

"What is?"

"Didn't you feel it? I know you did."

"You just won," she said.

"Watch what's going to happen with these cards."

Sure enough, I lost the next six hands.

I laughed. I wasn't going to leave blood on the table. Not today. I pushed fifty thousand dollars in chips at the dealer and got up.

"It's yours," I said. "Thanks."

On my way out, I took the pit boss aside and got his address. A few days later, I sent his crew Cartier watches from Trabert Hoeffer, one of Chicago's finest jewelry stores, as a thank-you for my big win. But I had trouble leaving the casino. Casino execs had quietly positioned themselves at various turns and corners on the different floors, making it impossible for me to walk more than ten steps without one of them stepping forward to shake my hand and ask if I'd enjoyed myself. They knew my germ phobia; were they so devious that they wanted to shake hands because they knew I'd go to the bathroom and wash my hands, thus tricking me into walking back through the casino?

I'd never know. The truth was, they didn't want me to leave with a million dollars of their money. They knew I was an addict. They knew that if they got me back to the tables they had a damn good chance of getting their money back.

"Mr. R, you're on a run," one executive, standing by the door, said. "Are you sure you're ready to go?"

"Yeah, I'm out of here," I said.

I don't know why I left. It was harder to leave than to stay. Forty minutes later, I parked my car and walked inside our beautiful two-story home. I heard Ariel and Sam playing in the family room off the kitchen. I paused in the foyer and casually lowered to the floor my leather shoulder bag containing $2.2 million in cash and the $1 million check I'd found in my pocket. Meredith was on the phone. I breathed in the clean air of family life, fresh after the smoke and noise of the casino.

"Adam? Is that you?" Meredith called.

Mr. R no longer existed.

"Yes, honey, it's me. Did you expect someone else?"

Maybe subconsciously she wished I was.

"What's up?"

"Nothing."

We ate dinner at 5:00, and, as much as I loved my family, sitting through it was torture. I found it was impossible to transition from hours of high-stakes gambling to normal dinner conversation with an unsuspecting wife and two active children ages three and one. I checked my watch every two minutes. I'd trained my family to eat in ten.

At 5:30, I bolted from the table, putting my dishes in the sink and grabbing the dog's leash. Harley, our eight-year-old bichon frise, waited for me by the kitchen door. It was such a ritual when I was home early for dinner that Meredith didn't even ask where I was going. I also purposely forgot my cell phone on the table. Once outside, I pulled a secret cell from my pocket. There were three numbers programmed into my cell phone, the three B's— Bookie, the Bellagio, Binion's.

I pressed Bookie.

"It's 5:33," Luciano said. "What took you so long?"

Lucky, as I called him, was being facetious. He didn't start taking action on the night games until 5:30.

I wanted to say "fuck off," but I didn't have time to respond. I was under the gun, with tension on the rise, feeling pressured to get my bets in before something unpredictable happened that exposed my double life. Suddenly I saw our front door open and heard my daughter telling Meredith that they wanted to walk with Daddy.

"What was that?" Lucky said.

I rattled off so many of that night's baseball games that my book warned that I'd gone the other way in parlays and couldn't possibly win some of my bets.

"I don't care," I said. "Just take 'em. I won't be able to get out of the house again until you close at 6:30."

"Whatever you say, boss," he said. "I want you to know I've started tap-ing these calls so there's no dispute when you come down from whatever crazy shit you're taking."

"Dude, I don't do drugs. I'm trying not to get caught by my wife."

I hung up, savoring the high of being back in action. Again, it didn't matter if I won or lost, just that I was engaged in the competition and had put myself at risk. I returned home and helped Meredith clean up and put the kids down. I read Ariel *Goodnight Moon,* as I did almost every night. She knew the words; I still can't remember what it was about because I wasn't present even though I was there. Afterward, I got into bed with Meredith. We talked and watched TV until 8:45 when she said good night and drifted into an easy sleep. She rarely stayed up past 9:00. By contrast, I never slept. I was a full-on insomniac.

To make sure she was sleeping soundly, I stuck my hand in her pants. When she didn't stir, it meant she was asleep or wanted nothing to do with me sexually, and probably both. Either way, I knew it was safe to get out of bed. I crept down the hall into the guest room. I sat down in front of the computer and logged onto an online gambling site. I checked the baseball scores and calculated that I'd lost five hundred eighty thousand dollars on the games that I'd bet on while walking the dog. Most of the crazy bets I made were to make up for equally crazy losses. From what I recall, I scrolled through the gambling website and scattered a couple hundred thousand dollars on horse races and soccer games, even though I didn't know a thing about the horses and couldn't name a European soccer player other than David Beckham.

I then clicked to a blackjack site, logged onto my account, and played until sunup. I didn't even really like online blackjack, for a variety of reasons. I had a slow Internet connection. The game lacked human interaction. I couldn't *feel* it. My gut was irrelevant. I couldn't get into the zone. It wasn't fast enough. If you wanted to deposit money, it took a long time to go through the process. And if you won, it took even longer—weeks—to collect. At one point, I actually told myself, "You have to be an absolute sick fuck to play online blackjack."

But that was the point.

I was very, very sick and had been my entire life. The proof was indisputable. This had been a day like so many others, a steady progression of constantly escalating events spanning my entire life. I had little idea of the Universal drama behind the scenes, but time had finally run out. A lifetime of lies and deception was about to catch up with me.

ACCOUNTABILITY AND CHOICE

Who says dead men don't tell tales?

After all the times I had told my story, to my wife, to my family, to FBI agents, and so on, I was telling it again. This time I was at my computer, pecking out the disturbing details of my gambling addiction and how it led me down a self-destructive path to ruin. This version was for a PSR—a presentencing report. With a few months before I went to prison, it would go to the probation department and then to the judge, who would digest the information and take it into account when determining the length of my prison sentence, up to thirty years.

> I fully accept responsibility for what occurred and entered a plea of guilty in this case in order to demonstrate that I acknowledge the wrongfulness of my actions. Furthermore, I do not feel that my acceptance of responsibility or my rehabilitation ends with these words or my punishment decided by Judge Andersen. I feel without continuing through therapy, speaking, restitution, and helping others (which I am in a public forum as well as intimate private circles) then I am setting myself up like other addicts to relapse. I choose now to make my life in part a cautionary tale so others can "break the pattern" before they end up in the extremely regrettable position I'm in.

> Very truly,
> Adam B. Resnick

After I finished those six pages of the PSR, tears spilled out of my eyes. The details were tragic: in the four years since the bank had collapsed, we'd lost our home, we were broke, and our marriage had challenges. But I was crying for what I hadn't said. A few days before I wrote the PSR, Meredith had taken Sam, the younger of our two children, to the doctor after he'd complained at school for several days about a stomachache. She'd called me after the checkup with the results. According to the doctor, Sammy was fine physically, but it turned out he was constipated.

"He told the doctor he didn't go to the bathroom because he didn't want to miss any of the fun in class or on the playground," Meredith told me.

"Oh my God," I replied.

The significance of that statement burned through to the center of my soul.

"Yeah. He's exactly like you."

That was all the confirmation I needed to believe something good might come from my plight. My gambling addiction stemmed from patterns of behavior established long before I was ever conceived, and then I continued them. No one broke the pattern until I got in trouble and had to deal with it myself. If nothing else, my son wouldn't find himself in the same regrettable position. Nor would my daughter. It would be different for them, and it could, I realized, be different for many others battling impulse control–related syndromes, not just gambling addicts, if I sucked up the courage to go beyond the accounts that had already appeared in papers and on TV and took my story public.

Everyone I knew told me I should write a book. They thought my story, from childhood to the bank's collapse, was a thrilling ride. But they mostly saw the glitz and gaming. To me, it wasn't about sexy Las Vegas stories or how I got a bank to give me access to hundreds of millions of dollars. It was a cautionary tale about family dynamics, insecurities, deception, and love. It was about the way people treat each other, excuse their mistakes, and often enable them. Most importantly, it was about accountability and choice.

The key to writing a book, I realized, was getting at the why—why this happened—and how I could have prevented it. I asked myself those questions every day, from early in the morning until late at night, as I waited for the judge to decide when and for how long I'd go to jail. The answers were what my children would want to know, and *need* to know. It's what anyone struggling with an addiction or dealing with a loved one with an addiction needs to know. Why did it happen? How could it have been prevented? That was the real story.

As I told the judge in my PSR, it began a long time ago . . .

I am a pathological gambling addict who began to engage in compulsive, addictive-related conduct when I was a small child. Actually, my first memory of life is a gambling activity . . .

3

CHASING LEAVES

"Who wants to bet I can catch more leaves than anybody else?"

There were five of us, and as we waited in front of David "Tippy Toes" Teplin's house for the school bus to come, I grabbed at leaves as they fluttered from the tree branches in the crisp morning air. We competed to catch the most leaves as they fell, a game I'd invented called Catch the Leaves. The game stopped when we heard the school bus approach. Whoever had the most leaves won.

"Look at how many I got!" I said, holding up my hands, which held gobs of red, yellow, orange, and brown leaves. "I have fourteen!"

None of the others were as excited as I was, but then I wasn't like the other six-year-olds in the Mequon, Wisconsin, neighborhood, where I grew up the second of three sons born to Alvin Resnick, an executive with Unicare Health Services, and Barbara, a homemaker. I was like a light switch—on or off; there was no middle ground. And mostly I was on, or trying to stay on. When it came to Catch the Leaves, I played with more enthusiasm and determination than anyone else.

But soon I felt the need to do more than just catch leaves. I needed there to be a point to the game. If that were true of me, it must be true of the others. Sensing that I needed to keep their interest piqued, I suggested playing for pieces of gum. Tippy's father was a dentist, so he always had packs of Trident bubble gum. Like poker chips, that would be our currency. The person with the most leaves would win the gum. I badgered my mother to buy me gum. I lost purposely many times to make sure the others won and stayed involved. If they wanted to play, I stayed in action.

I was the one who always needed more, more, more. I drove our wagers from individual pieces to packs to whole boxes of Trident.

I thought about playing Catch the Leaves as soon as I woke up. I was always the first to arrive at the bus stop at 7 AM and I kept going until the bus came at 7:30, and sometimes longer. One morning I got so absorbed in looking up at the sky and grabbing leaves that I lost track of everything else. I recall the others yelling, as they always did— "Adam, get on the bus" and "Come on, Adam, we're leaving"—but then their voices faded while I kept running around and chasing leaves in my own world until they stopped falling.

Then I woke up. When I looked around, Tippy and my friends were gone. I was by myself. The school bus had come and gone without my ever knowing it.

I walked home, and when my mom asked why I wasn't in school, I said everyone had disappeared.

"What do you mean?" she asked.

I honestly didn't have an explanation, and she let it go—the story of my life.

The next morning I found out what had happened when my mother received a call from Shirley Chan, a friend's mom. She wanted to make sure I was okay. She told my mother that I'd been so consumed by running around and catching the leaves that I hadn't heard the other kids yelling at me to get on the bus. Even the bus driver had stepped halfway down the stairs and called to me. I was probably fifty yards away, clearly within hearing distance, but I didn't respond.

After hanging up with Mrs. Chan, my mother asked if I'd heard them yelling my name. I shook my head no. I didn't know how to say it, but I'd gotten into a zone where nothing else mattered except chasing leaves. Finally the bus had pulled away. According to Mrs. Chan, the kids in the back of the bus kept screaming at me; staring out the window and sensing something was wrong, one girl started to cry.

In one way or another, I never stopped chasing the leaves.

My second grade teacher, Mrs. Nelson, gave out Snoopy dollars as an incentive for good work. If you got a good grade or tried hard, she handed out Snoopy dollars. You could also earn them by doing jobs, such as cleaning the sink after art or wiping up the floors on rainy days. I accumulated more Snoopy dollars than half the class in the aggregate. Once Mrs. Nelson literally had to drag me out of the classroom to get me to stop scrubbing the floors. She thought I was a superstar.

In third grade, we played a math game once a week called Around the World. A student would stand up next to someone and attempt to answer a question (addition, subtraction, multiplication, division) that the teacher, Mrs. Fisher, held up on a flash card. If you answered correctly, you advanced to the next desk. If you missed, they traded places with the person in the desk nearest them, and the winner continued on. The goal was to advance all the way around the room.

I was very good at the game—too good in fact. One day, after I'd gone weeks without an error, Mrs. Fisher took me aside after class.

"Adam, we have a problem," she said. "The teachers and I are really concerned about you."

I was mystified. I hadn't done anything wrong. I never got in trouble, not like some kids. I paid attention. I got good marks.

"What do you mean?"

"Adam, I don't know how long it's been, but you haven't lost once when we've played Around the World."

I shrugged.

"I know you're very good with numbers, but it's not fair to the other students. You're way too competitive."

I can't remember verbatim how I responded, but I can clearly see myself looking at her with a puzzled expression as I tried to find the right words—words that would unfortunately elude me for the next twenty-three years. She had me wrong, I tried to explain. I wasn't competitive. I tried so hard to win simply because I was afraid of losing and then having to wait another twenty-two rounds before my turn came again.

I needed the action. I didn't want to wait for anyone else to take their turn.

The spelling bee had the same magic combination of ingredients. I won on the word *supercalifragilisticexpialidocious*.

A year earlier—when I was almost seven—my mother gave birth to my younger brother, Joshua, who arrived on the Sunday of Super Bowl XIV, the afternoon the Steelers defeated the Rams. It was an exciting addition to the tri-level stone and cedar home whose backyard backed up to the green grass of a country club golf course. Both my parents had grown up poor in Pittsburgh. They met on a blind date when my dad was in medical school. My father's dad died at age forty-two of a broken heart during his second year there, and he transferred to law school, no longer interested being around sick people. His mother had died four years earlier at thirty-eight, and the combined loss cast a pall over my father. Though he was ambitious, he never thought he'd live past forty. He and my mother had moved to Milwaukee by the time I was born. He'd vowed not to be poor and was rising in the health care industry.

My mother was glad for a fresh start in Milwaukee. Stability was foremost on her mind after a childhood of constantly changing addresses while her father attempted to stay ahead of bill collectors. Her parents' divorce further angered her. I didn't know my grandmother was alive until I was fourteen years old. According to my father, my mother wrote her off when she refused to visit after I was born. My mom had argued that she owed it to her grandchildren to give them a grandmother. She replied that she told people she didn't have any grandchildren.

"Then I'll tell people I don't have a mother," my mom had said. As far as I know, they never spoke again.

Between 1976 and 1981, my father was among the state's highest paid executives. His success made it easy for them to ignore old family issues and rewrite their own history. They wanted their children to have easier, better lives, which may have made them too permissive and forgiving. Once, I broke a ceiling light in the school gym by kicking a ball on a bet with my gym teacher, Mrs. Brodie. My parents excused the three hundred seventy-five dollar bill the principal sent home.

"It's not a lot of money," my father said. "Don't worry about it."

Stricter parents might've made me do chores to earn money and pay the damages.

Both of my parents were fragile in their own ways. My dad was a hypochondriac, and my mom was prone to withdrawing from situations she didn't want to face. But they did express concern when I started complaining about stomachaches. I was eight years old, and up till then I wasn't known for complaining. But I had a problem that I didn't tell anyone about. When I played ball with the neighborhood kids, I didn't like to take a break for lunch or even the bathroom because it meant missing out on the action.

It began innocently. If I had to pee, I'd run behind a tree in the woods. But if I had to poop, I squatted and held it in until the urge passed. It worked once, then it worked again, and by the third time I was all about exercising the control. It was my private game. I was master of my universe. Little did I know that I was obstructing my bowels. Then one day I dropped to the kitchen floor in agony. An excruciating pain shot through my stomach. My mother rushed me to the hospital. The ER doctor literally pulled the doody out of me and declared that I had one of the worst cases of constipation he'd ever seen.

Instead of pulling the shit out of me, someone should've investigated why I kept it inside. The condition became chronic. I made more trips to the hospital. One doctor prescribed a chocolate-flavored drink to keep my stools loose. Another doctor told my mom to give me suppositories. I was traumatized after the first time my mother approached me with that little white capsule in her hand. It looked like a piece of chalk. I put up a fight when she told me to pull down my pants. I didn't want anyone shoving a pill an inch long up my ass. My mom and dad and brother literally had to tackle me in the kitchen.

Afterward, my father wiped his hands as if to say, well, that's done. My mother looked drained. My brother snickered behind the door.

At ten, after two years of such battles, I quit getting constipated. Our pediatrician told my parents that, as he'd predicted, I'd outgrown it.

He was wrong. The truth was, I discovered something else that allowed me to let go.

4

A CHIP OFF THE OLD BLOCK

"You got the cards, kiddo?"

Those were always my grandfather's first words to me when he visited. He drove in once a year from Pittsburgh with his girlfriend, Shirley. He and my mother got along, but it was clear they never talked about life in any depth or honesty. Theirs was a relationship of denial. They never discussed their issues. I don't know if she wanted a more honest relationship or if she was content to pretend it was something it wasn't, buying him clothes and presents whenever he came. Outside of our home, he was the only family she had.

Papa Ruben called me "a chip off the old block." I was more like a boulder. He taught me how to play cards—first gin rummy and then poker—and I took to it instantly. We turned the educational game HiQ into a gambling contest. I looked forward to his visits. My mother enjoyed how much I liked her father. I counted down the days and then the hours. I parked myself by the six-foot windows in the family room that overlooked the driveway and watched for his car. I wouldn't even go into the kitchen for lunch. I ate my ham, cheese, and mayo sandwich looking out the window.

"How much longer?" I asked my mother every few minutes.

When Papa Ruben finally came in, he gave everyone a kiss and then stared at me. There was a sparkle in his eye as he caught sight of my hand holding a brand-new deck. We had the connection my mother imagined.

"Papa, do you want to play right now?" I asked.

"You *bet*, kiddo."

We played through the night. Around midnight, he'd start to nod off. I'd wake him up.

"Papa, play the hand," I said, nudging his arm. "Don't go to sleep yet."

"I need to take my dentures out."

"Not yet. Let's play a couple more hands."

My grandfather's visit gave my parents a chance to entertain other couples, and after dinner they always played cards. They invited me to play, too. I was the only kid invited to sit at the table with the adults, and I was the only kid that *wanted* to be at their table. I added energy and excitement. I went in on every pot.

The Hansons lived next door. Their two kids, Michael and Beverly, introduced a bunch of us neighborhood kids to strip poker. I was the youngest by a few years. I was always the one that ended up naked. Translation: I always lost. Was there any subconscious desire on my part for humiliation? I've wondered. Still, I was never deterred from playing.

I responded to the rhythm and action of being at a card table. It did something to my internal chemistry that made me feel good. I played poker with Adam Fisher (Fish), Jason Devorkin (Devo), and other friends. My dad would give me a couple of twenties for the night, and my friends and I wagered stacks of nickels, dimes, and quarters at the kitchen table.

It was one thing to bet Trident gum—which came sanitized and wrapped—but even at a young age, I found money disgusting. Thousands of people might have touched any one coin or bill, but there they were, on my kitchen table, where my family ate. When I wasn't gambling, I would go to great lengths not to touch the money—but gambling had the power to override my incipient OCD.

My gambling wasn't limited to cards. At school, we played a game called rolling quarters at lunchtime. I also organized fifty-yard dashes—mostly pitting me against whoever wanted to race—and bet on them. I bet on the school's Campbell's Soup fund-raiser. Once I spotted two men walking down the fairway on the golf course near our house and bet my friend which one would reach the green first. The game didn't matter.

People thought my gambling was cute. They were amused by playing cards with a kid. It wasn't like watching a twelve-year-old smoke pot or crack or open a Budweiser. Nor was it as disturbing as watching an overweight kid shovel Twinkies in his mouth. Gambling is much more subversive and insidious. I entertained people by splitting eights and doubling on ten and eleven. They thought it was harmless fun.

But I'd already established a pattern of behavior that would continue until it was too late.

I loved sleepovers at Josh Shon's house. With a basement full of games, he had the perfect setup for fun. He'd have three or four of us over, and we'd play Nerf ping-pong with wild abandon for hours. We swung at the spongy ball with all our might because it only went so far and so fast and it wouldn't break anything. I played in every round, all night. I worked up such a sweat that I'd bring four T-shirts.

I dreaded that time of night when the other guys would want to settle down. There was no way I could lay down in my sleeping bag. As I did a few years earlier while playing Catch the Leaves, I cooked up ways to keep everyone interested. We played for movie tickets, CDs, and McDonald's game pieces, and eventually I took out cash and asked who wanted to play. After I lost that, I issued a new challenge.

"Double or nothing!"

That was my mantra whether I won or lost. I just wanted to keep going.

"Resnick, it's over," Shony Boy would say.

"Dude, take my money. I don't care. I just want to PLAY!"

Finally, to shut me up, one of the guys would rise from his sleeping bag and take hold of the Nerf paddle. "Okay, one more."

The one thing that kept me relatively grounded was soccer. I was a big kid, fast, strong, and smart. I turned out to be a natural fútbol player. Something about the team aspect appealed to me, and I fought with my father to let me play. I had tried the individual sports, like tennis, which I was pretty good at, too. But one time I was trouncing a kid and my dad came onto the court and told me to take it easy. He suggested I lose. I didn't understand.

"Why do you want me to lose?" I asked.

"I feel bad for the other kid," he said. "It'll make him feel better."

That happened several times. I never liked the way it felt. Why did he want me to lose? Were these the seeds of future self-destruction?

Soccer was different. I excelled from the first time I sprinted up and down the field as a ten-year-old for the Vipers in the Milwaukee Kickers Soccer Association. Soccer suited my personality. It was endless running. There were no time-outs. It was nonstop action. I begged the coach to schedule more practices. At practices, I pleaded to play games.

On the day before games, I checked the weather reports two, three, and four times a night. I did the same in the morning. I prayed it wouldn't rain or thunderstorm—anything that might cancel the game. When a game was cancelled, I crashed and burned. My reaction was abnormal. After two games were canceled when the referees didn't show up, I asked my coach for the name of the ref scheduled to work our next game and called him from a pay phone at school to confirm he was coming. I can't imagine what he thought after hanging up—a kid calling him at work.

The highlight of my season was supposed to be the day my grandfather came to see me play. I was so excited. Before the game, I bet him that I'd score six goals that game, and he took the bet. Even I knew that six goals was a preposterous number, absolutely unrealistic. But I put that out of my mind and instead ran up and down the field with a sense of purpose and determination beyond my normal effort. I tried to score every time I had the ball. Unfortunately, the other team was much better.

As the clock ran down, they were kicking our ass. We weren't going to win the game, so I focused on my bet. With a couple minutes left, we had a free kick from midfield and the coach told me to kick it. I got an idea. I ran to my grandpa on the sidelines and said, "Forget about the six goals. I'm going to score on this one. How about double or nothing?"

My confidence amused the old man.

"You got it," he said.

I ran to the ball, reared my right leg back, and thrust it with every ounce of strength and fury I possessed. I kicked the shit out of it. And then I cried out in terrible pain and went down, holding my hip. The game stopped. My dad, along with my grandfather and older brother, Jonathan, rushed me to Milwaukee Medical Center. Dr. Stephen Nord, an orthopedist, determined that I'd torn a ligament, ripped it right off the bone.

Dr. Nord gave me the choice of surgery or crutches for six months to see if the ligament would reattach by itself. My dad looked at me.

"Crutches," I said.

"Surgery may help him heal faster," the doctor said to my father.

"No!" I screamed.

I didn't want to be put under. I feared the idea of being unconscious. It was like a time-out. Darkness, loss of control, nothingness. . . . All that was the antithesis of my life.

As soon as I was up and able to get around on crutches, I returned to school, and on my first day back I hobbled onto the basketball court, balanced myself at the free-throw line, and bet my friend Clarence Rayhill Jr. that I could make a basket. I nailed it and had to bet him again. Once wasn't enough.

Without soccer, I was restless. I had to fill the void. I got into card games with some high school guys, who played for higher stakes. I started taking money from the roll of hundred dollar bills my dad always carried and placed on his dresser after he came home. He never missed them. If he did, he never said so.

I was allowed to do my thing. My independence often made my friends delirious with envy. One weekend Fish saw me walking in town and pushed me into a store. He was strong, with curly black hair and an athlete's build. With exasperation painted across his face, he simply blurted, "Don't your parents care?"

I laughed hard. I knew exactly what he meant. My parents had gone out of town with my two brothers and left me alone with a babysitter, a sixteen-year-old girl. Fish described how he'd seen me going to breakfast that morning in the babysitter's car—except I'd been in the driver's seat. She'd been riding shotgun.

"Dude, you're twelve!" he shouted. "You can't drive! What's going on?"

The thing with me was, I never thought I'd get in trouble. I never considered the ramifications.

In eighth grade, I dated Kristen Schreiber. On Valentine's Day, we wanted to see each other for dinner. But there were obstacles to overcome. She lived in a different neighborhood. My parents went out. And the weather was crap. There was half an inch of snow that turned into a sheet of ice, and the temperature, with the windchill, was below zero. I paced around, determined to think of a way I could get to her house. I decided to drive. I got in my mother's 1983 silver 380 SEL Mercedes, a four-door sedan with blue leather interior, and started out for Kristen's house.

Kristen lived eight and a half miles away. An adult would've had trouble driving in the conditions that night. At thirteen, I had no business behind the wheel of a car and certainly even less business driving in such hazardous weather. I was underage. I hadn't taken driver's ed. But somehow I made it safely all the way to her street. I had her house in sight when I turned the corner onto her block and hit an icy patch.

"Fuck!"

I knew what was going to happen, and then it did. The car spun out of control and went into a slide. I didn't know that you're supposed to turn the wheel into the skid. Nonetheless I remained calm throughout the ordeal. I had a premonition, more like a picture that flashed in my head, that things would be okay. I held onto the wheel and didn't breathe until the car came to an anticlimactic stop halfway in a ditch. I sat there for a moment, listening to the wind outside.

"Shit, shit, shit . . ."

But then my brain kicked into overdrive, breaking down the situation. I knew I had to call a tow truck. I also knew that if a cop happened to come by, as was likely after hearing a tow truck call in this weather, he'd want to meet the driver and see a driver's license.

I ran to Kristen's house, explained what had happened, and called the one person I knew with a driver's license—a girl named Stephanie I'd dated two years earlier. I begged her to help. Fortunately she lived nearby and said she'd be right over. Then I called a tow truck. Everyone arrived at the same time—the tow truck, Steph, and, just as I feared, the cops.

There were two officers, neither of whom looked like he wanted to spend much time in the nasty weather conditions. They assessed the scene, then asked who the car belonged to. Just then Steph walked up, having parked her car at Kristen's house. Thinking fast, I pointed to her and said it was her mother's car. They asked what I was doing there.

"I was in the passenger seat," I said.

I don't know why, but they believed me. The ruse worked, and it left me feeling even bolder. I went to Kristen's house and made out as planned. I drove back home without incident, making sure I got back well before my parents. In the garage, I started to wipe down the car when I discovered a problem. The side of the car that had fallen into the ditch was completely iced over. For the second time that night, I exclaimed, "Oh shit," and had to think fast as my parents were due back within the half hour.

Hurrying, I ran inside and got my mom's handheld hairdryer and six bath towels, and went to work on the iced-over car. Afterward, I dumped the dirty towels in the laundry and told my parents that water had leaked through the skylight in our Florida room. They thanked me for cleaning it up.

Six months later, I got into a fight with my brother Jonathan and he told my parents what had really happened that night. It was a Saturday afternoon. I was at my friend Andy's house, getting my ass kicked in a poker game with high school sophomores. My mother tracked me down and ordered me home. I knew by the tone of her voice that I was in trouble. But I didn't know why.

She and my father were at the kitchen table when I walked in. They glared at me, their expressions confirming my suspicion of trouble. I joined them at the table. I remained quiet as they recounted the story my brother told them about me wrecking the car. I felt confident that I'd be able to argue my way out of trouble.

But I didn't have to. In the midst of their lecture, my father got a business call and left the table. My mother stopped talking to me. She listened to his side of the conversation and watched as he paced back and forth across the kitchen. Since selling his business two years earlier, he'd started experiencing tough times. There'd been a lot of phone calls like this one. They filled the room with uneasiness.

I had gotten so I could tell by the look on his face whether it was a good or a bad call. This one, judging from his expression, was a bad one.

My mother didn't say anything until he hung up the receiver. Then she looked at him. He frowned. And they deciphered the call in concerned whispers. At that point, I skirted out of the room. I knew the thing with my mother's car no longer mattered. It was never mentioned again.

THEY THOUGHT I WAS EIGHTEEN

"Here's five hundred dollars. Spend it any way you want."

It was December 1986. My father, my brother Jonathan, and I had just boarded *The Festival*, part of the Carnival Cruise fleet of ships. My father was losing his money but continued to live as if he still had a hefty six-figure income, as evidenced by this holiday cruise. I didn't want to know about the dent this was going to make on his credit card, but I was happy to take the cash he offered. I knew how I was going to use it.

Chief among the ship's amenities was a Vegas-style casino, with all the games. You had to be eighteen to gamble. My brother handed me his college ID, and I got inside without a hitch. I sat at the blackjack table, where the maximum was two hundred dollars a hand. I didn't start out at that level, but something happened to me as I sat there, trading wisecracks with the dealer and flirting with the cocktail waitresses. I came alive. I was entertaining, energized, and the center of attention.

They say the worst thing that can happen to a gambler is to win the first time out. It's a thrill that stays with you, like a drug user's initial high. I can't deny it. After winning a couple of twenty-five-dollar hands, I wanted more. So I laid the max, two hundred dollars, on a single hand. The large amount caused a stir among the adults at the table. They were shocked, but, as usually was the case, they also seemed to be entertained by my recklessness with money. What was more fun than watching a kid (they thought I was eighteen) throw money around?

On top of it, I was red hot. I ripped off a couple of runs that put me ahead almost four thousand dollars. Men and women cheered. My parents stood behind me, approvingly.

"Everyone's telling us you're a star," my father said later.

"You're a fucking king," my brother said.

The casino was only open for limited hours a night. I was always the first one in, the last one out, and as my Latin friends on the cruise said, I was *en fuego*—on fire. Women shoved money into my hand and asked me to play for them. Men gave me high fives. At dinner, strangers stopped by my family's table to shake my hand and take my picture. They congratulated my parents. I bought meals for my family when we stopped at ports of call. In St. Thomas, I picked up the bar bill.

On the last night of the cruise, I left the casino with seventy-eight hundred dollars. The people who had been there every night stood up and applauded.

I never understood why we went on that cruise. That was another subject none of us discussed. My father's bills were piling up in inverse proportion to my father's declining income. He was always on the phone, whispering. When he and my mother talked, they went into their bedroom and shut the door. The atmosphere was fraught with pending trouble. Sometimes I picked up the phone and listened in. I figured out that the troubles began in 1983 when my father and his partners sold their business. It was confirmed when I discovered that he leased a Cadillac Seville in '82 instead of buying a new one as he'd always done. In '85, he re-leased the same car. Who did that?

I came across my parents' credit card bills and was surprised to find that they had more than one card and balances due on each one. My mom, I learned, paid the minimums. I found out other things too. But my father would never get mad at me for prying.

"Don't tell your mother," he'd say. "She might crumble."

But I don't think he was trying to protect my mother. He was protecting himself from being exposed to his failures or what he perceived to be his failures.

In the '80s, he got a doctor to prescribe him Xanax; he kept taking the pills till I got out of rehab in 2002. He checked himself out of reality. In retrospect, I see that he was my mentor—and I was an amazing pupil. I was channeling my fears into gambling, and later as it got me into trouble I knew not to tell my wife.

"You were always ahead of everyone our same age," my friend Fisher reminisced years later when I asked him to write a letter on my behalf to the judge weighing my prison sentence. "You were hands down the most fun, entertaining, and likeable guy any of us knew. You were never boring."

In sixth grade, I got blow jobs from two junior high school girls from another town, Becky and Lisa. Most of my friends didn't even have pubic hair then. In eighth grade, the year I was elected school treasurer, I sat behind two hot girls and spent the days rubbing their butts with my knee and thinking about my erection.

On the last day of eighth grade, I challenged the fastest girl in the school, whom I'll call Joanne, to a race in the fifty-yard dash. Not only was she the queen of speed, she was one of the hottest girls in school. We'd raced before, and she'd beaten me every time. But I wanted one more try before we went to high school, and I suggested an interesting wager.

"If you lose, you have to give me head by the time we graduate high school," I said.

"And if I win?" she asked.

"I'll do favors for you for a year."

"Deal."

We shook hands, said ready-set-go, and sprinted down the track. We were even until the last couple yards, when I pulled ahead and won.

There was no gloating and neither of us mentioned it for years. We stayed good friends. Our lockers were next to each other through high school. Everyone thought she was one of the hottest chicks in high school. On the day before we graduated, Joanne called and asked if I'd buy her and her girlfriend Maggie a case of beer. She knew, as did everyone else, that I had a fake ID.

The truth was, it wasn't 100 percent fake. On July 19, 1989, the day my brother Jonathan turned twenty-one, I took his birth certificate to the

DMV and applied for a replacement driver's license. I even took, and passed, the written test. Although we didn't look anything alike, I got the license. It had my photo. Most kids try to get by on fake IDs. I tried the ballsiest thing I could think of, and it worked. I was legal.

"Yeah, no problem," I told her. "I'll get you a case. Swing by my house in thirty minutes."

"You're the best."

A short time later, I heard Joanne and Maggie pull up in front of our house and my mother let Joanne inside. She followed me to the basement. We were near the bottom of the stairs when I suddenly turned around, smiled devilishly, and looked in her eyes as if I'd just remembered something.

"We've got two days before we graduate high school," I said. "You can't welch on your bet."

She shook her head as if she thought being a guy was pathetic and looked at me as if she had other things to do.

"Hurry up," she said. "Take down your pants."

I stared out the window and saw her friend Maggie waiting in the car. My mom was at the top of the stairs. I told Joanne that she was a phenomenal girl. It felt so dangerous and good. Joanne didn't say anything. Afterward she gave me a kiss, grabbed the beer, and left.

My first true love was a cute, petite, dark-haired girl named Jamie, an Alyssa Milano type. She was a junior at Nicolet, where the majority of my friends went. I went to Homestead. We knew each other only slightly, having crossed paths at a few parties. I realized she really was into me in August 1987 when I came down with a twenty-four-hour flu after a soccer tryout and she surprised me with a giant cookie from the Original Cookie Company at the Grand Avenue Mall. The top of the cookie said, I LOVE YOU, ADAM. I HOPE YOU FEEL BETTER.

"Who is this girl?" my mother asked.

"Just a girl," I said, downplaying the gift.

Friends teased me.

"She got her grandmother to bring you a cookie?" my buddy Aaron asked.

"Yeah."

"Is she a stalker?"

"Maybe. It's a little bizarre," I said. "But I love the cookie."

On October 14, she got her driver's license and picked me up in her new white '88 VW Cabriolet. It was one of those teenage moments when all the stars aligned. Steve Winwood's hit song "Higher Love" was on the radio. Jamie drove to the park. I stared at her the whole time, feeling a closeness that was new to me. I was used to being with girls, but she was different. I thought, *Wow, I've already lived a hard life. Had liked lots of girls. I really need to settle down. She could be the one.*

Jamie had on Liz Claiborne perfume and a leather jacket. We made out, and for the first time in my life, I fell in love.

That weekend, my friends found out I was dating her. They were surprised. They were used to me fooling around with a bunch of different girls. Jamie wasn't like those girls. They knew that I wasn't going to do the bone dance with her, and they didn't get the relationship.

The truth was, as much as I fell for Jamie, I fell even harder for her family. She took me to her house for dinner the next time we got together. She was a homebody. She wanted me to meet her family. She was the oldest of three children, with a younger sister and brother. Her father was a successful attorney and real estate developer; her mother ran her own business. When I sat down at the table, they already knew everything about me. Everyone asked questions. They laughed at my jokes. They were my fantasy of an ideal family.

When I left, Jamie's mother gave me a hug.

"Adam, I know we're going to see you again," she said.

The next night Jamie and her father came to my soccer game at Shorewood High School. Afterward, he invited me to the Milwaukee Bucks' home opener a few weeks later. I showed up at their house almost every day for the next month until Jamie and I had our first fight. We were on the phone when she lied to me about having spoken to an ex-boyfriend. I knew she had when she said she hadn't. I couldn't deal with the lie, even though in other ways I was a liar myself. It triggered a feeling of pain and abandonment that I couldn't explain.

"We're through," I said. "We're breaking up."

"What?" she screamed.

"I don't lie," I said. "People don't lie to me. Don't *you* lie to me."

Jamie called back in tears. I heard her mother in the background saying, "You broke up? When? What happened?"

I stayed on the phone with her for the next four or five hours, talking, arguing, crying, and laughing. By the middle of the night, we were sharing new secrets and discovering new reasons we were meant for each other. After that night, our relationship was tighter than ever.

From that November until Valentine's Day of my senior year—the next two-and-a-half years—I spent 95 percent of my free time at their house. Jamie's family treated me like a member of the family. Actually, we were like two married couples, plus two children, under one roof: Jamie's parents, us, and her siblings. We even had a routine: we ate dinner, then Jamie and I watched videotapes of *Days of Our Lives* until she fell asleep, and then I shot pool with her sister till 10:30, when I finally went home.

There were few boundaries in any of these relationships. After a few months, I was allowed to sleep over on weekends. I picked up food with her parents' credit cards. I used their cell phone. After I got my driver's license in March 1988, I was stopped multiple times for speeding to my two favorite destinations, Jamie's house and the Arlington Race Track, in Arlington Heights, Illinois; Jamie's uncle, a successful criminal defense attorney, got me off the tickets. (Years later, after the Universal collapse, he would become my second attorney. Quite a leap from going 50 in a 25-mph zone.)

On one of the few occasions we hung out with my family, we went to the horse races at Arlington. It was a hot summer day, and we had a sit-down lunch with my parents in the Millionaires Club. I hit a huge quiniela, which netted me almost seven hundred dollars for the day. On the way home, Jamie and I heard a blurb on radio station WKTI that *Major League,* a Hollywood movie starring Charlie Sheen, was being filmed at County Stadium and the producers wanted people to fill sections of the stands.

"Can we go?" Jamie begged me. "I would love to be in a movie. That would be so cool."

She was fascinated by movies. Her favorite movie in the world was

About Last Night. She pretended that we were Demi Moore and Rob Lowe, even though I told her that I was closer to Jim Belushi.

"It's over a hundred degrees outside and humid," I said. "It's miserable. Let's just go home."

She convinced me to at least check out the stadium. When we pulled up, the lines to get in stretched halfway through the parking lot. People had camped out for days to get their shot at fame. We got out and asked what the deal was. Everyone said we were too late and would never get in.

"You want to bet?" I said to the last person who told us that.

I grabbed Jamie's hand and marched us to the front of the line. I saw a woman and her son. I held out four crisp one hundred dollar bills from the Arlington race track.

"No way," the boy said. "We've been here for thirty-six hours."

His mother took the money and gave us their spot.

"I would've done it for two hundred dollars," she said.

What did I care? At sixteen, I didn't know the value of a dollar, and it was gambling money, to make things worse.

We got inside in the stadium. We sat about five or six rows behind the first base dugout. We were one row in front of Rene Russo, the lead actress. Jamie's wish came true. She was in the movie. The final scene was being shot that night. At the end of the film, Jamie and I are clearly visible, celebrating on the field with Sheen, Corbin Bernsen, Wesley Snipes, and the rest of the cast and extras.

I told Jamie things about myself that I didn't share with anyone else. She was the first person outside my immediate family who I opened up to about my greatest insecurity—that I was losing my hair. It started when I was fifteen. I remember feeling an electric current at the top of my head and from then on I could feel the hairs walking away strand by strand. The implications were dramatic. I've met men in their fifties who are traumatized when their hair starts coming out. I was fifteen!

I eventually saw Dr. Anthony Bonfiglio, a dermatologist. He didn't hide his astonishment. He prescribed Rogaine, the topical hair growth stimulant.

"I've never had to give this to anyone so young," he said.

That was real comforting. I counted the strands that came out daily. I was constantly touching the top of my head, feeling for the bald spot, trying to gauge whether it was bigger or perhaps, hopefully, not any larger. I had my eight-year-old brother, Joshua, measure my bald spot every day for months.

"I don't want to," he said.

"Do it," I ordered. "I'll give you five bucks."

I already thought people could be bought or compromised by money.

"Okay," he said.

I sat on my bed. He climbed up and stood over me. I made him draw a circle with a pencil so I could feel it.

"Tell me if it's gotten bigger since the last time," I said.

"When was the last time?"

"This morning."

"It doesn't seem to be bigger."

I traumatized the kid, I'm sure. I hadn't yet mastered the art of holding a mirror with one hand and measuring the growth of my bald spot.

The best and simplest option turned out to be a hat. Other than Jamie's senior prom, when she treated me to her hairstylist, who gelled my hair and combed it back so you couldn't see the bald spot, I don't remember a day passing for the next five years when I didn't wear a baseball cap. It was an effective cover-up, a trademark as well, but in reality nothing could forestall the progress of genetics and anxiety. I wonder, in retrospect, how beneficial it was in the long term, even though it was only a hat, to become comfortable living a lie.

6

BIG LOSSES

Not yet eighteen, I was in college.

Before starting my senior year of high school, Jamie started her freshman year at the University of Wisconsin, in Madison, and I helped move her into her dorm. We drove up in her car. On the day she rushed sororities I was sprawled on her bed, wrapped in her comforter, and on the phone with a student bookie I'd met the day before by the cereal dispenser in the cafeteria. I overheard a conversation and sought him out. He was taking my bet on the Arlington Million Dollar Horse Race.

It was a lark. My gambling had been mostly in check since I'd met Jamie. The urges weren't as strong or as frequent. I think it was due to Jamie's family, their acceptance, and the love they gave me. With Jamie going away, I started to feel anxious, and I channeled those feelings into gambling. I could've easily done drugs, alcohol, or food, but because of my character traits I chose gambling as my escape from dealing with reality.

Later that night, while everyone else on campus, it seemed, was partying, Jamie and I ordered Chinese food for delivery. I had the sense that I had dropped my wife off at a new job in a different city. Jamie didn't go out once her first semester. In October, her mother called me and asked me to come to their house to help move something. As I drove up, the garage opened and Jamie was standing there, beaming and waiting for me to take her in my arms. She took the next ten days off from school to be with me.

The Madison campus was ninety miles from my house, and sometimes I drove there after dinner to spend the night with Jamie. There was one stint when I went back and forth three or four times in a week. We arranged times when she'd call the pay phone at my high school so we could talk during the day. We called each other before going to bed and slept with the phone line connected. One month my dad's long-distance bill was over fourteen hundred dollars.

Over winter break, our families vacationed in the Caribbean. Mine went on a cruise, as was our tradition; and Jamie's family went to St. Martin. Our paths crossed in St. Martin, where we hung out for eight hours. All of us ended up in Miami, and then Jamie and I spent a week together with her grandparents in Boca Raton. But I'd started to feel like I needed more space.

"You should try to live a little more in college," I said to her one afternoon in Boca West. "Go out and party more."

"I don't want to," she said. "I'm happy being with you."

Jump ahead to Valentine's Day 1990. I sent Jamie flowers, a dozen roses, and didn't hear from her. When I called her, she said she couldn't talk.

"I'm going to a Valentine's Day formal," she said.

"With your sorority?"

"No," she said, pausing for a moment that in retrospect I knew she'd rehearsed. "With a guy."

There'd been no precursor, no warning. I went berserk.

"What are you talking about?" I screamed.

"I want to break up," she said. "You said I should live. I want to live."

I wanted to throw up. How could she be so cold? How could she drop me like that, after all we'd been through and shared, with no warning or emotion?

I fell onto my bed and went into shock. My mother came into my room and sat next to me while I twisted and shifted positions. She took hold of my arm and tried to comfort me. I looked up at her with eyes full of tears. I didn't believe her when she said things would eventually be okay. I called Jamie all night, something like every thirty seconds. She refused to answer. I believed I stood a chance of changing her mind if I could just get a hold of her.

At 1 AM, I got in the car and drove to Madison. The highway was dark and empty. For one fifteen-mile stretch, I set the cruise control on my 1988 Honda Prelude at the highest setting. I cranked the radio so I couldn't hear myself moan. I arrived at 2:30 AM.

Jamie's dorm, the Towers, was closed and locked. I shook the front door and banged on it with a hysterical fury until the janitor answered. He looked as if I'd woken him up. I paid him forty dollars to let me inside and then to unlock Jamie's room, 920 West. She was sleeping when I walked in and tapped her on the shoulder.

"How can you do this to me after three years?" I said.

She freaked.

"Adam! What are you doing here?"

"You know what I'm doing. How can you do this to me?"

The whole exchange was like a flash of white-hot anger. I was distraught and bleeding from being abandoned. She didn't want anything to do with me. In reality, there was nothing for either of us to say. I left after less than five minutes and drove back home.

I saw her sister at a party the next night. She turned away and wouldn't talk to me. I called Jamie's mother. She shut me out, too. She would've been justified if she'd told me off for paying the janitor forty dollars to break into her daughter's dorm room in the middle of the night. I drove to their house and tried to talk to someone. But I was locked out. Ultimately, that hurt more than the breakup with Jamie.

In the aftermath, I smoked weed nonstop. I didn't eat for nearly two days, and then I went to the other extreme and binged on everything, including Jagermeister shots, bong hits three times a day, and gambling. I rolled quarters with my teacher, who threatened to fail me. I went to Off-Track Betting four or five times a week. I played cards. I flipped quarters at school. At the horse track one day, I bet Fish that I could pee longer than he could pee.

I confided in my friend Tobias Coffman. Toby was my lockermate. Among all my friends, he was alone in having a serious girlfriend. Toby had spent part of the first semester in rehab for drug addiction. I drove him to school almost every morning. I told him about my breakup with Jamie over breakfast at Chuck's Place.

"Are you okay?" he asked.

"I'm totally fucked up," I said.

"Here's the thing. Jamie's a nice girl. But she's—"

"I know," I interrupted. "She's in college. We've got our own lives."

"Adam, I'm going to tell you the thing I learned in rehab."

"What?"

"Life is short. You have to enjoy it while you can."

It was such a cliché, we had to laugh. But Toby meant it. He was an artistic kid, more sensitive and spiritual than other guys in my world. He was like a mellow album in a collection of hard rock and rap—almost melancholy—and I loved him for it.

He had moved to Mequon from Frederick, Maryland, in sixth grade. We got friendly because he seemed to know a lot about chicks. He was the first guy I ever got drunk with. We were at his house, and his sister, a high school sophomore, had a party. We got obliterated. Before he went to rehab, he was doing large quantities of drugs, mostly weed and cocaine, and it changed him. He lost his spark and got depressed. He also got busted.

Following rehab, he was better. At least he was sober. But he suffered a big setback when school officials told him that he couldn't graduate because he'd missed so much school. They said he had to repeat at least a semester, if not more. That bummed him out, along with his girlfriend breaking up with him, though none of us knew how hard he actually took it.

On Friday, May 18, we drove to school as usual. We stopped at Hardee's for a Sunrise—a great Canadian bacon breakfast sandwich. I told him I wouldn't be able to pick him up the following Monday because I was going to Madison for my brother's college graduation and didn't know if the weekend festivities would run late. I ended up getting back early and drove to school that Monday, albeit late, thinking I'd see him at our locker and fill him in on the partying I'd done with the college kids.

I walked down the hallway, looking through the tiny windows on the classroom doors at classes in progress. Students at their desks looked back at me, shaking their heads. *There's Resnick, late again.* I heard footsteps behind me and turned my head enough to glance backward. It was the assistant principal, Mr. Jensen. A cool guy who liked me well enough, probably more than warranted. He caught up to me; he looked tired or upset. He put his head down and said, "Adam, I need to talk to you."

I followed him to his office. He sat behind his desk and took a deep breath. I knew it was going to be terrible, and it was.

"Toby has died," he said.

"What are you talking about?" I asked. "What happened?"

"Toby hung himself. His father found him in their basement."

I cried, of course, but I don't remember what happened next. I went into shock. I wanted to know more details. I wanted to know what Toby had been thinking that led him so desperately and sadly through the door of no return. What kind of pain must that have been?

Toby left a note that none of us ever got to see. The only detail I heard was that he'd quoted a New Order song in it. His funeral drew hundreds of people. Afterward, back at their house, I wandered around as if looking for my friend. It was hard being there knowing that Toby was dead. As I traded stories about him, I felt a profound emptiness that was beyond any high school senior's ability to understand.

Finally I hugged Toby's sister and his father and left in tears, trying to make sense of the fact that I'd never see or speak to him again. I paid my own tribute many mornings by playing his favorite music as I drove to school. I stopped at Chuck's Place and ordered breakfast. I drove by some of our old hangouts, including the skate park where he liked to board when we were younger, and at each place I said, "Hey, Toby, remember when . . ."

When yearbooks were handed out at the end of the year, I turned to find his photo. It wasn't there. I remembered that he'd been in rehab on picture day. I found that eerie, maybe prophetic. Was he fated not to make it, whether or not he went to rehab? Was our future already written?

Thinking back, mine seemed to be. I was voted Most Likely to Be a Millionaire and Most Dreamed About. But look where I ended up. Why? If there had been a category called Most Likely to Lose All His Money and Ruin His Life, I think I would've run away with that too.

I was in a dark place as graduation neared. I was mourning for my friend and still distraught from breaking up with Jamie. I wasn't in the mood for graduation parties. Everyone I knew spoke excitedly about college plans. I wasn't stoked about anything except getting away from home until I heard about the Dairyland Greyhound Dog Track in Kenosha, Wisconsin. It opened in June, and I was there the first night.

"Why the hell are you going to the dog track?" my friend Devo asked. "There are parties. We're graduating."

"From what I understand, the dogs run every eight minutes," I said.

He grinned, as if to say *of course.*

"Rezzie, say no more."

I was going to the dog track; I was sacrificing something I loved— namely, the horse track. As a leading scorer on my high-school soccer team, I'd given up a promising future in order to spend more time at the horse track. Dairyland was more fun than either soccer or the horses. The dog races were fast, and I didn't have to wait long between races. It was heroin for an action junkie.

I also had a valuable connection there that proved useful. Fish's father owned a piece of the track. One day I ran out of money after betting on long shots and crazy parlays. (My dogs always collapsed on the final turn.) I wanted to keep going and asked Fish if I could cash a check. He persuaded one of the track employees to cash one for me. I was amazed. Not only wasn't the track supposed to cash checks; mine was from my father's account. I didn't have my own checking account.

A few weeks later, the shit hit the fan. I wrote another check, this time for five hundred dollars, and it was returned for insufficient funds. Fish's father read us the riot act after first asking how the hell I'd been able to cash a check that didn't even belong to me. He was a smart man who lectured us about getting on the other side of the game. He made me pay back the money, too. That was nothing compared to the embarrassment I felt that my father didn't have five hundred dollars in his checking account and everyone knew it. My father? Never said a word to me, incidentally.

But worse than everything, after going to Dairyland for almost thirty days straight, trying to forget about my pain at losing Toby and Jamie, I was banned from the track.

I had no place to go. It was the end of July, and it was time for me to leave home.

SO WASSA MATTER, SWEETHEART?

"Resnick, you want to go to New York?"

I did. It was the middle of July 1990, six weeks after graduation, and my friend Fabs, like me, was going to the University of Arizona, in Tucson, in the fall. He needed to switch cars with his sister, who lived in New York. He was giving her his Pulsar and getting an MX6 in exchange. He asked me to drive with him. A road trip felt like the tonic I needed.

I brought fifteen hundred dollars for the trip. The minute we arrived in New York City, we went to Chinatown. For hundreds of miles, I'd talked about how I'd heard they had great games in Chinatown, and I was psyched to try them. We parked his car and walked into the colorful neighborhood. Halfway down the first street we were on, I saw a couple of young guys running a shell game—three shells and a hidden stone. Excited, I turned to Fabs and said, "I can guess where it is."

"You're going to get screwed," he said. "These games are fixed."

We watched for a minute or two.

"No way. I got this figured out."

I lost five hundred dollars before Fabs pulled me away from the table.

We walked further into Chinatown until I spotted a dice game outside a little store that sold souvenirs, T-shirts, pajamas, and incense. I won the first two games and gave Fabs an I-told-you-so look.

"They always let you win the first so you keep playing," he said.

"I don't give a shit. I'm playing."

Within ten minutes, I was down another five hundred dollars. Fabs literally pulled me from the game.

It wasn't the first time I'd been physically yanked from a game. A year earlier my brother Jonathan, his friend Mark, my friend Aaron, and I had gone to the Oneida casino outside Green Bay. I lost a lot of money and kept borrowing more until my brother and Aaron each grabbed one of my arms and dragged me from the blackjack table to the car in the parking lot, then drove away.

Fabs did the same thing, and then we went to his sister's apartment in the Village. His sister and her husband, Greg, both in their mid-twenties, picked up on my dark, dreary mood and suggested getting a drink. They took us to McSorley's, the city's oldest bar, on 7th Street. We got wasted on Guinness. Everyone in the bar was drunk, too, and singing old TV theme songs.

After returning to the apartment around midnight, Fabs and his sister fell asleep. Greg and I were still buzzed and chatty. He asked if I wanted to play gin. All of a sudden I perked up even more. When Fabs and his sister woke up the next morning, the two of us were still at the kitchen table, playing cards. She asked when we got up. Without looking up, I said, "We never went to bed." For the next three days, I played gin with him every night. By the end of the trip, I owed him thirty-two hundred dollars.

It was a disaster. Even though I gave the impression of being a spoiled kid from a privileged family, I didn't have that kind of money, not even close. Sitting at their kitchen table, while Fabs watched nervously from the doorway, I explained as much to Greg and Fabs's sister. I said I had five hundred bucks. Fabs's sister suggested reducing the sum to a thousand dollars, then looked at her husband for approval. Greg said he'd "cut the debt," a new term in my vocabulary, and one I'd hear often in the future. He said that I could give him the five hundred dollars I had on me and put another five hundred in the mail.

I had no choice. I made the deal. Then Fabs and I packed up and drove home to Milwaukee.

At home, I got ready for college. I didn't know it, but Dad had to go to his sources and borrow money to pay the out-of-state tuition. Before I left, he took me to the bank to get a checking account and a credit card in my name. We filled out the paperwork. Then the guy helping us asked my father to cosign because I didn't have an address in Tucson.

My dad shook his head and stood up.

"Let's go, Adam," he said.

Outside, he appeared frustrated.

"You can set up an account when you get to Tucson," he said.

I saw his frustration and knew he wasn't telling me the whole story. I didn't want to embarrass him by asking about it.

In the middle of August, Fabs and I loaded his MX6 with our stuff and drove it to Tucson. Before leaving home, my dad handed me his Bank One credit card. Driving through "the Hatch," a two-lane stretch between New Mexico and Arizona in the middle of the night, Fabs and I hit a coyote and freaked out. Alone, in the desert, with a dead animal next to the car—it was like a horror movie.

"Where are the people who are going to murder us?" I asked.

"Shut the fuck up," he said.

"But you know it's true. In the movies, something happens, the people get out of their car, and then it happens."

"Shut the fuck up. All we did was hit a coyote."

We stood by the side of the road and debated what to do with the coyote. I talked myself into a state where I had us looking every which way for a murderer. Finally, scared shitless, we left the coyote for the buzzards, got in the car, and drove even faster toward Tucson.

Once there, I found an apartment off-campus. I was one of two freshmen I knew of who didn't live in a dorm. I was supposed to be in a dorm, like every other freshman, but the buildings looked gross and dirty. I was a clean freak and modest. I wanted my own space, including a private bathroom. I should've been made to live with the other freshmen. I mean, who did I think I was? But no one forced me to have any boundaries.

I decided to go to Las Vegas the day after I got my new apartment. I didn't even unpack. I took the bus to Phoenix, caught an America West flight to Vegas, and went to Caesar's Palace in the center of the fabled strip. It's funny, but I didn't even have to think about where I wanted to go. Caesar's *was* Vegas to me. It was the Rat Pack. It was Evel Knievel. It was action.

I'd been to Vegas once before. My family had gone there for a vacation when I was five years old. We stayed at Circus Circus. I could still hear the clanging bells of winning machines. I posed for a family photograph wearing a silver swimsuit and matching top, with my brother, beside the MGM lion. I had no other recollections of what that trip was as I walked into Caesar's thirteen years later and began to rewrite my history.

I planted myself at the twenty-five dollar blackjack table. After twenty-four hours, I won seventeen hundred dollars. I left town feeling like I owned Vegas.

Back in Tucson, I signed up for English 101, sociology, and astronomy. When I thought about the future, I saw myself becoming an entertainment attorney in Los Angeles. We'd vacationed there once when I was little and I'd fallen in love with the city. Now I had to work toward that goal. I needed books and supplies. I drove to the University of Arizona bookstore and picked out the books on the course syllabi. I handed the cashier the credit card that my dad had given me before I left home. The girl gave it back a moment later.

"I'm sorry," she said. "It was refused."

I was surprised and mortified.

"What? It's brand new. My dad just gave it to me. Let me make a call."

I knew what had happened, and I didn't want to stand there and face what I knew would be embarrassment. I left the books there; I would never buy another book through my entire college career.

When I got back to my apartment, I called the credit card company. A woman on the other end informed me that the card had an eight thousand dollar credit line, but there were already seventy-eight hundred dollars of charges on it. The three hundred dollars worth of books I'd tried to charge had put it over the limit. I was glad I hadn't called from the counter. Incensed, I hung up and called home.

"What's the story with the credit card you gave me?" I asked my father.

"I'm having some issues," he said. "I don't want to tell your mother or your brothers."

I knew there were problems, but I hadn't realized the extent. My father probably didn't either. He never kept a checkbook or wrote down the check numbers or the amounts he had written. He had loose checks all over the house. I despised him for putting me in such a compromised position.

Socially, I fared much better. I rushed the ZBT fraternity, and within days of being accepted I organized a trip to Vegas with my new fraternity brothers. While they gambled, drank, and went to a strip club, I stayed at the blackjack table and lost everything I had, and then some—including the seventeen hundred dollars I'd won earlier, all the cash my dad had given me, and the two hundred dollars left on the credit card.

The debacle made me an instant legend among my frat brothers.

"Resnick, do you ever go to class?" a guy asked as we played cards at night in the frat house.

"I go to class," I said, pretending to be insulted. "You take psychology, econ, and whatever. I take blackjack, roulette, and slots."

He laughed.

"Dude, you're nuts."

"Seriously. Who needs school? My father went to medical and law school and he isn't faring so well." I'd say this so often, it was like my mantra. I used it as my rationale for my lack of ambition. "I need street smarts."

My education began a week after I opened a checking account at Valley National Bank. I went there with Matthew Rudnick, a Chicago kid in my fraternity. We'd been sent each other's checks by mistake, and the mix-up made us instant best friends. We shared many similarities. We loved sports, girls, and gambled—he nearly as much as me. But there was an important difference between us. Matt's father was a powerful, hardworking, responsible attorney. Matt had to answer to him. I didn't have to answer to anyone.

When Matt and I took our mixed-up checks in to Valley National, we were helped by Charlotte Baly, a personal banker who was used to wealthy students from the Midwest whose families put ten or twenty grand in an account at the start of the school year. Matt was genuinely one of those kids. She thought I was too, and I didn't do anything to dispel her notion.

Charlotte apologized for the mistake. After Matt left, I stayed and talked with her for about an hour. She was in her twenties, open and personable. Her husband traveled a lot on business, and she seemed to live vicariously through the students. Our conversation ran the gamut. The thing about me was that I genuinely enjoyed talking to people. Years later, they'd call me a con artist and wonder how I convinced people to do special favors for me. But whatever convincing I did was inadvertent. People offered to help me. I never had to ask. I was just friendly. I treated everyone the same, whether they were busboys at a restaurant or corporate CEOs. Charlotte was one example.

"Anything you need, Adam," she said. "Let me know."

We spoke again less than a week later when I bounced my first check. It was for a couple hundred dollars. I sweated bullets that my account would be closed. But Charlotte called and said that she'd cover the check with overdraft protection. She let me know that she was sympathetic to students away from home for the first time and taking care of their own finances. I was relieved.

The bank was like a watercooler. All the fraternity boys and sorority girls and everyone else on campus flowed through there daily. Sometimes I sat in the bank to watch the chicks float through. Charlotte began to hear stories about my gambling, and after I bounced several more checks we met and I clarified the stories she'd heard.

I was surprised but relieved to hear Charlotte say that she knew other students who gambled. I felt even better when she promised to help me through tough times.

"I'm so sorry," I said. "I can't apologize or thank you enough."

"Adam, I'm here to help you."

"It's such a comfort to know there's someone in my life who wants to help. I mean that."

My freshman year, I made twenty-three trips to Las Vegas—twenty-two times more than I showed up in any of my classes. I never had trouble getting a crew from the frat house up for a twenty-four-hour jaunt to

Vegas. Our frat house was an old hotel with a central courtyard—a perfect spot for keggers and barbecues. Before leaving for Las Vegas, we huddled there and worked up a lather by shouting "Gamby! Gamby! Gamby!" as Kenny Rogers's song "The Gambler" blasted in synchronicity from stereo speakers in windows.

Pumped up, we piled into cars, drove to Phoenix, and caught the America West flight to Vegas.

The moment the plane landed, we turned to each other and said, "City of Lights, baby! Let's hit the City of Lights!"

I also discovered the Tucson Greyhound Park. The races started every night at 7:30. I went there whenever I couldn't find a card game or get up a trip to Vegas. Around that time a fraternity brother told me that he'd started gambling with a bookie. This was exciting stuff for a college student, and as the resident gambling expert he wanted my approval. I didn't know much about bookies yet, but I'd bet a hundred here and there on games.

"I'm paying a thousand dollars to a betting service run by a guy named Russo out of Jersey," he said.

"And?" I asked.

"He gives me picks to the football games. You want me to introduce you? Get in on the action?"

"You jackass," I said. "Don't you see what's going on?"

No, he didn't. But it was absolutely clear to me. Russo had a betting service; he wasn't a bookie. He picked games. If the Packers were playing the Bears, he gave the first fifty people who called the Packers and then he gave the next fifty people the Bears. At the end of the game, he had fifty happy customers.

Early on I understood the differences between bookies and gamblers. Bookies were businessmen and most of them were very savvy. Gamblers, specifically compulsive gamblers, came in every shape, size, and variation of intelligence, but they were bound by a common pursuit: action. Traditionally, their motivation has been seen as money, which has, I think, created a misperception that's made compulsive gamblers less sympathetic than drug addicts or alcoholics. But it's not about the money. It's about the high that comes with playing.

And hence the reason, despite what I knew about Russo, I was in. But I just went in that one week. We lost. *I told you so*, I thought.

Through different friends, I learned about two other bookies, Arturo and David, two students from wealthy, connected families in Mexico City. Seniors, they worked as a team, servicing all the major action on campus from their apartments. Their runner was a stocky, dark-haired kid from the Midwest nicknamed Jake the Snake. I started out betting five hundred dollars a game—money I obviously didn't have—and I fell behind the first week. I bet against myself with another bookie, a bartender in a Tucson sports bar, just so I could stay in the action. I gladly paid the juice.

Betting against myself—the epitome of sickness. And the juice was starting to add up.

Then Bobby disappeared, and Arturo and David lowered my bets to two hundred fifty dollars. They said my lack of self-control was a liability. It didn't stop me. A few weeks later, I skidded through a two-week losing streak and owed them four thousand dollars. I'd never been that deep in the hole. When Jake called to arrange payment, I stammered through some lame excuse. There was silence on the other end.

"Hello?" I said finally.

"I'm furious with you, Resnick," he said.

"I'm sorry."

"You'll be hearing from us."

The next night I walked into my apartment from dinner and the phone rang. It was David and Arturo wanting their money. I told them the truth. I only had a thousand dollars. I offered it to them.

"No fucking way," they said. "It's four grand."

A few days later, I lost that last thousand bucks trying to win the four I needed. I was screwed.

Desperate, I racked my brain for a way out. One name kept popping up, and I didn't get why. But I went to Valley National anyway and sat down opposite Charlotte Baly. I muttered something about applying for a loan, but she said that wasn't an option. After thinking for a few minutes, she looked straight into my eyes.

"Listen, you're a good-looking kid," she said. "There are a lot of wealthy women up in the foothills in Tucson."

"What?"

"I don't have any other suggestions." She sighed. "Do you know the Tack Room?"

"No."

"It's a nice restaurant, and there are women . . . they're older . . . in their fifties. I know it sounds crazy, but some of them would pay to sleep with you."

I leaned back and laughed. Her suggestion was nothing if not crazy. It took me by surprise. I know she was trying to help because I was desperate, but she was suggesting prostitution. Now, in retrospect, I wonder if the scenario aroused Charlotte, if she was fantasizing out loud. If that was the case, I didn't pick up on it.

"Charlotte, I'm not a porn star. I don't work out. I'm not a body-builder. I'm—"

"It doesn't matter," she interrupted. "You're an eighteen-year-old guy. Those women, for whatever reason, don't have a sex life. They'll pay a guy like you for sex."

"Get out of here."

"I'm just telling you what happens at a lot of nice restaurants like this. It's one way to get some money if you really need it."

I left there confused and thinking whether I really had any options besides going down on a Social Security candidate. I didn't want to imagine that view.

The next day I went for a drive with Rod and Mike. Rod was a pretty funny guy. I took them into the hills in my brother's 1984 Pontiac Sunbird, which my father had recently shipped me. We rolled a few joints and enjoyed the night. As we came down the hill, the car conked out. I parked it on the side and we walked to the nearest gas station.

I called my father and asked what I should do.

"You deal with it," he said.

I dealt with it by calling my friend Darren to pick us up and leaving the car up in the hills. As far as I was concerned, it could stay there.

Three weeks later, my friend John saw the car at the Pontiac dealer. They were fixing it up. They probably sold it, but I don't know, neither I nor my father ever bothered to check on it.

I was out of control. Given that mind-set, it's no wonder I decided to check out the scene at the Tack Room. I was scared to death, but I was out of options. I drove a Honda from some bullshit rental car place that gave me a car without having the proper credit. The Tack Room was Tucson's only five-star restaurant. It was perched on the hillside with a spectacular view of the valley. I walked in wearing a sport coat. I'd also taken off my hat and combed back my hair. I looked thirty-eight, not eighteen.

The restaurant was a dimly lit, older, classy restaurant. I went to the bar, ordered a drink, and started up a conversation with the lady next to me. She was receptive, friendly, and . . . in her fifties. Her name was Priscilla. I quickly found out the basics about her: she wasn't married, her family owned a car dealership, and she was lonely. I was about to order a second drink when she asked if I'd like to go back to her house. I turned toward her as if surprised. In reality, I was petrified.

Maybe she picked up on that. She smiled.

"I have beautiful views of Tucson."

I felt my stomach lurch.

"Let's go," I answered.

We walked to the parking lot and I got into her Mercedes. She turned the radio on to the soft rock station. As she drove down the hill, her hand brushed my thigh. I retreated by inching closer to the door. Then I cracked the window after catching a whiff of her perfume. It was the same as my mother's. Could there have been any bigger turnoff? I loathed myself for getting in this situation.

"I've got to tell you something," I said as she wound down the hillside from the restaurant. "You're probably wondering what I was doing up there. I've never been there before. But I'm in a situation and—"

I caught myself trembling.

"You don't need to pay me for sex," I said. "It's not going to happen anyway."

I didn't know how to read her expression. She pulled the car over to the side of the road and listened as I told her my life's story. She took me back to my car in the restaurant parking lot. Before I got out, she wrote me a check for twenty-five hundred dollars and gave me a kiss on the cheek.

"I hope things get better," she said.

They didn't. Despite my need for money, my conscience wouldn't let me cash the check. On the surface, it didn't make sense. But people who knew me would've understood. I got myself into trouble; at my core was a sense of decency. Over the years I've recoiled in horror every time I've thought of myself sitting next to Priscilla.

A few days later, Jake the Snake left a threatening message on my answering machine. Since I wasn't picking up my calls, he also let my friends know that he was looking for me.

One day I got to my friend Peter's apartment. He had me stand by his answering machine. He shook his head in disbelief as he hit the play button.

"So wassa matter, sweetheart? You don't wanna to talk to me?"

I shook my head and was about to say something, but Peter put his finger to his lips.

"We *will* find you," Jake finished.

I preferred they didn't find me. So I abandoned my apartment and slept with friends. I was a good houseguest. While my friends were in classes, I straightened up their places, answered phones, ran errands, and cooked. A pal jokingly dubbed me "the butler." Every few days, I changed apartments. One day, as I left Fabs's place, I was grabbed by two guys who ID'd themselves as associates of Arturo and David.

"What the fu—"

"Shut up, Resnick," one of them said.

I tried to shake them off and one of them pointed what I assumed to be a gun in his jacket pocket. I couldn't believe it.

"What the hell are you doing?"

"Shut the fuck up."

They hustled me into the parking lot and threw me into the trunk of a car. They breathed heavily as they wrestled with my heavier frame. I didn't resist. Even if they didn't intend to shoot me, I didn't want the gun going off by accident. Once I was in the trunk, though, I felt the gun.

"We're going to kill you if you don't pay up," one guy said.

I was silent for about twenty seconds while I thought. The other two guys obviously didn't know what to do either.

"You're going to kill me over three grand?" I finally said.

"You're already dead, man," one guy said.

"Come on, you aren't *really* going to kill me for three thousand bucks," I said. "You guys are graduating in a little bit and don't want to fuck it up, right?"

The tough-guy expressions on their faces softened.

"So here's the deal," I continued. "Get the gun off my fucking head because you're not really going to kill me. Then get me out of this trunk. Let me come up with the money. I need to bet the games tonight."

They stepped back. Their expressions relaxed. They'd gotten their point across.

"Of course we weren't going to kill you," one guy said. "We want our money."

"You're really sick," the other added.

After they were gone, I climbed out of the trunk and exhaled. Meanwhile, Jake the Snake had called my father on his private number at home. It was unlisted. How they got that number was beyond me. My father took their threat to kill me seriously. I received a call from him in the middle of the night. He sounded very scared. I confirmed Jake's story and filled him in on the details.

"I don't have the money," he said.

"You don't have three grand?" I asked, surprised.

"No. I have to try to borrow it. Don't tell your mother or your brothers. I'll try to find a way to help you."

Two anguish-filled days later, my father called back and said he had the money. I held back tears as he told me. He tried not to cry, too. There were a lot of fucked-up feelings on both our sides going unspoken at that moment. They were covered up by the business at hand. He had no way of knowing whether the threat on my life was true, and so he took it seriously. He probably called everyone he knew until he came up with the three thousand dollars. I'm sure he felt guilty and responsible as he made those calls. He hadn't parented me properly, and that was probably one of the moments reality set in. I was, at the core of my DNA, a product of my parents.

I picked up the money at Western Union and paid Arturo and David. I was done with them as far as I was concerned. I went back to my apartment and collapsed on the sofa. I don't know how long I spent there. Hours. I hadn't slept for days, and then with the drama over I collapsed.

The phone woke me up. It was my father, checking in. He'd decided that was the moment to fill me in on a family secret.

"Your grandfather had a gambling problem."

"Papa Ruben?"

"Your mother doesn't talk about it."

I thought about our family history and how I was fourteen when I first heard that her mother, my grandmother, was still alive in Pittsburgh.

"She doesn't talk about anything," I said.

I thought about Papa Ruben, how he had taught me to play cards, and how he would sit at the table with me all night, the only person I'd ever encountered whose stamina and interest in playing equaled mine. At that point I didn't know he'd lost everything he had and moved my mother while she was growing up more times than she could recall. But I saw that we were very much alike.

"Adam, maybe your gambling is out of control," my father said. "Maybe you need some help."

I thought about what he'd said.

"I think you're right. I probably do."

Later that night, with nothing to do, I walked to one of the dorms on campus in search of a card game.

8

FINANCIAL AID

"How about going to Atlantic City?"

"I'm ready," I said.

It was the summer after my freshman year, and I had a job as a counselor at a camp in the Poconos, a bucolic sweep of mountainous countryside that runs through western New York and Pennsylvania. I went with my friend Aaron, who'd finished his first year at Penn. I enjoyed supervising games, kicking around a soccer ball, and physical activity in general. At night, I played cards with my campers. By week two, I'd lost all my money. How pathetic. They were eleven and twelve years old.

Camp ran for eight weeks. We got time off at the end of the third week, and a bunch of the counselors planned a trip to Atlantic City. I signed up right away and persuaded the camp director to advance me money on my paycheck. I didn't explain that I'd lost all my money playing poker with Harold "Goober" Luber and Freddie "The Piano Prodigy" Krone.

Aaron and I drove there in his Pontiac Grand Prix. He parked in front of Bally's and I jumped out, feeling a surge of excitement and anticipation that literally created a different energy in my brain. One of the ten diagnostic criteria of gambling addiction—in fact the most basic of the criteria—is a preoccupation with gambling. Reliving past experiences, planning the next gambling opportunity, and scheming to get more money. I was preoccupied with my own preoccupation.

Bally's was bustling. Outside, buses parked out front and let off hundreds of people of all ages and ethnicities from every point across the East Coast. I counted more than half a dozen different bus lines, and I was sure there were at least double that running trips to the Boardwalk. Real estate and gambling moguls were trying to update Atlantic City from its dilapidated past. Another reminder of how gambling was accepted as entertainment and fun.

I entered the hotel and walked straight to the front desk. I asked for a room and paid for it with my credit card. I also cashed the paycheck I'd gotten from camp. I sussed out the blackjack tables and sat down at an empty table. Within six hours, I'd lost all the advance money and taken a cash advance off the credit that remained on my credit card. After losing that, I found Aaron and persuaded him to let me borrow a thousand off his mother's credit card. I lost that, too.

Now I was in a situation where I needed to gamble again, with even more on the line, to pay my debt. I was a live wire of anxiety.

I went to the front desk and asked for the money back from my room. In cash.

"I changed my mind," I said. "I'm not staying."

"We will refund it, minus the three percent fee from MasterCard."

"Fine. I just want the cash."

That had been part of my initial plan, converting the credit for the room into cash if I needed it. In my head, I'd put that money aside for an emergency. Now I had the emergency. I placed the entire sum on a single hand and busted on the fourth card. Aaron was pissed at me for losing a grand against his mom's credit card. He didn't have that kind of money and didn't know how he was going to explain it to her.

"What can I tell you?" I said, apologetically. "I feel terrible. I'll make it up to you. Just give me a little more."

"Dude, I can't. My mom's going to kill me as it is. You lost a thousand bucks!"

"If you can get a little more, I'll win it back. I know it. I'll even pay you interest. You can pay your mom back and make a little for yourself."

"No."

"All right. But I'm really, really sorry. I feel awful."

That night we slept in his car in front of Bally's. In the morning, I began talking about ways I might come up with more cash. He told me to shut up. He didn't want anything to do with my gambling. We tried to sleep in the car, which we parked beyond the Boardwalk. Aaron complained endlessly, as he had a right to do. I felt so guilty for his misery that I called one of the female counselors who'd taken some of the girl counselors to her parents' summer home in Margate, a vacation town on the Jersey shore. She let us stay there overnight on the sofa.

The next day Aaron and I drove back to camp and I quit my job. Atlantic City had wiped me out, emotionally as well as financially. I was so down in the dumps I had no enthusiasm for playing games, managing campers, and organizing campfire sing-alongs and stories. I told the camp director I'd make good on the advance. I also talked Aaron into quitting his job. It was selfish on my part. He was my ride back to Milwaukee, and I wanted to get out of there ASAP. We packed up that day, cranked the radio, and hit the road.

I hated being home. I felt suffocated there. Even though it was mid-July, I drove the 1,937 miles to Tucson by myself. I did it without stopping by sticking my head outside the window to stay awake. My father sent me a couple thousand dollars for the summer. In mid-August, Tucson began to fill up with students. One day, as I was waiting for a FedEx from my father with my tuition money, I got a distressing call from him.

"Hey, I'm waiting for your FedEx," I said.

"I didn't get my carry," he replied.

I knew what he meant. He hadn't sent the money. Nor was it going to come, as it turned out.

"I've already checked things out with the financial aid office," he said. "You go there and it will be fine."

I was mortified. I'd grown up in a wealthy suburb among kids with expectations. I was, in many ways, no different. Maybe if my father had warned me that I needed to get financial aid, like so many other people, my reaction wouldn't have been irrational. But there was a lot of subtext left unsaid. He may as well have told me to apply for food stamps.

"What is the problem?" I asked.

"I've had some issues," he said. "You don't know the extent. I'm heavily in debt."

"How much?"

"Too much." He paused and I could hear his heavy exhale. "It's temporary. I have some balls up in the air. I'm telling this to you, Adam, because you can handle it. But please don't tell anyone, especially your mother or your brothers. Just get the loans. I'll pay them back when the time comes."

"Sure."

"Meanwhile, I sent you two thousand dollars to help you start off the year."

What? If I had to get loans, why was he still sending me money? I didn't bother to ask and he didn't explain. Maybe he could only get the two grand, not the ten that I needed. It was beyond either of us to hash out and so, like everything else between us, we left it at that.

I registered for just enough courses to stay enrolled. I often thought about my father and tried to relate him to my education. He'd studied law and medicine and risen to a position of power as head of one of the largest companies in the state. He'd dreamed of having money and got it. Then his world came apart, and now he was broke. He'd never planned to live past forty-two, and suddenly he was fifty without a plan. He was tortured by his failures, and his inability to deal with them tortured me.

Matt Rudnick, and I hosted our fraternity's freshman pledge party on the top floor of our two-bedroom apartment at Euclid Terrace. About thirty guys participated in this crazy night of gambling, beer, and hits off a six-foot-tall glass bong. Some of the pledges also brought Quaaludes, cocaine, and whippets. Personally, I never did any illegal drugs other than pot. I was high enough.

The debauchery was like a scene from *Animal House* as if directed by Hunter Thompson. Matt and I got deep into a card game of rat's ass with some pledges when there was a pounding on the front door so forceful that it rose above the music, which was pumping hard enough to vibrate the floor. A pledge opened the door at my direction and there stood two uniformed Tucson police officers. One was older, maybe in his thirties, and the other looked relatively new to the force.

"Whose place is this?" they asked.

I walked over to them. If I hadn't been stoned out of my mind, I would've freaked out. Instead I showed them my legal fake ID stating that I was twenty-one.

"We're having a pledge party," I explained.

"Come with me," the older cop said.

I followed his lead as he walked into the apartment and glanced from side to side. It was like slogging through muck in a swamp of college depravity. He picked up a plastic bag of weed and threw it down. He brushed some remnants of cocaine off from the dining room table and chucked the razor blade out the open sliding glass door. He bent the six-foot bong to eye level, looked in, and shook his head. He walked to the table where we'd been playing cards and counted the money.

I'd started estimating the number of years that I was going to have to spend in jail when I gave up, figuring that I was fried for life. By then, Matt was right behind me, presumably because he felt obligated to share some of the heat. Finally the cop pulled us into the kitchen.

"Listen, guys," he said. "I don't give a shit about your gambling. I don't care about your pot smoking. As a matter of fact, I don't give a shit about the cocaine and whatever else is happening here. But do me a favor. Get rid of those beer cans right now or that's going to get you into a hell of a lot of trouble."

"Yes, sir," I said.

The cops left. Matt and I lit up a joint and, without saying anything, began to pick up beer cans and throw them away. About two minutes later, the significance of what we'd escaped hit us. We stopped picking up cans, turned, and looked at each other with astonishment.

"That was a trip," he said.

"Very," I said.

"He was either the world's coolest cop, or else he couldn't believe that you stood there like we had a right to be doing all this shit."

"It was insane."

The insanity was just beginning. That fall I made thirteen trips to Vegas and gambled more heavily than ever. In October, I had a garage sale out of my apartment to raise money because I was broke. As friends buckled down, I felt lost. I didn't have anything going for me. Rather than clean up my act, I found a new one. A week before Thanksgiving, I decided to transfer to the University of Wisconsin in Madison. I told my parents that I wanted to be closer to home. They backed me 100 percent.

"You're going to be in-state," my father said. "The tuition will be a lot less. It's good for you."

"I think so too," I agreed.

But in order to transfer, I needed a 3.0 GPA and twenty-five credits. I was enrolled in three classes: Journalism, Poli Sci, and Theater Appreciation. The last was a clap for credit-type class and not a problem. I started going to my Poli Sci class and realized that the four people I knew in that class all cheated off the same Milwaukee girl. I became the fifth. She gave me the answers for the final exam, and I cavalierly taped them to the wall next to my desk.

My friends laughed at my brazenness. I argued that it was less obvious to be obvious rather than constantly glancing at a cheat-sheet in my lap.

I was right. I got a B.

Journalism was more of a problem. It was a difficult class, requiring real work, and I hadn't gone once. Nor did I know anyone in the class. I didn't have a chance of passing, never mind getting a B. However, I knew what I had to do because I'd been through a similar situation my freshman year that was like something out of a movie, and even then it was hard to believe.

All freshmen had to take English 101. It was mandatory, and attendance was required. I ignored the rules and withdrew because I couldn't get my ass to class. I planned to re-enroll the second semester. But while flying home during Thanksgiving break, I met a guy who taught English at the college. Tommy Mulholland was heading someplace back East, but like me, he had a stopover in Minneapolis. After I found out what he taught, I asked if he wanted to get a drink.

We went into the bar and I told him my situation, changing a few details to make myself more sympathetic.

"Actually, I need an A," I said, and then, with a nervous laugh, added, "But get this. I've never been to class."

"Man, there's no way you're going to pass."

"I know."

He considered my situation, then he shook his head in disbelief. He didn't know what to say as he looked around the bar.

I kept on talking in the hope that I'd hit on something that would work on him.

"Okay, I'm going to give you my number," he said. "After Thanksgiving break give me a call and I will find someone to tutor you."

Perfect. I thanked him and we finished our beers.

After the break, I got him on the phone. He remembered our conversation at the airport. We met at his apartment early the next evening. He answered the door right away. His place was a one-bedroom, with a tiny eating area in his kitchen and a couple of chairs in his living room. We sat down. I went straight for the kill.

"I'm going to pay you five hundred dollars a month for the next four months and then a thousand dollars for the exam if you give me an A. But *you have to give me an A.*"

His jaw dropped slightly. He froze, staring at me.

"I can't," he said. "Oh my God. I can't do that."

"It's a total of three thousand dollars."

He shook his head as if shaking an Etch-A-Sketch screen clear. He got up, went into the kitchen, paced around, and came back with a beer.

"You aren't even in my class," he said.

"I'll transfer."

He was silent for a moment. Then he said, "You need to register for second semester English 101. Then you have to request a transfer into my class and tell the registrar's office you have a scheduling conflict, because you're assigned randomly and probably won't get into my class automatically. Then I'll sign off on the transfer."

I did it. We did it. I got my A.

That episode gave me confidence when it came to getting an A in my sophomore journalism class. It was Journalism 151. I went to class for the first time two weeks before the final exam. I sat in the back of the lecture hall and listened to the professor discuss the final exam and term paper. As he spoke, I noticed a T.A. working at a desk near his podium. I thought, no way, that's never going to happen again, and so I concentrated on surveying the other people in the class, looking for someone who might help me cheat. Unfortunately, I was unable to find any takers.

That night I did my laundry. Ordinarily I went to Wildcat Wash, on Speedway, but instead, for some reason, I wandered off campus, and I carried my sack of dirty clothes to another Laundromat on Sixth Street. After loading two machines, I looked around and saw a guy in a black leather jacket doing his wash nearby.

"Aren't you the T.A. in my journalism lecture?" I asked.

I thought he looked familiar. But he didn't share that same memory of me.

"Yes," he said. "But I don't recognize you."

"That's because I've only gone to class once." I paused and let that settle in for a moment. "We need to talk."

The Laundromat was mostly empty. The hum of the machines ensured that no one could hear as I pitched the T.A. on a plan. Afterward he scratched his head and leaned against the machines in thought. When he didn't refuse immediately, I knew I had a chance. It turned out that he was in some financial trouble.

"I want a day to think about it," he said. "I also have to see if I'm the one who will be entering the grades."

We met the next night at an off-campus bar, Danny's Baboquivari. Nervous, we ordered beers and shot pool. Both of us were lousy pool players. I purposely lost twenty bucks, knowing he was hard up for cash, and then, as we stood around and talked, I laid two hundred dollars in hundreds on the table.

"They're yours—no strings attached," I said. "And there are thirteen more of these waiting for you if I get an A on the exam and an A in the class."

He paced back and forth. Then he put his hands on the side of his head, squeezed, and said, "Arrrrrrrgh!"

"I need the money but I don't know what to do," he said.

"It's not going to hurt anyone," I said. "I need to transfer."

"Why?"

"My family has money problems."

For whatever reason, whether it was nerves or greed, he didn't see the absurdity of someone with money problems paying him all that cash.

"Come on," I continued. "You get some cash. We never see each other again."

He leaned against the wall.

"I can't promise anything," he said. "I still don't even know if I'm the one entering the final grades."

"Just say you'll do it if you can."

I called him on the day of the exam. He told me to skip the class and meet him later that night at the same bar. I was at a corner table when he came in and sat down. He took a piece of paper out of his jacket pocket and put it on the table. It was a photocopy of the final grade report. He pointed to my name. It said, "Resnick, Adam," and next to my name was an A.

"Fuck yeah," I said. "Thanks."

I gave him the money, drove back to my apartment, packed everything up, and went home to Milwaukee.

I had a 3.04 GPA and exactly twenty-five credits. I was done in Tucson. In a year and a half, I had, among other things, traveled back and forth to Vegas more than twenty times, been stuffed in a car trunk at gunpoint, and bought myself two A's. I looked forward to a fresh start in Madison. I needed one.

9

BOOKS, BOOKIES, AND BLACKJACK

In mid-January, after a five-week winter break at home, I drove to Madison and got a two-bedroom apartment about two hundred yards away from the state capitol building. I furnished my new place during a single twenty-five hundred dollar spree at the American TV megastore with winnings from the OTB.

The University of Wisconsin was a comfortable fit. I fell in with Devo, one of my closest friends from home, also a sophomore. That first day he introduced me to Bino, a guy who said, "I've heard about you. Devo says you're a wild man." My friend Darren, who'd let me sleep on his sofa when I was hiding from Jake the Snake in Tucson, hooked me up with his younger brother, Chris, a freshman.

The next day I opened a checking account at Firstar Bank. It was approved without any issues, even though I was a few hundred overdrawn at Valley National Bank in Tucson. My father had once told me that as long as you had cash and made money, you could always fix problems, so I didn't worry.

That afternoon, as I walked across campus, I saw one of my new friends and he asked if I knew anything about a new Indian casino that I believe was called the Golden Nickel. It was forty-five minutes from campus. I hadn't heard about it until then, but I was there that night. I lost nearly a thousand dollars at the blackjack table—a couple hundred in cash and the five hundred dollar credit I somehow still had left on a student Chase card issued me the previous year at the U. of A. It had only been thirty-six hours, and I was right back into gambling mode.

I tried telling myself that was an exception, but who was I fooling? It was typical addict behavior: escape one bad situation for a worse situation. It was two weeks before the Super Bowl. I was anticipating the game as if it was a national holiday. For me, it was. Super Sunday was the one game when you could get action equal to thirty games. The bookies took bets on everything from the first field goal to third quarter over-under.

On the Friday before the game, I was at the student union when a friend introduced me to a bookie who worked the campus.

Although his real name was Bill, he went by Roy. It fit him better. In his mid-twenties, he had short black hair, dressed preppie, and looked like an accountant. But when I looked into his eyes I saw that he was like every other bookie, all business, 100 percent greed. He preyed on students who thought they were players and hooked them for a couple thousand a semester. If he got a couple dozen, he made a great living through the school year.

He knew that I was different. I knew the lingo. But that didn't make me any better or more likely to win. By March 1, I owed Roy seventeen hundred dollars.

Broke, I took in a roommate to help me pay half of the seven hundred and eighty dollars a month rent. My new roommate was from Encino, California, and friendly with an old fraternity brother of mine from U. of A. But after moving in, he confessed to being flat broke and asked if I could spot him two months. I didn't care.

But I still needed to pay Roy. I could think of only one place to get that kind of money quickly.

I took Chris to the Golden Nickel. The Nickel was a ramshackle card club with room for bingo and a half dozen blackjack tables. They served food at a counter on paper plates and poured drinks in Styrofoam cups.

The clientele consisted of bingo junkies and hardcore card players whose idea of a time well spent was being hunched over a card table chain smoking for five hours.

I had several hundred dollars in my pocket, cash I'd raised by selling CDs that I'd collected since seventh grade and brought with me to Madison. I walked inside the casino feeling confident that I was going to multiply those hundreds at least tenfold, into enough to pay my bills and buy some room to breathe.

I'd never had such consistently bad cards dealt to me in my entire life. There wasn't a face card in the deck. I lost seventeen hands in a row.

I told the dealer that I was going to throw the table upside down if I lost one more hand. He gave me my next two cards, a six and a seven, and then said, "I think you're going to bust."

"Don't taunt me," I said. "Just give me a card. But I'm warning you, if I bust on something funny I'm going to grab your fucking neck."

"Okay," he said, grinning.

He gave me a ten. He turned up his cards. He had a six and a two. He then pulled five straight twos for an eighteen. He looked at me and laughed.

I immediately lunged over the table, attempted to grab his neck, and shoved him to the side. Then I started lifting my side of the table. Chris grabbed me before I was able to completely upend it and told me to get a grip. The pit boss ran over and threw me out of the casino. He said I was banned forever. It was messy.

I was shaken afterward. Since childhood, I'd always been quick to blow up and also to calm down. But I wasn't a violent individual. I'd never hit anyone in my life. However, something about that dealer's behavior set me off, and later I figured out what it had been. I couldn't tolerate being lied to. I hated when my father lied, when Jamie lied, and when this inconsequential dealer and the pit boss deceived me. The crazy part was that I would end up the biggest liar of all.

I went back to the Nickel two days later with one hundred dollars. The same pit boss saw me and hurried over to the table where I was about to settle myself. He took me aside.

"Are you calmed down yet?"

"Yes."

"Good."

"Just one question," I said. "Why doesn't it appear this is a straight game? There are no face cards."

He laughed, and I proceeded to lose my hundred dollars.

In the meantime, Roy began looking for me. He wanted his seventeen hundred dollars. Without any options, I went underground. I left my apartment and slept in Chris's dorm room. A year earlier, I'd slept on his brother Darren's sofa as I hid from the bookie Jake the Snake, who'd left an oily phone message saying, "So wassa matter, sweetheart? You don't wanna talk to me?" Roy found Chris and threatened to break his legs if I didn't pay. Chris relayed that to me with a worried look. I shrugged it off. I didn't think Roy would make good on his threat.

"He doesn't want to go to jail," I said.

"Can't you just come up with the money and shut him up?" Chris asked.

"Don't worry. Don't freak out. I'll come up with something."

Then, randomly, my father sent me three thousand dollars. I hadn't mentioned a thing about my situation during the few conversations we'd had. His check arrived unexpectedly in the mail with a brief note. He knew I could use it. Unsaid was the fact that he'd borrowed it. I preferred not to think about that. I was just irresponsibly grateful.

Flush, I rallied my friends Fish, Aaron, and a couple of others from different schools to take the Carnival Cruise Jubilee on the Mexican route for spring break. Why a cruise instead of South Padre Island or Daytona Beach? The cruise had gambling. The trip coincided with my birthday. One of the guys videotaped me that night in bed, totally baked, and muttering with half-opened eyes, "It's my birthday and all I've done is smoke weed and gamble . . . oh yeah, and gamble."

There's also a clip that same night of a girl named Nancy. She was from New Jersey and had wandered into my room after screwing my friend Brian from Penn. She pointed the longest, cheesiest, hot pink fake fingernail at me and in a thickly accented voice said, "Adam Resnick, you're going to get into trouble one day with that gambling. I've known you four hours and I can tell."

I laughed nervously at her remark. My friends began telling stories about me in high school. They painted me as everyone's good time. It was clear that I hadn't changed, though the stakes had.

"What have we done so far on this cruise?" Fish asked.

"I don't know," I said.

"We've chased girls," he said. "And what have you done every night?"

"I've played blackjack." I paused to think if I could come up with anything else. "I went out to dinner with you guys when we were in port."

"Only because the casino's closed when we're in port, jackass."

I was content. I didn't start losing until the last night of the week-long cruise. That night nothing came up right. I'd win one and lose three. My money was disappearing fast. The pit boss was a five-ten beauty from London named Samantha. We'd flirted the entire cruise. She stood behind the dealer and began to signal me subtly whether to hit or to stay. Fish joined in for a few hands and left with a fistful of cash. I still lost.

At nearly 2 AM, moments before the casino closed, Samantha left her post behind the dealer without saying anything to me. She swept through the casino, pausing to say goodnight to an energetic group still at the roulette table and a couple of other regulars at the slots. I didn't notice her slide up behind me until I felt a hand on my shoulder. I looked up. She smiled and let her fingernails tickle my neck.

"You haven't had any fun yet," she said. "Let's get a drink."

We went to the bar. Samantha was hands-down the hottest female on the ship, but at the time I was unaware of the coincidence that the only chick I'd picked up the whole week was connected to the cards.

"How many cruises have you been on?" she asked.

"This is my third," I said.

"Have you ever seen where the crew sleeps?"

"No."

Her face softened. I noticed her eyes were large and turquoise blue and her lips were full.

"Would you like to?" she asked in a softer tone.

"Of course."

I was nervous as I followed her downstairs. I kept my nerves in check by staring at her perfect ass. We got to her room without anyone noticing, but first I had to pee. When I came out of the bathroom after washing my hands three times from the grime of the poker chips, Samantha was lying flat on her bed completely naked and smiling at me. I crept out at 6:30 AM after one of the best sexual experiences of my life. I was on a flight to Madison at eleven.

In April, I started to bet baseball with Roy. He took up to a thousand dollars a game, and I won fourteen games in a row betting the limit. He was pissed. He wanted to know if I had inside info, if I was on the straight. I reminded him that I lost 90 percent of the time. My hot streak was an anomaly.

"Bro, let me enjoy this for a fucking second," I said.

He paid promptly, and all in hundreds—one hundred forty of them. It felt heavy. I rolled it up, and the roll had heft. I'd never held that much money. Fourteen thousand dollars. To me, it was the equivalent of four or five cocktails or an ounce of coke. I was intoxicated by the possibilities it afforded.

But only one possibility made any sense to me. I rallied five guys from campus, including Bino and Brett, for a four-day getaway to Las Vegas. We drove the hundred miles to Chicago, where we caught the flight to Vegas. I was the only one of us who'd been to Vegas. I told stories and created an exciting picture of the Strip. Not that I'd seen much beyond the casino. I gambled thirty to forty hours straight, then left, burnt.

"One thing," I told the guys. "While we're in Vegas, I'm Jonathan Resnick."

"Jonathan?" Bino asked.

"My older brother," I said. "I have a fake ID. I'm not twenty-one yet."

"You're not twenty-one? Shit, you live like you're forty-two."

I put my hand up.

"Enough said. I'm Jonathan."

Once in Vegas, Jonathan Resnick signed for a top-floor suite at Caesar's. Amid excited shouts of "livin' large," I led my friends into the enormous suite, which boasted a Jacuzzi tub in the center of the living room and mirrors above the beds. Lighting up cigars, which I'd also bought for them (I didn't smoke), they fantasized about a *Risky Business*–type weekend. I promised them a great time.

There was one problem. Within four hours, I lost my entire fourteen grand at the blackjack table. I left the table determined to find a way to keep playing; I wasn't finished. I sought out Bino and the others in the casino. They couldn't believe I'd run through all my money. I asked them for some credit off their credit cards. Most had cards that were paid for by their parents. They were reluctant to turn over their credit, if they even knew how. I tried jawing them into submission.

"No fucking way, Resnick," Brett said. "My father would kill me. Then he would kill you."

"Don't be a pussy," I said. "I'm going to pay you back."

"You're going to lose it."

After ranting for twenty minutes, I ended up with two thousand dollars from Bino's Amex. I went back to the table, promptly lost every cent, and cut our trip short.

My friends were doubly pissed off at me. One for losing the money, and two for ruining the trip.

On the way back, I got Roy on the phone and tried to make back my losses. By the time we landed, I owed him four thousand dollars. I was whacked, and I knew it. I tried to think how I could pay off Roy so I could continue to play. I was out of options. He called two days later and said he was coming by to pick up the money.

"I don't have it," I said.

"You better have it," he said.

"I don't."

He didn't say anything for the longest time. I could hear him breathe.

"You little fucking rat," he said finally. "I just gave you fourteen grand. I am going to kill you. Have it by Friday or you're dead."

As the panic wore off, I spiraled into a funk. I laid down on the bed in my apartment with the lights off. It seemed hopeless. I was overdrawn at the bank, I'd used up my credit card, and I'd put friendships on the line by using their credit cards. With no place else to turn, I called my father and told him that I needed money. I knew if he had the cash he'd give it to me without asking for an explanation, and I was right. He wired the money the next day.

For the rest of my sophomore year and into June 1992, other than card game at a frat house or dorm, I limited my gambling to the Golden Nickel. I stayed in Madison for the summer and went to the casino every day. My father gave me rent, so I didn't have to work. I also won more than I lost at the Nickel. It was a good time.

In July, I met my future wife, Meredith Siegel. I was hanging out with two other girls at the time, Abby, a freshman, and Nicole, a senior, when I saw Meredith at my friend Bino's apartment. It was a warm summer night, and he was having a barbecue. There were about twenty-five people at his place. Meredith was in the kitchen. I was in his living room. I spotted her from across the room. She was blond, with a great figure and a bright smile. She wore a T-shirt and jeans. She looked fantastic. Our eyes met, and we smiled at each other.

"That girl Meredith likes you," Bino's roommate told me later. "She remembered seeing you before."

"Yeah, it was last fall when I visited Devo."

Meredith and I hung out several times over the next couple weeks. We always went out with a group of friends, but the two of us paired up by the end of the evening. She was the oldest of three children from a close Chicago family. Her father was a successful attorney and her mother was a homemaker. Meredith had a nice way that put me at ease within myself. I wanted to be around her. Even when I was out with Abby or Nicole, I wondered what Meredith was doing.

Toward the end of July, Meredith went home to Chicago to have foot surgery. As soon as she left, I began going to the Nickel again, filling my emptiness with blackjack. Then Roy disappeared on me. He owed me two thousand dollars. When I got hold of him, he told me to fuck off. I never heard from him again.

In August, as students returned for the start of school, I still hadn't found a new bookie. One night, I was playing darts for dough at the Kollege

Klub, longtime favorite bar for students in Madison. The KK was a typical college bar, with wood-paneled walls, a dart board, and a long wood bar with neon signs for Lite, Miller, Old Style, and Bacardi.

After darts, I sat down with some friends. The KK was packed, and a fight broke out between several varsity football players and some drunken fraternity assholes. I heard shouting, then a commotion right behind me. As I turned to see what was going on, I was hit on the side of my head. The blow was so hard it spun me out of my chair and onto the floor.

I felt woozy when I tried to get up, like there was a massive blood rush into my head. I stayed down for a few minutes and felt my face, which pulsed with pain. Luckily, I didn't appear to be bleeding. I felt the top of my head and my Los Angeles Lakers hat was gone. That freaked me out more than getting hit.

"Where's my hat?" I asked various friends standing over me.

A girl I knew rushed over sweetly and gave it to me.

"I was waiting for you to come to," she said. "Are you okay?"

After applying a bag of ice, I started to feel better. Then my food, along with the stuff my friends had ordered, was brought out from the kitchen. I was finishing my burger when I spied a flash of blond hair, like a burst of light, and cautiously turned to look. I didn't know if I was dreaming or had a concussion or a sense that I was about to get hit again.

It was more a combination of all of the above. I hadn't seen Meredith since she went home to have foot surgery at the end of July, and suddenly there she was, entering the KK. She arrived with two girlfriends, both of whom sashayed down the stairs and into the crowd. Meredith paused at the top, either inspecting the scene or just taking her time after foot surgery. She wore a clunky boot on her right foot.

The moment I saw her, I knew I wanted her. I realized how much I'd missed her, how deeply intrigued I was by her, and also how uninterested I was in Abby and Nicole. Nothing against them. They were hot in their own right. But Meredith made me feel something different.

I stood up at my table, leaving my friends in mid-conversation, and intercepted Meredith before she got all the way down the stairs. I put my hand on her shoulder, said hello, and with only a slight tilt of my head said, "Come with me." Without saying a word, she turned around, followed me outside, into a cab, and we went back to my apartment.

Though we didn't complete our intimacy for several months, Meredith ended up in my bedroom and spent the night. Most of that time we talked, deeply, personally, endlessly. I took her clothes off slowly. I wanted to prolong the unveiling of a picture that had occupied my fantasies since the night we'd exchanged smiles nearly three months ago. She had the smoothest skin I'd seen in my life, like porcelain, but with a creamy tan. She also smelled so good.

I fell asleep knowing that I was in love. It took Meredith longer. The more time we spent together, the more stories she heard about me. Most were gambling related. They weren't necessarily funny, but they were entertaining. What other college student had had his life threatened by bookies not once but twice? She'd listen, sometimes amused, sometimes incredulous, but more often than not she'd ask me to clarify fact from fiction. I assured her it was all true.

Between the two of us, she was the first to say I love you. We were in a bowling alley with Bino and his girlfriend Ellen (who would later marry my friend Matt Rudnick). The four of us were wasted from drinking sake bombs at a Japanese steak house beforehand. After I rolled a gutter ball, Meredith threw her arms around me and said, "I love you."

I kissed her, then playfully held her at arm's length.

"Don't tell me that when you're drunk," I said. "Tell me in the morning."

I hugged her, and she laughed.

"No, I really love you."

"You're drunk."

"But I love you."

"Let's see in the morning."

We crashed at my place and slept late. I saw her looking at me when I opened my eyes the next day.

"Well?" I said.

She looked confused. "What?"

"Well?"

"What are you talking about?" she said.

"What you said last night."

"Just kidding," she cracked up. "I love you."

I wrapped my arms around her.

"I love you too."

But there was competition. In fall 1992 a new bigger, brighter casino opened in the Wisconsin Dells. Called Ho-Chunk, it was forty-five minutes from campus. Ho-Chunk advertised all over school. I went the opening night after picking up Meredith at the library and dropping her off at her apartment. I went the next night too. Soon, hooked by the excitement and newness, I made it a matter of routine. I waited until Meredith fell asleep, then I split. Once football season started, I found a new bookie. I got into trouble that first weekend. Nothing serious, just in over my head.

The problem was that Meredith had never witnessed me in action, or struggling to stay in action, and I had never been involved with anyone who I wanted to be with almost as much as I wanted to gamble. I felt the conflict internally. I had no idea if it was obvious to anyone else. I'd never before given a moment's pause to see how anyone perceived me, my gambling, or the situation in which I put myself by owing money.

Did my mood change? Did I talk incessantly? Did I worry out loud? Did I turn into a liar? A manipulator?

I didn't have any idea. Nor had I thought about it.

I told her about the money I owed the bookie and my scramble to come up with the cash to pay him.

"Why would you do that?" she asked.

"It's not like I planned it. That stuff just happens."

"But the risk doesn't seem worth it."

"Sometimes it is."

"I don't understand the lure or why you think it's fun when it puts you in this spot where you're freaking out."

"Am I freaking out? I don't think I am."

Cut to the next night, a Friday and the start of the weekend. Meredith slid into the front seat of my car looking drop-dead gorgeous. Pick any Hollywood blond and I thought my girlfriend was hotter. I'd pulled up in front of her place at night for what was officially our second actual date. Date—as in going out on the town by ourselves for a romantic evening. I had an 8 PM dinner reservation at the Blue Marlin, the nicest seafood restaurant in town. I had a Caesar salad and Australian carpetbag steak. Meredith ordered a salad and salmon, even though I tried to talk her into the lobster. For dessert, we shared a chocolate soufflé.

"With me, it's always chocolate," I said, smiling, as I plunged my spoon into the hot dish. "Awwwwwh."

"It is good," she said. "I didn't eat dessert until I met you."

I took another spoonful and let it sit on my tongue.

"I'm in ecstasy."

We spent another half hour enjoying each other's company. I paid the bill, but I wasn't ready for the evening to end. If we went back to my place, we'd fool around and then Meredith would fall asleep. It was too early for that. I asked what she wanted to do after dinner.

"Something new," she said.

"What?"

"We're going someplace new. I already looked into it."

"You won't tell me?"

"Trust me."

"Just tell me."

Meredith leaned forward and put her hand on top of mine. She said she hadn't slept all night after hearing that I owed money to a bookie. It scared her. In the morning, she'd researched gambling addiction, realized I fit several of the criteria (preoccupation, chasing), and found a Gambler's Anonymous meeting on campus. That was the "someplace new" we were going.

"I'm not saying I won't go, but what if I don't want to?" I asked.

"You have a problem. You're out of control for a kid in college. I don't know anyone who even *knows* a bookie."

"You may and not know it."

"Adam, that's beside the point. I care about you. I love you. You should try to help yourself before you get any more out of control."

"Let's go," I said.

We got in the car and Meredith directed me back onto campus. The GA meeting was in an old building on University Avenue. We smelled the cigarette smoke from far down the hallway as we approached the designated room, which was filled with an acrid, gray cloud when we walked in. Meredith, an occasional social puffer, glanced at me, knowing I despised the smell of cigarette smoke. I winced. We sat next to each other on brown metal folding chairs and looked around. A man appearing to be in his early forties said hi as he took a seat nearby. We tried to gauge what we'd gotten ourselves into; it felt like we had walked into the wrong bar.

About twenty-five people showed up for the meeting. They were mostly male; they were all older than us; and they lacked the resilient glint of youth that Meredith and I had at twenty years of age. I felt like I was at a meeting for crack addicts.

"I don't like this," I mumbled to Meredith.

She nodded. She was freaked out. Three minutes into the meeting we looked at each other, got up, and left. Once we were back in the car, I thanked her for caring enough about me to have taken me to a GA meeting. No one else had ever done or said as much, including my parents. I gave her a kiss.

"I'm just not like those people in that room," I said. "The last thing in the world I want is to end up like those losers."

I didn't realize that I was the biggest one in the room.

10

THIS ISN'T NORMAL

I didn't see what the big deal was; I just wanted to cheat off her paper.

It was the end of October of my junior year, and Meredith and I were scheduled to take a midterm in a class we had together. She was already in class when I arrived, talking to friends. It was one of the few times I'd been to the class. I took the empty seat next to her and asked if I could cheat off her paper.

I should've known better. Before the first time we had sex, she made me call my internist in Milwaukee and prove that I had an AIDS test that came back negative. Not romantic, but definitely responsible.

Meredith looked at me as if I should have known her better—and I should have. She was a serious student, on track to graduate in three-and-a-half years. She didn't cheat. Never. Period. She sat back and shook her head, letting me know she was insulted that I'd asked and disappointed that I hadn't prepared.

I didn't care. I slammed my hand on top of the desk.

"You're a freaking idiot," I said. "I'm so much smarter than you. You think you know everything."

"Adam. Stop it."

Her friends sitting nearby turned away or looked down at their desks, embarrassed for her.

"School doesn't mean shit," I continued. "My father went to law school and medical school and look where it got him."

"Please stop, Adam."

"Don't shush me. I drive you to classes. I take you to nice dinners. I sleep with you. And you won't let me copy off your paper?"

She wanted to die. And I didn't stop my tirade until I'd demonstrated to everyone that I was a jerk. I went back to my apartment and planned a trip to Tucson. Using Continental Airlines vouchers Bino had given me, I booked a route from Milwaukee to Houston to Tucson and left the next day without having said a word to Meredith. I couldn't remember the last time I'd gone twenty-four hours without talking to her.

This time I was mad at her and I was not going to call. I wanted her to apologize to me. For what? For not helping me cheat?

I fought the urge to call her the four days I was in Tucson even though I wanted to hear her voice more than anything. The desire was almost crippling. I knew that she would chastise me, I'd argue, she'd prove me wrong, and eventually we'd make up. That's how our fights had played out before, and I was ready to go through it.

I decided to fly back on November 4. I went to the airport early and called Meredith from the pay phone. She hung up the second she heard my voice. I called again with the same result. And again and again and again. It seemed as if I called her a thousand times. Finally she let me talk.

"I'm on my way back," I said.

"I don't know where you've been," she said. "But don't rush home for me. We are finished."

Click.

I called back another dozen or so times without getting an answer. I finally gave up. I slammed the receiver down and stood in front of the bank pay phones, trying to cool off. A middle-aged couple seated across from me stared. I must've been louder than I realized. I glanced up at the list of departing flights and saw mine was on time. I still needed to check in, I realized.

I gave the ticket agent my name and certificate/ticket and waited while she looked me up on the computer. She shook her head, letting me know there was a problem.

"Your name doesn't match the name on the certificate," she said.

"It belongs to my friend, and he let me use it," I explained, trying not to lose the last shreds of patience I had left. "It wasn't a problem when I flew out here from Milwaukee. It shouldn't be a problem now. I just want to fly home. The ticket is good, right?"

"The ticket is valid, but it's not your name," she said.

"That shouldn't matter."

"But it does."

"So you aren't giving me a ticket."

"Not with this." She tapped her finger on the certificate and pushed it toward me. "You can buy a new ticket for eight hundred and fifty dollars if you want."

"That's bullshit," I said. "It doesn't cost you anything to give me the ticket. And I paid for the fee."

I slapped the side of her computer terminal. I could feel myself starting to lose control. All I could think about was getting back to Meredith, so I could get some control over the situation.

"You'd better calm down," she said.

"I don't care," I said. "You'd better get me on the fucking plane."

The ticket agent summoned a supervisor, who was more adamant about not letting me on the flight unless I had a new ticket. I didn't understand why they were being such major league assholes. Nor did I have the patience to take it. I was obsessed with getting home and talk sense to my girlfriend, and these people were making that impossible. I lost control. I picked up their computer and threw it on the floor. It shattered with a startling crash that caused heads to turn and people to stop. I started to walk away from the counter when I was blindsided by three large sheriffs. They picked me up and, as one of them squeezed my nut sack, they body-slammed me to the ground.

"Police brutality!" I screamed. "I need a witness."

They took me to the Pima County Jail and locked me up. I sat on the floor in the cell for a while, nursing a painful right shoulder, which the deputies had separated when they slammed me down. I stared at the concrete floor and decompressed. I couldn't believe Meredith had broken up with me . . . then the scene at the airport . . . and now I was in jail! What had I done to deserve this?

After about an hour, a cop called my name and led me into a private room. The room was bare, with cold, white walls, a table and chairs, a large bulletin board, and a couple stacks of paper coffee cups on a counter. He told me to sit on one of the four metal chairs at the table. I felt like I was on a TV set. Everything thus far had seemed surreal, so why not the room? The cop, who looked to be in his late thirties, was affable as he asked about where I lived and what I'd been doing in Tucson.

I went along respectfully, but in the midst of answering I thought of something that might possibly get me out of jail.

"Look officer, I admit what I did was wrong, absolutely, 100 percent wrong and I'm willing to pay for any damages," I said. "But I need to go home today."

"I don't know if that's possible," he replied.

"Let's talk about it for a second. I'm thinking that I won't press charges against the sheriff's department for police brutality if the charges against me are dropped."

"What are you talking about?"

"I didn't resist arrest. I was never told to stop, halt, or anything. I was standing in the terminal when I was tackled and roughed up by your deputies. There are witnesses who heard me scream 'police brutality' and call for help. Plus, my face is cut, I have blood all over my shirt, I'm bruised, and my shoulder is separated. If I were you, I'd at least talk this over with your supervisor."

He stopped and stared at me in sheer disbelief. I looked back with a stern poker face. I wasn't kidding.

"You're serious?"

"They beat the living shit out of me," I said. "Look, I'm bleeding. My shirt is torn. I'm dead fucking serious."

"I'll be right back," he said.

Two hours later I got into a taxi in front of the Pima County Jail. Case number CR 92 513155, charges of disorderly conduct against Adam B. Resnick, had been dropped. I went to my friend Gary's and stayed another day in Tucson, cooling off and making proper flight arrangements.

Gary and my other friends found a bright side to the matter.

"Now, thank God, you have to throw out that crappy T-shirt you wear every day," he said.

He was referring to the black and white tie-dyed reggae T-shirt I was wearing. I must have worn that shirt four times a week. It was paper-thin from having being washed and worn so often. I looked down at how badly my favorite shirt had been ripped and bloodied in the scuffle.

"I'll have it sewn and it'll wash out," I said.

"You're an idiot," he said.

Before Thanksgiving break, Meredith had warmed up enough for me to talk my way back into our relationship. But there was no mistaking that I was on trial with her. During the make-up process, she hit me with a litany of grievances that gave me pause. She made it clear that she knew I was a wonderful guy, a person she loved deeply, but she also said her love wasn't unconditional and I had to make some drastic changes if we were to stay together.

I knew she was right, and I vowed to quit gambling. I knew my gambling was at the root of our problems. I loved Meredith. I'd do whatever was necessary.

I decided to go abroad for the rest of my junior year. Though the deadline for applying had passed, I talked my way into the university's program in Spain. I knew a handful of people going, Seville sounded nice, and Spanish had been one of the few courses I'd enjoyed in high school. My teacher, Mrs. Schulte, had been warm and affectionate. Her husband had had the first heart transplant in the state's history. I'd gone to his funeral.

In the back of my head, I had an ulterior motive for signing up. I wanted, hoped, and half-expected Meredith to ask me not to go. I wanted to hear her say she was going to miss me too much. Instead she encouraged me to have fun, attend classes, and stay out of trouble.

"I don't think they have gambling there," I said.

"Good," she replied.

Two days before leaving, I had to scramble to get an emergency passport. The one I'd used since childhood had expired. Though I made it on the plane, I had a severe anxiety attack the minute the plane took off. I thought about summoning the flight attendant and telling her I was having a heart attack so the pilot would turn the plane around. Instead I took a Xanax my father had slipped me at the airport when I'd mentioned being nervous. He was like a magician. I could've used a couple more after the plane landed in Seville.

"What the fuck am I doing here?" I said to no one in particular as I stood outside the airport.

I never figured it out.

The program was supposed to last a semester, from January through June. I was supposed to live with a Spanish family. I found the house assigned to me, a walk-up owned by a woman with an older son who was away. It was old, dirty, and very cold. Every room had a draft, her one heater in the kitchen was broken, and there was no hot water. I didn't want to touch anything.

I didn't like my bunkmate. We spent thirty minutes getting to know each other, and another thirty minutes realizing we had nothing in common.

School started immediately. I registered for one class, as opposed to the three that comprised a full load. I missed the second day of class. On the third day, I received a note saying I needed to sign up for more classes. Homesick, I'd spent the day in the El Corte Englais department store, scouring the place for anything that would make me feel better. I found American-style Linzer cookies in the basement and walked around the store eating them by the box. I filled up on them because I hated the food prepared by the woman I lived with.

I called Meredith four times a day.

"It's not working for me," I complained between cookies.

"You need to try," she said.

"The food where I'm living disgusts me. Everything has ham or ham-flavoring in it. They even make potato chips with ham flavoring in Spain. How much ham can a man eat? I ate three boxes of Linzer cookies yesterday."

"Buy some food."

"I miss you. You're all I think about."

"I miss you too. But it's good for you to have some space."

"How much do you miss me?"

"Adam, you've called me two times today. We've already gone through this."

I was talking to her from a pay phone in a dingy area of Seville, lined with decrepit apartment buildings, on a street that was half paved and half dirt, when suddenly I heard a gunshot. I'd never heard a real gunshot before, but the sound was unmistakable. It scared the crap out of me, too. It was the only thing that made me stop talking to her.

Without a word to Meredith, I slammed the phone and ran for safety. Ten minutes later, I called her back. I told her what happened, making it appear that I'd come close to losing my life in an effort to talk with her. I wanted her to know the lengths I'd go to just to hear her voice.

"Be careful, Adam," she said. "I want to go back to sleep. It's still early in the morning here."

I felt unloved and uncomfortable. I had to do something about my living situation if I had any hope of staying in Spain for the next six months. I walked around a commercial area of the city until dark. It seemed every fifth store I passed had a sign in the window or out front saying La Rebajas. At a restaurant/bar that night with some other American students I asked if they knew where people like the Rebajases lived. If they owned all those stores with their name in the window, I figured they had to be rich, and I wanted to find a place to live in their neighborhood.

"Do you know what *rebajas* means?" a girl asked.

"It's the name of some wealthy family."

"No it's not," she said, laughing. "It means they're having a sale. Those signs you've seen all over mean those stores are having a sale."

That was it. The next day I called Meredith's roommate, Karen, and told her I was coming back early.

"When?" she asked.

"Tomorrow."

"Oh my God. Does Meredith know?"

"No, and don't tell her, okay? I want to surprise her."

I didn't realize that when I'd said "don't tell her" I was echoing my father's oft-used refrain, "Don't tell your mother." I also didn't realize that by leaving Spain I was repeating a pattern of escaping problematic situations rather than solving them, as I'd done by leaving home for Tucson, then Tucson for Madison, then Madison for Seville, and now Seville for Madison. I bought a one-way plane ticket for fourteen hundred dollars and left without telling anyone in the program.

After landing in Chicago, I took a bus to Madison, went to my apartment, which I'd kept, showered and changed into nice clothes I'd bought in Spain, and drove to Meredith's. She was studying when I walked in, her head buried in a book, a yellow highlighter in her hand. It was snowing very heavily outside, and Meredith had on a heavy blue sweater. I thought she looked gorgeous. She saw me out of the corner of her eye, looked up, and froze for thirty seconds.

"What are you doing *here*?"

"I came back. I wanted to surprise you."

"This isn't normal."

"That's not exactly the reaction I'd hoped to get. I thought you'd be happy to see me. Isn't this what you want?"

She buried her head in her hands and rubbed her eyes before turning her attention back to me.

"Adam, I don't know what to say. You were supposed to be gone six months. You're back after six days. Honestly, I don't know what I want."

There was a long silence. I felt like shit, but I didn't want to fight with Meredith. I lied and told her I had to go meet Bino.

"That's good," she said. "I'm kind of freaked out. Let's talk tomorrow. I need to get used to the idea that you're back."

We kissed good-bye. It was icy.

I saw Bino later that night. I slipped on his front walk and popped my shoulder again. I ended up at the University Medical Center with my arm in a sling. It was a terrible night. My parents were angry the next day when I called from my kitchen to tell them I'd returned from Spain.

"You never follow through on anything," my mother said.

"Neither do you guys," I said, shoveling ice cream into my mouth straight from the container.

I gave Meredith space. We talked on the phone and then saw each other. Within a couple of weeks, we were back in a good place. I re-registered for classes, but I didn't have any purpose or direction other than Meredith. By February, I was back at Ho-Chunk most days and some nights. I also found a new bookie, a student from New York. Steve Green was a year older than me and in a fraternity. We hung out at a local bar, where he made it a habit to pay for drinks and food. It made him feel less guilty about the thousands of dollars he took from me.

But at the end of May, as school wound down, I was up nearly thirty-two hundred dollars. It was a huge reversal of fortune from the previous months. The timing was perfect. With summer ahead, that money would enable me to stay in Madison without having to get a job. I called Green to arrange a place where he could pay me.

"Sorry, but I already went home for the summer," he said. "I'll pay you when I get back."

"Are you fucking nuts?" I screamed. "I lost eight weeks in a row and paid you. Now you're not paying me the one week you owe me. That's bull-shit."

"Sorry, dude. I'm gone."

"Your answer is totally unacceptable. I need this money."

"What the fuck are you going to do about it?"

"I don't know," I said. "I'll figure out something."

I don't know why, but I had a feeling that Green had lied to me about being home. It was early afternoon, and I drove to his place on Gilman Avenue. He lived in a two-story brick apartment building. He and his two roommates had the three bedrooms on the ground floor. Fortunately for me, Green's room was by the street. I looked through his window and saw his stuff was still in his room. I saw a couple of boxes and a steamer trunk on the floor. The window was open a crack. I yelled inside.

"Green, are you here, you dick?"

When no one answered, I opened the window and crawled inside, and decided I was going to take anything of value and sell it. Nothing jumped out at first glance. I opened one of his desk drawers and a slender red UW checkbook cover sat in the front. I picked it up and saw it was full of checks. I used his phone to call the bank and found there was enough in his account to clear what he owed me. I wrote a check for that exact amount and cashed it.

Amazingly, it cleared, and I called Green to let him know.

"What's your fucking problem?" he asked.

"Why don't you check your checking account balance, you piece of shit?"

We never spoke again.

11

A GOOD GUY

April 26, 2003.

I was at my brother-in-law's wedding at the Ritz Carlton Hotel in Palm Beach, Florida. Someone came up behind me and put his arm around me. I turned and recognized Green. It was the first time I'd seen or spoken to him since I'd settled his debt to me. I think he still feared me. But we laughed about old times. He ran a successful investment company. I was awaiting trial after the collapse of Universal Federal Savings and Loan. He'd read about my situation in the newspaper.

"I knew you were a good guy," he said. "I knew you were sick. I should've done something about it. Maybe you wouldn't have been in this situation."

He felt awful. I saw it in his eyes.

I didn't want him to feel responsible.

"Hey, I was the one making the choices," I said. I put a hand on his shoulder and squeezed. "It's inherently more natural, and easier, to be an enabler then an intervener. If the opposite were true, society would be better off."

12

THE HEART OF THE MATTER

I lied to Meredith about signing up for classes.

Following a summer in Madison during which gambling dominated my time, energy, and thoughts—and my roommates couldn't stop making snide comments about my problem—I was glad for the return of fall and the influx of students. It was as if the changing colors of the leaves signaled a fresh start. With more people in town, there was life on the streets. Restaurants and bars were full at night, and the campus was a fun place to hang out in the daytime.

Meredith's and my friends were talking about graduation in June. Meredith had worked hard enough to graduate ahead of schedule in December. I joked my way through those conversations. I didn't want to face my reality. I had credits equivalent to a sophomore. My parents never asked to see my grades. I never had to answer to anyone about school—anyone other than Meredith, that is.

"Did you sign up for classes?" she asked.

"Yeah," I said, naming a bunch of courses.

The truth was, I'd pocketed the two thousand dollars my father had sent for tuition and skipped registration. I'd thrown in the towel on my education without telling anyone. I felt terribly guilty for lying to Meredith. Telling her that I hadn't been to the casino when I had was one thing. It was another, more serious thing to make her believe that I was on track to graduate and move on to the next phase of life when that wasn't true. But I didn't feel like I had a choice. I didn't know how to tell the truth. I didn't know what the truth was. If I did, I wasn't going to admit it.

I got depressed whenever I thought about the future. After graduation, Meredith planned on moving to Chicago, where she had a job lined up with her father's law firm before going to graduate school. Where did that leave us? What was I going to do? I didn't have plans. I didn't know how to communicate these concerns. The issues piled up and turned into anxiety. I ended up dealing with them at Ho-Chunk.

Meredith was too busy to keep track of my whereabouts, and I always found one thing or another to say that kept us from the truth. There was one time I 'fessed up. I needed five hundred dollars to cover some checks, and I didn't have anyplace to get it quickly. I turned to Meredith when she came over that night. She was a rational, responsible girl. Overdrawing on a checking account was common among college students, but it wasn't something she did.

"I need, uh, five hundred dollars," I said.

She sat down on the sofa and straightened a pile of books and magazines on the coffee table.

"I'm going to let you borrow it," she said. "I have that in my checking account. My father gave it to me for a cushion. I haven't used it."

"I don't want to take your money," I said. "I've never taken any money from you and I don't want to start now."

"It's okay," she said.

"You seem apprehensive."

"This isn't going to one of your gambling things, is it?"

"You mean a casino or a bookie?"

"Yeah, that's what I mean. It's not going to one of them, is it?"

"No, I swear," I said. "It's going to cover checks."

Why I needed to cover the checks was another story. But technically, I told myself, I hadn't lied.

The next day we drove together to the bank. Meredith wanted to make sure that the money ended up at the bank, not at Ho-Chunk. Knowing she didn't trust me was devastating, and yet it confirmed the deep-seated fear that I wasn't worth trusting because I wasn't good. I paid Meredith back from a day's winning at Ho-Chunk. I didn't tell her where I'd gotten the money. She didn't ask either. I felt like I'd proved a point. But she was so entrenched in her final exams and planning for her family to attend her graduation that I felt like she didn't appreciate my effort.

"You're not normal," she said at dinner after I'd accused her of seeming distant and cold. "Everyone goes to class. You drive them to class."

"Yeah."

"It's weird. It's not right. You have to do something. You can't gamble all day every day. It's not a life."

"Thank you for the lecture," I snapped. "I know it's not a life. It's not how I'm going to spend the rest of my life. I'm in college now."

"We're almost done with college and you aren't planning for the future. It's like everyone else has grown up except you. You're still in high school."

"It'll work out."

By December, Meredith was fed up with me. The closer her graduation got, the more problems I created. As for graduation itself, her parents were coming up for the ceremony and hosting a small dinner afterward. I planned on sitting with her family and sharing in the celebration. I was a pain in the ass the night before, obviously embarrassed by my own failures and subconsciously taking it out on Meredith. I went AWOL the next day. Another quick escape. I started out at Ho-Chunk, then watched the Green Bay Packers playoff game from a bar. The Packers were my team. I'd made a large bet and was glued to the TV. I never made it to her graduation.

Before leaving Madison, Meredith gave me an ultimatum—it was gambling or her.

I celebrated New Year's alone. "1994," I told myself flipping the calendar. "Happy New Year!"

I stayed in my apartment and worked on fixing my credit. After a month-long hiatus, Meredith came up on weekends and we had some romantic nights. It was a perfect arrangement—no school, gambling on weeknights without having to lie to Meredith, and sleeping with her on weekends—and it lasted until June when she dropped the breakup bomb again. It turned out that her parents wanted her to take a break, especially from me, before starting graduate school in the fall, so she'd arranged to spend the summer traveling around Europe with some girlfriends.

On the day before she left, I "accidentally" bumped into her inside the tunnel of the Prudential Tower where she worked. It was lunchtime, and Meredith was a creature of habit. I knew where she ate, the route she took, and I made sure I was on that same path at that hour so we'd run into each other. She might not have wanted to see me, but I knew she wouldn't be able to resist, and I was right.

We had a good visit over lunch, but she made her intentions clear. She was going away, and that meant away from me. She didn't want to speak to me until she returned eight weeks later. She also warned me not to track her down in Europe, call obsessively, or do anything crazy.

I kissed her good-bye and wished her a fun time—but not *too* fun.

I flip-flopped between Milwaukee and Madison and worked as a tele-marketer selling insurance. I turned my first ten calls into sales. My boss, an acquaintance of my father from whom he'd borrowed a chunk of money, loved me. After my first call, he said, "You're unbelievable." But the quick success didn't sustain my interest. The combination of boredom, arrogance, and anxiety caused me to self-destruct on the job. I quit.

I was trying to figure out what else I could do with myself when I got into a fight with my parents. My father was pissed that I'd quit on a guy who'd bailed him out numerous times. They were also furious at me for my lack of direction and ambition. For all their shortcomings, my parents had a point. I was always criticizing them, and yet what was I doing with my life?

Fine. I'd show them. I took everything I owned, crammed it all into a white Toyota Camry that belonged to my parents, and drove to my brother's in Chicago. I parked outside his apartment building, on the east side of Clark Street, in front of the Mercedes dealership, Loeber Motors. He'd recently started his first job out of law school, so he was gone all day and didn't get home until late at night. I laid out by the pool, got sunburned à la John Candy in *Summer Rental*, and slept on his couch.

The next morning I went outside to get a bag of clothes out of my car so I could shower and change, and I found that the windshield was smashed. I didn't even have to look inside to know what had happened. Everything was stolen except for a few CDs. All my clothes, photographs, stereo—everything—it was all gone.

I called my father feeling like an injured dog, done and defeated. I stared at the floor as I told him what happened.

"It may not be that bad," he said.

"Uh, why? Everything I had is gone."

"I have a homeowner's policy that will probably cover it."

He was right. I called his carrier, American Family Insurance, and a helpful agent took down every item that had been stolen. Within forty-eight hours, I had a check for thirteen thousand dollars. It was an auspicious reversal of fortune. My father advised me to get an apartment and enjoy the summer before I looked for a job. That's what kids did after four hard years of college.

Of course my college experience had been a joke. But who was I to argue? With clean credit, new cards, and this unforeseen windfall, it was a fresh start. I opened a checking account at First Chicago Bank and rented an apartment in my brother's building, the Clark Elm Apartments at 1122 North Clark. I spent my first month in the apartment on the sofa, watching the O.J. Simpson saga unravel on TV. I tore myself away from the drama when my dad tipped me off to a small company looking for a salesperson for a medical device used by cancer patients.

It turned out not to be a company but a guy in his forties who subcontracted sales of a lymphedema pump, a device doctors prescribed to patients with chronic, intractable lymphedema, a swelling in soft tissue areas in arms and legs from an accumulation of lymphatic fluids. It occurs after lymph nodes in those areas have been removed or damaged in surgery or radiation. Fifteen to 20 percent of breast cancer patients develop lymphedema following removal of their lymph nodes.

My boss hired me as an independent contractor and agreed to pay four hundred dollars for every pump I sold.

That sounded good—until I learned that the average sales guy sold fifty to sixty pumps a year. That equaled twenty-four thousand dollars annually. I couldn't live on so little. It would've taken me two or three years just to cover a year's worth of rent and utilities.

But my boss was successful. I asked myself where all the money was.

I did my due diligence and found that I could buy the pumps for twelve hundred dollars apiece, for net-thirty terms, meaning I had thirty days to pay. I could get reimbursed fifty-two hundred dollars per pump from the government, for a profit of four thousand dollars a pump. The best part was the Indianapolis-based DMERC—Durable Medical Equipment Regional Carrier—would pay within fourteen days after I submitted a doctor's prescription. It was like clockwork.

I decided to start my own business selling pumps. I approached my brother's friend Craig about investing in it. Craig was a trader at the Mercantile Exchange. His family had once owned part of the Chicago White Sox. He was also as big a gambler as I was. The two of us regularly played cards together at the Empress Casino in Joliet, Illinois. One night I told him about my idea.

"I can start this business," I said. "I don't know what the hell I'm doing. I need a computer. I need to get a Medicare billing number. I don't exactly know what that is. I'll try to figure it out. But I need thirty thousand bucks to get it all going. In exchange, I'll give you 25 percent of my business."

"Now you're talking," he said.

We shook hands.

"You want to go to the casino?" he added.

Craig didn't just write me a check for thirty thousand dollars. Some of the money came from his credit card, some from a check, some came from chips he had at the casino, and some came from money he won playing gin rummy against me. But we got enough to start the business.

I was told it would take three months to acquire a DMERC provider number. I got mine in two weeks by pushing doggedly through every road-block the system threw at me.

I had business cards printed and set up an account through the Bank One branch located on the ground floor of my apartment building. I worked out of my apartment. My overhead was my rent (one thousand and forty dollars a month), the cost of the equipment (I had thirty days to pay), and a nurse, Regina Rutkowski, to help set up patients with their pump. I sold seven pumps within the first two months and cleared more money than I would have by selling sixty-five pumps for my previous boss.

With four good referral sources, I soon realized that I could expand by hiring people as independent contractors like the other guy. Except that I wasn't as greedy as him. I split sales 50–50 with my guys. What did I care? It wasn't costing me anything. I signed up salespeople in multiple states. The money rolled in. Within a year, I'd made a fortune for a twenty-two-year-old without a college degree and no burning direction.

It was exciting. I loved checking the mail. Large checks from the government and private insurance carriers arrived in spurts. I never knew how much money came in. Although I declared my income, I was completely unorganized with my taxes. I commingled all my money just as my father had done with his—the only difference being the added chaos factor of gambling.

I ran all my activities from the same Bank One. I don't think the money ever sat in the bank for more than forty-eight hours before I dumped it into card games at the Empress casino, OTB (the horse track), lottery tickets, and eventually a new bookie named Jimmy Black. Friends from Highland Park introduced us. His entrance in my life was perfectly timed—for him. He handled five thousand dollars a game, and by late spring of 1995, I saw that the money in my account had shrunk to less than forty thousand dollars.

Still, the money was flowing in. I still felt rich and successful. And I decided to reward myself with some fun.

13

THE BIRTH OF MR. R

"I'm going to Las Vegas," I said to Meredith.

My older brother and his future wife were there on vacation, and I decided on the spur of the moment to meet them at Caesar's Palace.

Meredith, now completely entrenched in graduate school, didn't oppose or endorse the trip. She didn't think one weekend of partying was cause for concern. She had no reason to suspect I was gambling again. I had money coming in—big money. It was heady stuff at a time when all of our friends were either roughing it in graduate school or starting jobs that paid them a yearly salary equal to one of my checks. We were living high and having fun.

Then there was the truth. I arrived at Caesar's with fifteen thousand dollars in cash, which I lost at the blackjack table in the first hour. I withdrew the twenty-four thousand dollars left in my business account. That disappeared within two hours. The situation wasn't pretty. I'd cleaned out my bank account in three hours. I was broke.

What thoughts went through my brain? *I still have two days left. How am I going to play all weekend?*

It was like that all the time. Vegas was the latest stop.

I'd been gambling at Caesar's since I was an eighteen-year-old college freshman, but this was only the second time I'd been registered under my own name. I'd used my brother's name and fake ID the previous times because I'd been under twenty-one. Also, for the first time, I boasted clean credit. I thought about ways I could use this in my favor to cajole an advance from the casino. My brain was firing on high speed as I walked into the casino manager's office.

His secretary brought me in and told him my name. He was in his fifties and wore a dark suit. He sat behind a large desk. Some family photos and notebooks filled the shelves of a credenza. I sat in one of the two chairs facing his desk. He gave me a severe once-over while still seeming cordial.

"I have to ask you something right away," he said. "Your name is Resnick."

"Yes, it is."

"Any relation to Ashe Resnick?"

That surprised me. Ashe Resnick was a legendary Vegas character with strong underworld ties. He'd owned the Thunderbird Casino in the sixties. He was also close to heavyweight boxing champion Sonny Liston. Many speculated that Resnick may have convinced Liston to throw his second bout against Muhammad Ali. I'd seen his story told in a documentary on old Las Vegas.

"A very distant relation," I lied. "I never met him."

"Probably because he died when you were a young kid," the manager said. "But since you're a Resnick, and a pretty good player, I'm going to give you a credit line of five thousand dollars."

I walked back into the casino and lost the five grand at the same black-jack table in fifteen minutes.

Anyone in his right mind could've seen my self-destructive pattern—anyone except me. An alcoholic behaving like me would've been thrown out of the bar long ago. Casinos don't work that way.

"Let's take a look at your credit and see what you have in the bank," the manager said after I returned to his office and asked for additional funds.

I showed him my bank statement from earlier, when it still had twenty-four thousand dollars. He ran a check. We spoke for about twenty minutes, during which time I dropped a ton of names and paved the ground with a thick layer of bullshit. If he'd been paying attention to anything other than creating another high roller to play, he would've caught the sham,

"I'm going to extend you forty-five thousand dollars, with thirty-day terms," he said. "That puts us at fifty grand. Are we good, Mr. Resnick?"

"We're very good."

"Now go bury us, will you? Kill the house."

That was such a line of bullshit, the kind of crap reverse psychology casino hosts throw out to their best customers, who are also the most compulsive gamblers. Outside, in the casino, I calculated my debt: I already owed Jimmy Black $35K. Add to that a fifty thousand dollar marker to the casino. This was serious. I'd never borrowed that amount of money from a real business. I didn't consider there might be ramifications.

I told myself that I'd win it back as I sat back down at the blackjack table. I was calling football bets to Black. One way or another, I was going to win back the money, I told myself. Sweat piled up on my forehead. No matter how much I wiped my face, the sweat returned. I concentrated on the cards. I wanted to play fast. I felt frantic when others sat down at the table and I had to wait my turn.

My brother and his girlfriend stopped by the table. She was from a hard-working, conservative family. She'd recently graduated law school. She wasn't used to people squandering money, and her good cheer vanished when she saw that I was playing with five-hundred-dollar chips.

She turned to my brother and made a face that I can only imagine. He stepped forward and put a hand on my back.

"How's it going?" he asked.

I shook my head.

"No woman should witness this," I said.

After three straight quick losses, I made a face at my brother.

"Correction. No other human should have to witness this kind of ugliness."

They left, and two hours later I was down to my last twenty-five thousand dollars. I was despondent, at the point of "what-the-fuck" times ten, and then I gave up. That was it for me—mentally, physically, emotionally. I threw in the towel like a demoralized prize fighter. Fuck it. I fired off a five-thousand-dollar hand. I lost. Pissed off, I played another hand for five thousand dollars. I lost that too. I did that three more times. Then the money was gone.

I knew it was going to happen that way. I was a big fucking loser.

I staggered into my suite tallying my stupidity. I'd lost eighty-nine thousand dollars in half a day—the $39K I brought and $50K to the hotel. I was also into Black for forty-five thousand dollars. I felt thoroughly beat up, battered, and like I'd been tossed in the gutter. And I'd done it to myself.

I felt suicidal. I called my college friend Matt. I also spoke to my brother. As I talked I paced rapidly around the hot tub in my suite.

"We'll figure it out, man," Matt said. "We'll figure it out."

"This isn't Arturo and David from college," I said. "This is thirty times that."

"We'll figure it out."

"The fucking hot tub in my room is empty," I said. "I can't even drown myself."

"We'll figure it out. Just get it together."

The room was paneled in mirrors. I saw myself sweating like a pig in whatever direction I looked. It was torture.

I changed clothes and went downstairs to the manager's office again. He greeted me with familiarity. If he knew why I was back, he didn't let on. I assume that he'd dealt with my type before. I'm sure there were people who blew as much if not more at the tables as me. Then the booze wore off, the women went home, they snapped out of it, and said, "Fuck! What did I do? I need two years to pay this off."

I never snapped out of it. I kept digging the hole, deeper and wider, like a fat man preparing his grave between meals and snacks.

I had no reservations about asking the manager for more credit. How could I do that after having just lost fifty thousand dollars in credit? It's not hard when your self-esteem is smaller than a grain of sand in the Mojave. I expected rejection. More wasn't going to hurt me any further. I had no shame. Or shame was all I had left, depending on how one looked at me.

"I gave you a courtesy fifty thousand dollars," the manager said. "In memory of Ashe. I know you're good for it because of him. Let's leave it at that."

"But I'm here for another forty-eight hours," I said. "Now I want to get out of here right away. I need help taking care of that."

"Don't worry about it. We'll take care of it, Mr. R."

Thus was born Mr. R, my gambling alter-ego. Created from desperation and humiliation, he was a high roller who was given respect when none was warranted. Casinos lived on the careless behavior of such fictional characters. They comped drinks, meals, shows, and lavish hotel suites to lure people who had no business gambling to the tables. They made them more than they were worth so they'd spend more. It was no different than hustlers running a shell game letting someone win the first couple of rounds before taking all their money.

Adam had fucked up royally. After running through every single dollar in his bank account, he'd gone into serious debt.

But Mr. R didn't have to deal with that. He was given a free plane ticket home and a limo ride to the airport.

At home, I borrowed twenty thousand dollars from my partner and gave it to Black. I needed to be on his good side to stay in action. I had thirty days to pay back Caesar's. I thought I could win most, if not all of what I needed, by betting football. I also set up three different credit lines for ten thousand dollars each in local casinos. I was a textbook example of a pathological gambler chasing his losses, gambling to pay gambling debts, piling risk on top of risk, when the best solution would've been to earn the money back through my business.

My efforts fell short—I played about even—and the thirty-day deadline I had to pay back Caesar's came and went. Although concerned, I was used to deadlines passing without any immediate consequences. It usually took banks and creditors another month to send out a first warning. But the next morning at 10 AM, there was a knock on my apartment door, which was odd since my 640-square-foot apartment was on the thirty-second floor of a thirty-nine-story building, where visitors were buzzed in and mail and deliveries were handled on the ground floor.

It was probably some neighbors who has locked themselves out, I thought. I opened it without looking through the peephole, and found myself face to face with a mailman holding a registered letter.

"Lucky you're home," the mailman said, handing me a piece of paper. "Sign this and I'm out of here."

The letter was from the legal counsel and collections manager from Caesar's Palace. It stated that I'd missed my deadline, and then it went on to warn in severe language that if I didn't pay, as I'd promised, they would aggressively litigate and destroy my credit. I thought, why not just kill me? Maybe they would. Who knew? This wasn't Jake the Snake or Roy making a threat; it was Caesar's fucking Palace. I was gasping for breath.

I got my brother Jonathan, the recent law school graduate, on the phone. He ran up to my place from his apartment on the fifteenth floor.

"I can't believe a lawyer would write a letter like this," he said after scanning it.

"It sounds like it came from a fucking bookie, doesn't it?" I said.

"You're into them for a lot of money."

"I'm not denying that. I'm taking issue with the tone of the letter and the way they're threatening me."

"Bro, they want their money."

"I know! I know they want their fucking money. I don't have it." I paused and caught my breath. "Can you call the guy? See if you can work something out."

With the two-hour time difference, it was still morning in Las Vegas. The lawyer wouldn't be in his office yet. Jonathan went back to his place and called later that afternoon. He recounted the details to me immediately after.

"I was straight with the guy," he said.

"How were they?" I asked.

"Serious. They aren't joking around. This is serious."

"What'd you tell him?"

"The truth. I said you were having some financial difficulties now. I said you kind of have a gambling problem, and you got yourself into trouble."

"What'd he say? Bottom line?"

"Bottom line—they're giving you another ninety days."

"So you bought me three months."

"Yeah. Ninety days. You better get that dough together."

"Shit."

"Deep shit."

"Don't tell Meredith, okay?"

Meredith was involved in her graduate studies in audiology at Northwestern University. She had no idea that I was in trouble again from gambling. She didn't know that I was gambling, period. She slept over several times a week, but to her I was completely wrapped up in my business. I talked about the sales and numbers. Despite my sloppy business practices, money still came in. Then I gambled it away.

The irony was pitiful. Here she was, developing an expertise in hearing, but she couldn't see what was going on in front of her.

I had to come up with the money for Caesar's. The deadline arrived with a grim inevitability. I'd extended the credit on my Visa and other cards, but I was still short fifteen thousand dollars. Caesar's collection notices made the consequences of not paying clear; they'd ruin me.

I called my father for help. The safe thing about my father was that he rarely, if ever passed, judgment since he was usually in the same situation himself.

"I need fifty thousand dollars," I said.

He groaned.

"I'm also looking to get some cash," he said. "Give me the night to think."

He called back the next day and mentioned the name Al Hubbard. Al Hubbard? Mention of his name took me back to my childhood. Hubbard was an older man from the inner city who'd worked around our house and my dad's office as a handyman when I was growing up. We'd given him our extra food and clothes. He'd taken junk from our garage. He'd made ten bucks here, thirty bucks there, whatever.

"Al Hubbard?" I asked, surprised. "I haven't heard his name for years."

"He's loaning you the money," my father said.

"Al Hubbard?"

It was true. It turned out, our former handyman was loaded. He'd never spent a dollar. The contrast between him and my father was a stinging reminder that reality is often never the way it appears. My father, educated in medicine and law and once among the state's most prominent business executives, never planned for the future, never thought he'd live past forty-two, overspent, and consequently faltered as soon as his life hit a rough patch. Hubbard, who labored for blue-collar wages, was now very well off.

"I told him you needed money for your business," my dad explained. "You have to call him and make the arrangements."

"He's going to give me fifty thousand dollars?"

"Ask him for seventy-five thousand," my dad said.

I worked out a payment schedule with Hubbard, something like twenty-four hundred dollars a month, and signed a promissory note. It was the first time I'd had such a structured loan. The interest was extremely high, which also set a precedent. But I felt good about the arrangement. In my mind, it was a win-win. I was doing Hubbard a solid by making money for him. And he was helping me.

A few days later, the check came in the mail and I paid Caesar's. With them off my ass, I was profoundly and immediately relieved. I took Meredith out to a fancy restaurant. I needed to celebrate even if she didn't know it. Within the week I received another letter from Caesar's that appealed to my dark sense of humor. Arriving by regular mail, it was a large envelope containing a Caesar's T-shirt and a letter welcoming me to visit the hotel anytime. It also offered a small line of credit.

"What'd you get?" Meredith asked later that day when she saw the envelope.

"This ugly T-shirt," I said, grabbing it from my desk and tossing it to her. "Caesar's wants my business."

Meredith frowned.

"I know what that look means," I said. "I haven't gambled in a long time, and I'm not about to start."

WHAT'S GOING ON UP THERE?

"There's something I want to ask you," Meredith said as she propped herself up with an elbow and stared at me as if, after waking up together hundreds of times, I looked different this morning.

We were in bed on a lazy Sunday morning after a late night. The bed dominated my tiny apartment, which also managed to accommodate a kitchen, eating and sitting area, and bedroom. The apartment had an expansive view of Chicago, with a sliver of Lake Michigan visible from a corner window. The view was my favorite feature. From the bed, it appeared as if we were floating in the sky.

"What do you want to know?" I smiled. "I have no secrets."

Meredith ran her finger from the tip of my nose up my forehead. She stopped just under my hair.

"What's going on up there?" she asked softly.

"What do you mean?"

She looked away for a moment, then back at me, searchingly. Her face quivered. I saw her eyes fill with tears. In her nervousness, I saw beauty. I knew at that moment how much she cared about me, how curious she was to know as much about me as I was willing to share, and beyond. She was concerned about me in a way that I never imagined anyone else caring. I knew where she was headed, and I loved her more than I could have possibly imagined.

"I know something's going on up there," she said, using her eyes as pointers to shift our attention to the top of my head. "I think you have one."

I tried to look cool and in control, but nearly a decade of insecurity was swamping my brain. All of a sudden, I found my mind flashing back to the way my hair had started coming out when I was fifteen. I remembered my little brother measuring the advance of my bald spot, taking my secret bottle of Rogaine to Jamie's house when I slept over in high school, and all the baseball and knit hats I had worn since then. My heart pounded. I felt the urge to jump out of bed and grab a hat. The truth was, I already had a hat on—my toup, my lid, my piece, my rug. But I knew it was too late. She knew my secret. She'd probably known for a while but had chosen this morning as the right time to ask.

"What do you want to know about?" I smiled slyly to let her know that I knew the answer. "My hair? Is that what you're getting at?"

She inched closer. I felt like I was under a microscope.

"What exactly is it?" she asked. "I know you have something going on up there."

I responded with a single, crisp nod.

"Why didn't you tell me?"

"I've been losing my hair since I was fifteen years old. Do you know what that's like for a guy?"

"Do you know I never once thought our relationship hinged on your hair?"

Meredith let her fingers dance on top of my head and smiled. Then she leaned forward and kissed me. I pulled her close and wrapped myself around her so she wouldn't feel me trembling inside from all the years of anxiety about this moment. How much work and worry had I invested so that my secret wouldn't be found out? I lamented the energy and effort it took to hide this fact from her—hiding the glue under the bathroom sink, moving the tape from pocket to pocket . . .

And why? For what? At my most vulnerable, I was being loved.

I felt liberated, and said so.

"I feel better, too," she said.

"How long have you been wondering about it and not asked?"

"I don't know." She giggled. "A while."

"Why didn't you ask? You should ask things like that," I said. "Keep me honest."

"Can we try having honest sex?"

"What do you mean?"

"Let's do it without your hair."

Like most addicts, I lived with the specter of being a liar. Friends always said, "Resnick, tell the truth." Often I was lying. I felt like I had to. Other times, things that seemed incredible to other people were true. One Saturday that summer I was at my health club, the Gold Coast Multiplex. I was shooting baskets by myself when I heard the bounce of another ball on the other side of the court.

It was Michael Jordan. We were the only two people on the court. Me and His Royal Airness. Who would have believed it?

I dribbled to half-court and stared. But it wasn't enough for me to see Jordan. I wanted to talk to him. I needed interaction, an experience.

I spent a moment thinking of a good opener, something that he hadn't heard a million times, something that would immediately connect us.

"Hey, do you know Stephanie Vardavas?" I asked.

Yeah, of course he did. Vardavas worked with Jordan at Proserv, the powerful sports agency that represented him.

"What's up?" he asked.

It was a good story. I knew the name Vardavas from an idea that I'd had five years earlier. On January 6, 1990, I was at a Bulls-Bucks game with my high school girlfriend Jamie and her parents. They had courtside seats. Jordan flew into the front row seats near us as he chased a loose ball. I turned to Jamie's dad and said, "He's so marketable. He chews gum while he plays. We should make Michael Jordan gum."

It wasn't enough for me to just say that. I sketched out a Pez-like dispenser. Jamie's father did the legal work. And Bruce Wynn, the father of another friend of mine, invested ten thousand dollars in the project, which allowed me to get a prototype made in Hong Kong. Then the two men met with Jordan's agents at Proserv. There was some consideration, but ultimately it was turned down. Jordan remembered the idea, though, after I reminded him and he filled me in on why they'd passed.

"But then you came out with pouch gum," I said. Then I added, jokingly, "I should probably sue you."

"That bombed," he said. "There aren't any damages."

We laughed.

"You still owe me one," I joked.

"Anytime, man. What can I do for you?"

For some crazy reason I didn't have to think about it. I explained that no one in college had ever believed me when I told the story about the gum dispenser, and the biggest naysayer of all, my friend Darren, coincidentally lived in the residential tower of the building we were in. I asked Jordan if he would hang out for ten minutes while I ran up to Darren's apartment to see if he was there. Jordan, who by this time had been joined by his trainer/security guard, agreed.

I sprinted out of the gym and took the elevator to Darren's floor. He was watching the Cubs on WGNTV.

"Come with me," I said.

"For what?"

"Don't ask. It will be one of the greatest days of your life."

He shook his head all the way into the locker room, grousing that I was taking him on another wild goose chase for the umpteenth time in our friendship. Then he encountered Jordan. Michael had showered and was in his briefs. Darren, like almost every Chicagoan, worshipped Jordan. He froze, his mouth wide open.

"Michael, this is my friend Darren," I said.

Darren was tongue-tied as he shook hands. Before he could figure out what to say, Jordan chimed in.

"Darren, it's true. Don't ever call Adam a liar."

Needless to say, that went a long way. The story was told often and gave me a lot of credibility.

But I knew it was tenuous. Soon I had a close call that could've been disastrous to my relationship. It was early afternoon, and Meredith had run to the grocery store. I was at my desk, researching lymphedema-related issues on the computer when I was interrupted by a knock on the apartment door. That's strange, I thought. The building had a doorman. If it were Meredith without her key, she would've yelled to me, knowing I'd be able to hear her from anywhere in the apartment.

There was another knock, harder and more determined.

"Who's there?" I asked.

"Chicago police."

It was a detective named Harry McKenna. He was looking for information on a guy named Jimmy Black. Black was my bookie. The detective showed me a search warrant. I played dumb and called my brother, who came upstairs from his place, read the warrant, and challenged its validity. The detective left his card.

"If you know anything about this guy, give me a call," he said before departing down the hallway.

I was totally freaked out by the detective's incursion into my life. It wasn't that I had lied about knowing Black. I was a terrible liar, when it came down to it, and the cop probably knew it. I was upset by what would've happened if Meredith had been home. She would've found out about Black. She would've asked questions. If she'd found out the truth, it would've fucked up everything.

A week later, we left for a week-long cruise on the Royal Caribbean's ultra-luxury cruise ship *Sovereign of the Seas*. Then we planned to spend a week with my parents, who were renting a house for a month in Florida. I'd seen the *Sovereign of the Seas* when it launched in 1988, and I wanted to take it with Meredith. There was gambling on board, but I told Meredith emphatically that I wasn't going to gamble. She was wary but excited about the trip.

The ship stopped in Puerto Rico, St. Martin, and St. Thomas. It was an ideal rest, in an exquisite part of the world. The water was a gorgeous turquoise, and the air was warm at night. The ship was full of Midwesterners escaping winter and talking about the weather. On deck, following dinner, Meredith and I bought into a horse race. She had zero interest, but I couldn't resist. The horses were wooden, and they advanced around the track according to numbers that were drawn from a cage.

Our horse was named Rum Runner. I paid eight hundred dollars for it, more than eight times the price the others paid for their horses. I thought I could influence the odds for a greater payoff. But it didn't work that way, and our horse lost anyway. During the race, we struck up a conversation with another couple, an accountant, Stephen, and his wife, from Toronto. He joked about how much I'd paid for our horse and offered to throw ten dollars into the effort. We all laughed at my enthusiasm.

Almost nine years later, in 2004, Meredith and I took another cruise (somebody else paid), the only other one we'd taken since 1996. As we waited in line to board, we were next to another couple and their two children. They were staring at me.

"Is your name Adam?" the man finally said.

"Yes," I replied.

"You aren't going to believe this, but this is my wife right here, and the two of us were on a cruise with you in 1996."

"What?" I said, taken aback. "You were?"

"Did you bet eight hundred dollars on a horse at the start of that cruise?"

"Yeah, I did."

The meeting was a pleasant coincidence. I caught them up on my situation. They weren't surprised.

"We've talked about you for years," he said. "The crazy guy who bet all that money."

They had no idea what happened on that trip alone. We were on the *Sovereign* for five days, and I assured Meredith that I wouldn't gamble in the ship's casino. I didn't, and it was torture. The first night, after she fell asleep, I lay in bed thinking about the casino, battling the urge to sneak away to find a game. The next night the boat docked in San Juan, Puerto Rico, and Meredith and I got dressed up for a night on the town. We ate at the Chart House and then I suggested strolling to the El San Juan Hotel & Casino.

The El San Juan was a spectacular resort combining luxury and Old

World charm *and* the island's largest casino. Meredith and I took our time walking there from the restaurant. I put my hand on her ass and whispered the things I wanted to do to her in bed later that night. But I began to change as soon as we entered the hotel and I saw the flashing slot machines and card games in the casino. The pull was strong and immediate, like a craving that demanded satisfaction.

"I need to play a couple hands," I said.

"No," Meredith said. "Come on, let's keep walking and then go back to the ship."

I don't know what she thought, but I knew I wasn't going to the ship before I gambled. All I could think about was blackjack, getting a seat at the table, and feeling that rush of jumping into the action. The desire was all-consuming. I summoned every ounce of persuasive ability and charm and directed it at Meredith. I was like a force of nature, and eventually she caved.

"A couple minutes and that's it," she said reluctantly.

"Perfect," I said.

Meredith followed me into the casino and stood behind me. I kept my bets to the table's minimum except for the two times that Meredith went to the bathroom. In her absence, I immediately upped my play to five hundred dollars a hand (picture a coke fiend sneaking lines from his dealer) and held my breath. As I played, I hoped that, one, Meredith would take her time, and two, the dealer would sense my urgency and play faster.

I was so caught up in my little drama that I didn't notice Meredith return from the bathroom. She had to speak to me first.

"How are you doing?" she asked.

"You don't want to know," I replied.

"But I'm asking."

I heard the annoyance in her voice. She'd never seen me in action. She'd never witnessed the change—the other me.

"I'm down," I said in a clipped tone.

"How much?"

"Almost three."

"Three what? Three hundred?"

"Three thousand dollars."

Meredith froze, shocked. She couldn't fathom losing that amount of money. She gripped the back of my chair and squeezed till her knuckles turned white. She was too angry to speak. But with her eyes, she told me plainly and clearly that she wanted me to get up and leave.

But there was no way I was leaving the game. I couldn't explain it. I couldn't exactly shout that I was a gambling addict and unable to control myself.

Instead I got mad at Meredith.

"Lighten up, you stiff," I said. "We're in Puerto Rico. We're young. We're on vacation. I'm having fun. You don't get it."

"I get it all right," she said. "I didn't want to go on this cruise in the first place because there was gambling."

"I didn't gamble on the ship," I snapped. "I deserve this."

"I deserve better," she said.

I swiveled around in my chair so I could face her. Meredith was absolutely right, but I wasn't thinking about anything other than what I wanted.

"If you're not having a good time, then go someplace else," I said.

"You need to leave now, Adam."

"Mere, you're not getting it. This is fun. It's entertainment."

"It's not entertainment," she said. "It's torture."

People stared. Meredith turned and stormed out of the casino. I kept playing and walked into our stateroom an hour later. She was in bed, waiting for the confrontation. We fought that night, and continued fighting the remainder of the cruise. I tried to make her feel as if she'd overreacted at the El San Juan by reminding her that I wasn't gambling in the ship's casino. Wasn't that her big concern? She'd said as much at the El San Juan. *I didn't want to take a cruise because there was gambling . . .*

I should've apologized. It would've been the simple and easy thing to do. We might have been able to salvage the remainder of the cruise. But I was too grossly entrenched in denial to admit any wrong-doing, never mind that Meredith had seen me at the nadir of my sickness: seated at the blackjack table, unable to control my impulses, unable to choose her over the cards, losing thousands of dollars, and lying about it even as she stood there looking at me.

Furthermore, I was lying through my teeth when I swore to Meredith that I wasn't gambling in the ship's casino. The truth was, I went there every night as soon as she began to blow-dry her hair after taking a shower, an hour-long process that gave me plenty of time. Since we never went in the casino, I was safe. I also called Black and bet football from the ship-to-shore radio.

The fighting subsided from fatigue and boredom during the week we spent with my parents in Florida following the cruise. We avoided any mention of gambling and didn't talk about the cruise around my parents, who, as the king and queen of avoidance, didn't pry when we provided only surface details of the cruise in conversation and quickly changed the subject.

But the cease-fire crumpled when we returned home and Meredith overheard me playing a phone message from Black. I cringed the moment his wiry voice came through the answering machine's tinny speaker: "Where ya been hiding, kid? Are ya back from vacation? Ya owe me six grand. I haven't heard a peep from ya."

I knew that Meredith could hear. I turned, as if facing my firing squad, in time to see her gasp from surprise.

"What?" I said preemptively.

"What!?!"

She was shocked, horrified, disappointed, and mad. I wanted to say something, but I knew it was futile. I tried not to watch as Meredith gathered her things, but the damn apartment was so small I couldn't hide. I wondered how Black had found my home number. He should've called my cell. He knew the etiquette.

"This is it, the last straw," Meredith said. "I can't take it anymore. I don't know what to do."

"So you're leaving?"

"Yeah. I'm going to my parents'."

"You aren't going to give me a chance to prove myself?"

"Adam, you've proved yourself to be a gambler, a liar, and someone who has a problem. That's really what you've proven. Anything else, I don't know what you're talking about. I've given you so many chances. You've lied to me so many times. But it's the way you lie to yourself. You can't tell the difference anymore."

"I think you're being too harsh."

"I think I've been too forgiving. You need help."

"Why don't you help me?"

"It's more than I can handle," she said.

After Meredith moved in with her parents, I fell apart on every level. This was a new experience, being enemies with her. It didn't feel right. My gambling was crazy, but I knew losing Meredith was crazier. I loved her, but more important, she loved me. I couldn't imagine going on without her.

For the next two days, I sat in my apartment and replayed the terrible things I'd said to Meredith. I ignored my business, correspondence, and the ringing telephone. Half the time I felt like calling her and apologizing, but the other half of the time I fumed at her for expecting too much from me.

I'm a gambler, I told myself in a perfect example of the selfish, sick thinking of an addict. *If I hurt anyone, it's myself. And that's my right.*

Then New Year's arrived. January 1, 1996. It was the biggest football day of the year on TV, and my opportunity to put the fight with Meredith behind me and get back into action. Tired of being cooped up and cut off, I called Black and plugged into all the games, spreading money like peanut butter. My largest bet was on the Rose Bowl, which pitted Penn State against Oregon. Then I called Julie Ragin, a hot chick I'd dated for two weeks at U. of A., and invited myself to watch the game at her condo.

I hadn't spoken to Julie for a while, but I liked her company, I wanted to bang her, and above all else I wanted to make Meredith jealous.

Before leaving my apartment, I smoked a joint. It was a bad high. It brought all of my guilt and anxiety to the surface, kind of a free-floating mine field. I arrived at Julie's in a strange mood as I struggled internally to keep myself together. I didn't think she noticed as we caught up over beer, food, and football.

As I got fucked on my Rose Bowl bets, I realized that I wasn't into hanging out with Julie. Truth be told, I was struggling to keep myself together. I felt very jittery, fragile, and racy. While talking to Julie, I was also carrying on a separate dialogue with myself about Meredith, my life, my parents, and everything. I wondered whether the weed I'd smoked had been laced with something. Hmmm, is it my heart beating awfully fast?

Suddenly I couldn't think of anything but my heart rate. It seemed unusually fast. Ignoring Julie, I put a finger against my neck and counted my pulse. I felt sweat on my forehead. I thought I felt my left arm go numb. Or was it just tingling?

That's when the panic set in. I took several deep breaths in an effort to gain control, but it didn't work. I could barely breathe. *Get ready for the explosion, I told myself, you're about to have a heart attack and die.*

"Oh my God," I muttered.

"What?" Julie asked.

"Nothing." I reconsidered that statement. Why pretend now? "No, that's not true. I don't feel right," I said.

Julie nodded. She could see as much.

"I really don't feel right," I said again.

"Adam, you need to get to the doctor," she said.

"I know."

"Should I call an ambulance?"

"No, I'll take a cab," I said. "I'm going now."

I got up and like a robot headed for the door.

"I'll come with you," she said, grabbing her coat and purse.

"No."

"Adam?"

"NO."

If I was going to drop dead, I wanted to be alone. I didn't want Meredith to find me with another woman. I'd never be able to explain. I regretted going to Julie's, fighting with Meredith, my behavior . . . everything.

I left without saying good-bye or thanks and caught a cab in front of her building. The taxi let me off at the Northwestern Memorial emergency room. I walked into an empty waiting room. There was no delay as soon as I mentioned the words "heart attack." A nurse took my blood pressure and pulse and confirmed that both were out of control. I was put into a bed, hooked up to a heart monitor, and had blood drawn. I was able to call my brother between tests and tell him to hurry to the hospital.

The ER doctor stood over me. I was breathing through an oxygen mask. I'd been given nitroglycerin under my tongue.

"Your white blood count is twelve thousand," he said. "Normal is twelve hundred. You seem to be having a heart attack. We need to take you to the OR."

As surely as I thought I was dying an hour earlier, I knew I wasn't having a heart attack. My brother also walked into the room.

"Adam, what's going on?" he asked.

I kept my eyes on the doctor.

"I feel better," I said. "Here's the situation. Before I got here, I was anxious. I lost a lot of money. I lost my girlfriend. And I smoked some bad weed."

"Just another day in the life of Adam Resnick," my brother cracked.

No one laughed.

"I think I had an anxiety attack," I said, and then rambled nervously. "I have a fear of anesthesia. I've never had it. I don't want to die that way."

"Your blood pressure, heart rate, and tests are all at heart attack levels," the doc said. "You're young, but we've seen heart attacks at your age."

"Please run the tests again," I pleaded.

The second batch of tests indicated a lower enzyme count. It turned out the lab had misread the first blood tests. I wasn't having a heart attack, but they did find a previously unknown arrhythmia and kept me in the hospital the next two and a half days for observation. That first night a friend brought me dinner — a hot corned beef sandwich, a double-stuffed baked potato, and an ice cream pie. I was so grateful I didn't have a heart attack that I decided to test the cholesterol gods.

The next morning, knowing that Meredith was in class, I filled her answering machine with the details of my near-death ordeal—everything but the corned beef sandwich. I made it sound like I had one foot in the grave and was holding on in case she wanted to see me one last time.

"I know you're mad at me," I said in a soft, vulnerable voice. "I know we broke up. But the doctor thought I was having a heart attack. I could've died . . ."

I was eating another double-decker deli sandwich that afternoon when Meredith came in. She was with her girlfriend Francine.

I was sitting up in bed. The TV was on CNN. The newspaper and my cell phone were within reach. I had an open bag of chips, along with my sandwich.

Meredith looked repulsed but not surprised.

"I assume this is the Adam Resnick cardiac care plan and not the work of anyone affiliated with Northwestern Hospital," she said.

I laughed. "You're not normally that funny," I said.

"You're not normally this out of your mind," she replied.

She sat down on the bed and picked at the other half of my sandwich. A half hour later, she had to meet someone about school.

"So what do you think?" I asked. "Is there hope?"

"I think you'll get out of here alive," she said.

"No, I mean for us?"

Meredith and I met for dinner two days after my discharge from the hospital, and I knew from the conversation that we would get back together. More important, I listened to her when she demanded I not merely change my ways—"it's time, at almost twenty-five years old, for you to get your act together," she said—but seek professional help. My instinct was to deny it and argue, but she was right. I saw the reality. My gambling and lifestyle had taken a toll on my health. I needed to get my personal shit together. I also needed to make a living.

"What are you trying to become, Adam?" she asked. "Where are you going with your life?"

"What do you mean? I have a business."

"From the little information you've given me, you've let your business go to shit. You make fun of me studying to become an audiologist, but at least I'm learning something. I'll have a profession. I'll be able to get a job. What are you going to do?"

I exhaled. When I tried to picture the future, I didn't see anything. The screen was blank. Maybe the movie hadn't started.

"We've been going out almost five years," Meredith said. "It was only a month ago that I found out about your hairpiece."

"Is that my problem or yours?" I said defensively.

"It doesn't matter," she said. "It's more a symptom. I wonder what else there is about you that I don't know. I don't want to be a detective with the person I love. I really don't want to always look at you with suspicion. But I don't think it's about me. I think it's about you figuring out the lies you're telling yourself."

I leaned back in my chair and stared at the other couples in the restaurant. They all seemed to be enjoying themselves. I was miserable.

"What are you thinking?" Meredith asked.

"That maybe you're right."

15

BANKRUPTCY: JUST WHAT THE DOCTOR ORDERED

Meredith had ground rules.

"There are two things you have to do if we're going to get back together," she said.

I listened, feeling genuinely sorry and ready to change.

"One, you have to work every day. And two, you have to see a therapist."

In early 1996 I started weekly therapy sessions with Dr. Marjorie Bradley, and I continued on a regular basis through the year. It was the first time I'd ever gone to a therapist. Meredith had found her through a friend who gave her high marks. I liked her right away.

Dr. Bradley, in her sixties, greeted me with a firm handshake and invited me to sit down. She saw patients in an office in her twelfth floor condominium overlooking Lincoln Park. Dr. Bradley's office was decorated with the excellent taste of a sophisticated, learned, and well-traveled woman, and like her office, she was smart and warm. I enjoyed going there for the calm I felt from entering her refined world. She zeroed in on the reasons I'd sought therapy. I tried blaming Meredith, explaining that my girlfriend thought that I needed to see a professional, but she pared away that meager attempt at obfuscation and forced me to face the facts.

"My relationship is a mess," I said. "My business is a mess. And I gamble too much."

"Are you gambling now?" she asked.

"No," I said in a firm voice.

"When was the last time you gambled?"

"I can't remember."

"Why have you stopped?"

"Because it's ruining my life."

I had no problem opening up to Dr. Bradley. I felt safe with her. I knew whatever I said would stay in her office. I liked the idea of talking to an older, wiser, more experienced parental figure and receiving feedback and guidance, something thus far absent in my life. I enjoyed the attention, too. For an hour, the focus was on me. It was an intellectual exercise that appealed to my egotistic curiosity.

In the early sessions, as if my problem needed official confirmation, Dr. Bradley ran through the basic diagnostic criteria that defines a pathologic gambler:

★ **PREOCCUPATION** ("Every fucking breath I take contains some part of gambling," I said.)

★ **TOLERANCE** ("Did I need to gamble in increasing amounts to get the high that I needed? Well, I started at six years old with Trident bubble gum as my currency and now look at me. . . .")

★ **WITHDRAWAL** ("How am I when I'm not gambling? I'm angry, manic, an asshole. . . . Shall I go on? My nickname is ZT—Zero Tolerance.")

★ **ESCAPE** ("I changed schools, moved my home. . . . I am Harry fucking Houdini when it comes to dealing with my problems.")

She brought up other criteria, including chasing, lying, risking relationships, the loss of control, and so on. I remember throwing up my hands and saying, "All of the fucking above—and then some! This is not a mystery. I am a freaking gambling addict. I hit the trifecta of preconditions. I'm your poster boy."

At that point, what I needed was a no-holds-barred intervention, someone to get in my face and scream, "Hey, buddy, this is where you're going to end up if you don't start taking some major responsibility for your shit." Instead my therapist took a traditional therapeutic approach, exploring my family and searching for an understanding of the root causes of my addiction.

"Did you have family discussions?" she asked.

"Yeah. We watched *60 Minutes* together," I said. "We discussed politics. We talked about stuff. We just never addressed our problems."

"Why?"

" 'Cause it was easier not to."

"Do you think your parents had a happy marriage?"

"That's the sick part. They have an unbelievable marriage. But they don't address their money problems. They don't address their kids' problems. So they don't have any problems. They're perfect for each other."

"What about your brothers?"

"Jonathan is four years older. I don't have many memories of him. We have a good relationship, but he was ahead of me. Then there's my little brother—I feel like I raised him. I always made sure he had enough money. For example, I'd take him and his friends out to Smokey's in Madison for steak dinners. But I did so much more. He'd be the first to tell you I filled the void he felt from our parents."

Over time, Dr. Bradley focused on two issues—my business and my father. At the time both were inextricably woven into my life and causing serious stress. I told Dr. Bradley about my successful venture selling lymphedema pumps, about how my gambling binges in '95 and early '96 had caused me to lose focus on the business and set me back. In addition, I explained, the business was upended by investigations, including a national news story, into health care fraud that highlighted the huge profit margins being made off lymphedema pumps, which led me to get out permanently.

"So you're telling me that you have a conscience?" she asked, smiling at the way she was pushing me.

"Yes, I do," I said indignantly. "It wasn't against the law to bill five thousand dollars for a twelve hundred dollar pump when it was medically necessary. I saw a way to make money. But I don't know if you saw the national news story investigation."

"No, I didn't."

"Well, it was about people filing false claims. I never did that. It never crossed my mind. I had other issues. When I got the money, which was considerable, it went straight to casinos and bookies. It barely passed through the bank. And when I heard about the fraud, I lost interest in the business. I don't have any desire to rip off grandma and grandpa."

I told Dr. Bradley that without the cashflow from my business, I had serious money problems. I let her know that my father had contributed to those difficulties. I'd given him a platinum American Express card in my name and he'd rung up large bills without paying them. Since he didn't have credit, I'd also leased cars for both him and my mother, but he was ignoring the payments.

"Do you like the health care business?" she asked.

"I can't say it's fulfilling," I replied. "No, not really. I mean, I enjoy reading the *New England Journal of Medicine*. I also read tons of periodicals on health care, pharmacy services, cancer research, and topics across the board. But that's only for my edification. It's not a passion."

"Then why are you in that line of work?"

I paused.

"You know, since I was a kid when we took a vacation to Los Angeles and stayed in the Century Plaza Hotel, I said I wanted to be an entertainment lawyer," I said.

"And?"

"I went into health care because my dad was in it," I said. "It was there." I took a breath and reflected on my life till then. "My parents never pushed me to follow my dreams or passions," I mused. "I didn't have the drive to succeed in school. And then, of course, my addiction kicked in and had a big influence."

"Let's talk about your father," she said. "What did he do in health care?"

I answered with a description of my father's life. He built a nursing home company, which he and his partners sold. He went to medical school, but dropped out before he graduated. He graduated from law school, but didn't practice law. After selling the nursing home company, he jumped from one deal to another.

I paused.

"He has a history of quitting," I said.

Dr. Bradley raised her eyebrows as if I'd hit upon an important point. Over the next several sessions, she focused on his influence in my life. Her insights were simple, obvious, and profound. According to her, I worshipped my father. Despite all of his mistakes, he was my hero. But because of those mistakes, I was angry at him. Either way, I was determined to be like him, and do better than him. And therein was the trap that Dr. Bradley wanted me to see.

"He lost everything, and he's encouraging you to do the same," she said. "Didn't he recently bring up the idea of filing for bankruptcy?"

"Yes."

"You're subconsciously destroying your life as much if not more than he did," she said. "In a strange way you've felt uncomfortable when you're successful. You don't feel like you deserve it. You need to destroy yourself to be like him. Unless you can work on this and change it, you're going to end up destroying yourself even worse."

Dr. Bradley was, as it turned out, right. But so what? Though we had enlightening moments, she never gave me the tools I needed to help me after I said, "Okay, now what do I do to not be like him?" I never saw the direct connection to the harm and destruction my gambling caused. In other words, I wasn't held accountable for my actions, which is the only road to recovery.

Once I figured that out, my sessions with Dr. Bradley lost their meaning. By spring, I'd begun to gamble again. A few months later, I was gambling as ferociously as ever. Dr. Bradley didn't know, and I continued with our sessions only because Meredith wanted me to.

I was still seeing her regularly in December of '96 when I filed for bankruptcy with debts in excess of three hundred thousand dollars. I found it interesting that everyone, including Dr. Bradley, supported me when I filed. In some respect, it was another example of escaping culpability. According to the rules, I'd have my credit back in seven years. In May 1997, my bankruptcy case was terminated; $311,086 worth of debt was discharged. My father congratulated me and Meredith moved back in.

As far as Meredith knew, I was in therapy, I'd quit gambling, and I worked full time. However, only the latter was true. After shuttering my lymphedema business, I looked around the health care field for other opportunities. My friend Matt told me about Medline Industries, the largest privately held manufacturer and distributor of medical, surgical, and ancillary products to nursing homes in the United States. Matt was in their sales program.

After hearing about his job, I researched Medline, came up with some ideas for expanding their business, and then finagled a meeting with the company's cofounder, Jon Mills.

I went in well prepared. Step one was the overall plan. I saw that Medline had built its business by catering to the small, independent nursing home companies and long-term care facilities, a sector comprising almost 75 percent of the business. But Medline wasn't as strong with the major chains, the other 25 percent, and that's where I envisioned them finding new business.

Step two was sounding knowledgeable and plugged in. I went to Milwaukee, looked through my father's old files, and took down the names of his former executives, assuming they'd moved on to bigger positions. Though my father had never leveraged these relationships, I had an innate ability to envision ways people could work together. I spent a week locating people and sharing my ideas.

Then I met Mills, a man in his early sixties. Oozing confidence, I sounded like a veteran who knew everyone in the business. I sold him hard on my vision and ability to put these contacts to work. He signed me to an eight-year deal as an independent contractor. The deal called for me to get a percent of the gross sales I put together in year one and a sliding scale in succeeding years. Its potential was fantastic.

Following that first meeting, Mills took a liking to me. It was mutual.

He was the most understated gazillionaire I'd met. He invited me to his home for breakfast on weekends and we'd talk for hours. My energy was infectious. I landed in the boardroom the same way I sat at the blackjack table, aggressive and hopeful. I unveiled one plan after another. I did my research. I painted a landscape full of dollar signs. I swore I was going to make things happen, and I did.

One day I mentioned Integrated Health Services—IHS—a fast-growing, Fortune 500 company in the post-acute nursing care business. Dr. Robert Elkins, a psychiatrist who was previously in the rehab business, founded IHS in 1986. By 1996, IHS claimed more than forty-four thousand beds in nursing homes nationwide. The government was about to change the laws regarding Medicare's funding system, which had enabled IHS and other companies to fly so high. But that had yet to happen.

The Medline people loved the idea of working with IHS. They told me to make the deal my mission.

"If you do, you can retire," Mills said.

My father said he'd known Elkins a bit in the early '80s, and I played that slim connection on the phone into an in-person meeting with one of Elkins's top executives, Charles Murphy. We met for breakfast at a Hilton Hotel outside Baltimore. Murphy was young and happening. He juggled calls on three cell phones, none of which stopped ringing. I laid out my plan to create business between Medline and IHS and dropped a ton of names. Within fifteen minutes, he offered me ten thousand dollars a month for a year, plus a bonus, on a nonexclusive basis, to bring him deals.

That I didn't have a college degree or a resume didn't matter. It was my dream job—perfect for a gambler. All I had to do was connect people, marry them to possibilities, and let them do the work. Charles and I grew to be great friends. He flew me around the country to scout for new acquisitions, companies they could buy.

It was during one such flight that I picked up a copy of *Forbes* and saw a cover story on Abe Gosman. Gosman, who would go on to file personal bankruptcy in 2001 after amassing a fortune estimated at $480 million, was then known as the king of health care for having built the nation's largest health care real estate investment trust (REIT), Meditrust. He also oversaw

Carematrix, a booming assisted living company, and Phymatrix, a physician practice management company. *Forbes* put him at the top of the high-flying field.

After reading the story, I saw more opportunity for me along the lines of what I was trying to do with Medline and IHS. My father had met Gosman once. That was enough of a connection to get me through to Gosman's son when I cold-called the Meditrust headquarters in Boston. Andrew Gosman was his father's right hand in the assisted living business. We connected quickly. In a gust of sentences, I described everything I thought I could do for him. I had no clue what I was saying, but I knew I could make *something* happen.

At the end of the conversation, I brought up football. The Packers were playing the Patriots in the Super Bowl. Andrew and I made a bet on the game.

That gave me multiple amazing business relationships. I had the ear of two of the most powerful men in the health care industry in the United States. They listened to my ideas. They entertained me and flew me between cities. They drooled over the tens of millions of dollars in potential new business that I was going to stitch together. I cultivated the relationships with calls and dinners. The numbers were big and exciting. My stake would make me, unlike my father, the master of my own fate. It was heady stuff for anyone, never mind a fast-talking twenty-five-year-old. All or even just one of those relationships could've been developed into a lifetime of work and wealth. But for me, it didn't matter if it was business or blackjack. Nothing was ever enough . . . until I ruined it.

16

THE BOAT

Meredith's hints lacked subtlety.

She wanted to get married. If she'd known I was still gambling, she wouldn't have continued living together in my puny apartment, and planning a future together would've been beyond comprehension. But she had no idea that I was still dropping five G's a night with Black and spending free days at the Empress. As far as she knew, I spent my days reshaping America's health care landscape—which wasn't altogether incorrect—and she was proud that I'd begun to channel my natural talents for business and people in a positive direction.

Like so many people in their twenties, Meredith measured the progress she was making in life according to a mental checklist. Hers went like this: (a) finish school; (b) find a boyfriend; (c) land a job; (d) get engaged; (e) get married; and (f) start a family. In early 1997, she was on letter "d." Most of the couples in our social circle were already planning weddings. One of her girlfriends had recently come over to show off a diamond ring after dating a guy for little more than a year. We'd been together since 1992. Meredith knew that I loved her to pieces. Her doubts were different—whether she could trust me, and how she could tolerate herself when she didn't.

One night, as she stepped out of the shower in her pink towel cover looking like a Hollywood starlet, she stared at me as if I didn't fit in the picture.

"I was thinking about something," she said.

I turned from the TV.

"What's up?" I said.

"If we're going to live together, don't you think we should be engaged?"

"We've been living together for almost a year. What's so different all of a sudden?"

"Nothing. I was just thinking."

"Thinking?"

"You always said you wanted to start a family while you were young."

"I'm still a spring chicken."

"Adam! Why do you have to be such an ass?"

I yanked the towel off her. She was stark naked and gorgeous.

"Now there's a tush!" I said.

"It's going to stay covered," she said, laughing.

I wanted to pop the question, but I had to figure out the finances before I could do it. My bankruptcy had been discharged in May '97, which relieved more than three hundred thousand dollars of debt, including the expenses my father had accrued in my name. My retainers were more than enough to cover my monthly nut, but whatever cash I had went to gambling. I had money one day, then bounced checks the next. I had so much action in all aspects of my life that I couldn't keep track. Then I fell out with Black after I went to collect a week's worth of winnings and he paid me only a third of what I claimed was due to me. He maintained that he'd cut my limit to fifteen hundred dollars a game from five thousand dollars.

"Without telling me?" I asked.

"It's for your own protection," he said.

"Fuck my protection," I snapped. "You didn't protect me when I was losing week after week."

"Man, I'm doing you a favor and you don't even know it."

"I didn't ask for a favor," I said. "I asked for my money. There's a difference, a big difference, in case you don't know."

"I know you're going to destroy yourself one of these days."

I'd received the same advice from Dr. Bradley a year earlier and ignored that, too. Within two weeks, I had a new bookie. I met Gerry

Greenstein through a guy named Brett. Brett was the half-brother of an old college friend of mine. That guy, Danny, a broker, called after hearing me bitch about being out of action.

"Rez, my brother is struggling and needs to make some dough," he said. "Can you give him your business if he can get you higher limits?"

I gave my business to Brett, who, unbeknownst to me, fronted for Gerry. He did Gerry's pay and collect. I got murdered three weeks in a row: $25K, $37K, and $19K. It never dawned on me that my nightly juice was double or triple what I wouldn't spend on an engagement ring. Following my third losing weekend, I received a call from Gerry, who said he'd let Brett go (I found out he was accused of skimming) but wanted to keep my business. He suggested we meet in person.

A few days later, Gerry picked me up in front of my apartment. He was driven in a black SUV with tinted windows. He looked sixty-five years old, five foot ten, huge gut, and out of breath even when sitting down. His friend Marty was behind the wheel. Marty was a slimmer, younger version of the opera singer Andrea Bocelli. He was also a host at the Empress. "The riverboat," he called it. Or "the boat." As in "Let's go to the boat." The casino, which later became Binion's, paid him six figures annually to bring in high rollers.

The three of us started hanging out at lunchtime. They were genuine Chicago characters, veterans of the gambling scene, and they had access to the underworld. I was captivated. They talked about the day's games and betting, analyzing spreads, debating over and unders, sharing inside dope about teams and athletes; when there wasn't anything going on, they told stories about Chicago-area athletes, big-time gamblers, politicians, and people I read about in the newspaper. I felt privy to inside information about the way the city worked.

That was never truer than the day when I was lunching with them at Chicago's legendary Italian steak house, Gene and Georgetti. The dimly lit, wood-paneled restaurant was a reputed hangout for the city's old mobsters and mafia. Indeed, sitting in a booth with Gerry and Marty, I was over-whelmed with feelings of suspense, danger, and power as they pointed out an Illinois state senator, prominent lawyers, and businessmen. Afterward, I walked outside and rounded the corner leading to my car when two guys in black suits and sunglasses grabbed my arm.

"FBI," one of them said.

"Really?"

I didn't know what else to say. It was straight out of the movies. It didn't seem real.

They introduced themselves and showed me a photograph of myself from a few days before. I was at a table with seven other people. The photo showed a man who'd come over to our table to say hello to Gerry and Marty.

"Do you know that guy?" one of the agents asked.

"Nope," I said.

"What were you doing there?" the other agent asked.

"Eating lunch with friends," I said and pointed to Gerry and Marty. "Why? Am I doing anything wrong?"

"No. Just be careful, kid."

There were warning signs all around me, but I ignored them. Gerry and Marty were too much fun and too exciting. Like the men I'd met through Medline, IHS, and other business dealings, they launched me into a new world—in their case a level of gambling beyond my wildest dreams. With the start of baseball season, I was throwing down five thousand dollars a game. Some nights, I lost fifty thousand dollars or more. It didn't matter to me. Business was good, at least in theory. My deals looked as if they could earn me millions.

In June of '97, I wanted to finally ask Meredith to marry me. I was firing on all cylinders, in action 24/7; why shouldn't I take my personal life to the next level? There was one problem. I was broke. I'd given Gerry a chunk of money, something like thirty-five thousand dollars. I'd written a couple of bad checks. I was working my deals, but there wasn't anything to commission yet and I'd gone through my retainer ages ago.

I went into Jon Mills's office for help. The Medline cochair and I had grown close. I also played in a Thursday night poker game at his brother Jim's mansion.

"I have some pretty serious money problems," I confessed.

"Aren't we paying you enough, kid?" he joked.

"No, not really," I said with a faint smile. "Seriously, the timing couldn't be worse because I want to get engaged."

"What do you need?"

I made up some figures—a couple thousand for rent, ten grand for a ring, and then I allowed for expenses, explaining that I wanted to do it right while secretly thinking I could win back everything I'd lost if only I could get my hands on twenty-five thousand to thirty thousand dollars. Mills wrote me a check from his personal account for sixty thousand dollars.

Before I did anything stupid, I went to a fancy jewelry store on Oak Street—the Rodeo Drive of Chicago. A sharp salesman named Ed picked up on my obviously bewildered look as I walked slowly in front of the display cases, surveying diamond rings, all of which looked the same to me— ugly and gaudy. From past conversations, I knew that Meredith wanted her engagement ring to be different, a sapphire surrounded by diamonds, and with Ed's help, I designed a ring that I thought was beautiful and unique.

Ed said the ring, costing about twelve thousand dollars, would be ready in mid-July. I circled the expected date on my calendar. I rented a boat for that evening and planned a romantic summer night on Lake Michigan. But when the ring came back, it wasn't right. The diamonds were black and the sapphire was chipped. It was a complete fugazy. Furious, I got my money back and put my plans on hold.

Meredith knew nothing at that point. Later that night, as we watched television, she abruptly turned to me as if overpowered by a thought.

"Are we ever going to get engaged?" she asked with a tired sigh.

The coincidence of that remark, along with the anger I was struggling to conceal, was too much to let slide. I told Meredith about the ring and the plans I'd made. Her reaction was predictable: disappointment, then frustration, and then anticipation. I didn't (or I should say wouldn't) give her any more details.

"But have you already picked out another ring?" she asked.

"I have an amazing new jeweler named Izzy," I said.

And I did. A week later, I quietly picked up ring number two. It was perfect. I took it home, put it in my desk drawer, and began thinking of another romantic way to surprise Meredith. I didn't have to expend many brain cells. That afternoon Meredith came home from work wearing her scrubs and a funny look. Standing inside the doorway, she glanced around the apartment as if something was different and she was trying to figure it out.

"What are you looking for?" I asked.

"I had a feeling the ring came," she said.

I played coy. "What ring?"

"Just give it to me," she said.

Getting engaged wasn't the only memorable thing that happened that night. It was also the first time I lost more than a hundred thousand dollars in a single night. We had friends over for dinner. While Meredith showed off her ring, I repeatedly excused myself and called Sports Phone to get the latest scores. I was a nervous wreck. By the end of the night, I ended up losing a total of one hundred twenty thousand dollars. I was destroyed.

Meredith had no idea. I didn't say a word until our guests left.

"You weren't very fun," Meredith said.

"Sorry. I got sick in the middle of the dinner."

"I want you to know that I love my ring. You did a great job."

"Did I?" I offered a weak, tired smile.

Addictions are about losing—losing self-control, losing your ability to exercise better judgment, losing perspective, losing the conviction to hear the truth and the courage to tell the truth. My heart belonged to Meredith, but gambling was lord, king, and master over the rest of me.

17

I DON'T PLAN ON GOING DOWN

Gerry, Marty, and I became good friends.

I spent as much time as I could with them. They epitomized everything I loved, everything that turned me on. Gambling. Freedom. Connections. We hung out at steakhouses, told stories, met the city's powerful and influential. The Chicago police knew them, and by association the cops came to know me. I was able to park on streets at restaurants and not get tickets. I felt dialed in, like I'd arrived.

But true to form, I didn't stay in one place very long. Meredith and I set March 1, 1998, as our wedding date. As she threw herself into the preparations, I stepped up my gambling activities. In August, I came off a long winning streak in baseball wanting a bigger jolt from my bets, needing more risk, exactly like a pill popper doubling his dose after building up a tolerance.

I pushed Gerry to up my limit past the twenty thousand dollars per game that he was giving me. But he refused.

"It should be entertainment," he said. "It shouldn't ruin your life."

"My life is great," I said.

"I'm not budging, kid," he said. "I like you too much."

Fine, if Gerry didn't want my business, I'd find someone who did. It didn't take long.

Through my friend Craig, another gambling addict, I met Dimitri. If Gerry was a gentleman, Dimitri was like a character in a Martin Scorsese movie. Cocky and aggressive, he'd learned the ropes from Roger Riccio, an infamous Chicago bookie with underworld ties. He ran a small construction business. He wasn't as professional or personable as Gerry, but I didn't care. I started with him at ten thousand dollars a game and we got up to twenty thousand dollars by the second week.

Gerry didn't know about Dimitri. I bet with both of them through the fall, that magical time of year when baseball and football overlap. I won with Gerry and lost with Dimitri. In early November, though, I had a couple of lousy weeks and all of a sudden I was unable to pay Gerry and Dimitri. I walked around with a knot in my stomach and a feeling of continual anxiety. I didn't know what to do.

Fortunately, both of them unexpectedly closed down for a couple weeks—Gerry because he needed new "clean" phones, Dimitri because he was feeling the heat from local authorities—and I was able to scrape together enough money to keep me in their good graces.

At the end of January I had my bachelor party in Las Vegas. Where else was I going to celebrate? Twenty-one friends—how fitting was that number—flew in from Miami, New York, Los Angeles, and Chicago. We met at the Mirage, the Strip's newest temple of decadence and depravity. The agenda was gambling, drinking, strippers, drinking, strippers, and finally the Super Bowl, which featured my favorite team, the Packers, against the Denver Broncos.

I flew out on a Friday morning with eleven friends. Except for the three minutes it took to throw my bags in my suite after check-in, I sat at the blackjack table and didn't move until dinner when my friends, as had happened time and time again, physically dragged me away. You'd think my inability to stop would've shocked people, but no, it was treated as par for the course.

My friends had arranged a traditional strip-show in my suite following dinner. As a heterosexual male, I wanted to enjoy the private T&A display, but the degenerate gambler in me had no interest in anything but getting back to the table. My friends took me up to the room. They insisted that I stay for at least ten minutes. Through our bookie Black, they'd hired a stripper named Ella, who I recognized as a hooker he'd touted as his favorite Vegas fuck.

"You're going to love her," a buddy of mine said.

"How do you know?" I asked.

"Me and a couple other guys—I'm not going to point out who— sampled her all afternoon." He grinned. "We wanted to make sure she was worthy."

That was my only laugh all weekend. Ella started her show and looked bummed when I was clearly uninterested. I love women and worship their bodies, but I'm a germaphobe as well, so hookers were never on my list of vices. Few things in life are as torturous as looking into the eyes of a stripper as she straddles your lap and both of you know it's a waste of time. But I allowed the show to go on.

Another chick joined Ella, and they did a hot lesbian strip and make-out routine as the guys cheered their approval. It was a sexy scene by any measure. Yet I couldn't believe that Ella had banged Black. I couldn't think of anything else. He'd boasted that she'd given him the best head. The thought of that made me sick. He was a disgusting, obese, sixty-five-year-old schlub. Worse, I couldn't get over that my friends had banged this girl knowing that Jimmy Black had been there first.

As the music thumped, the girls moved over to me and tried to remove my shirt and pants. Even if I'd been interested, I wouldn't have allowed them to take off my clothes. They'd learn that the bulge in my pants was actually my gambling cash, eleven thousand dollars, an impressive roll, and I preferred to keep that my secret. So I let them think that I had an enormous package, but still didn't want to play.

"You're such a downer," Ella said.

I couldn't think of a polite way to tell her that (a) I wouldn't betray Meredith; (b) I wasn't into H-bags, as a friend called hookers; or (c) the thought of her banging my friends all afternoon grossed me out. Then there was the thing with Black. But more than all that, I wanted to get back to the tables. I was down twenty-two thousand dollars.

Fortunately, a spirited friend stepped in and set off the fun by ripping off his shirt. I snuck out of the room as he began grinding with the girls. I went downstairs and resumed my spot at the blackjack table. I had the worst string of luck for a few hours. I blamed it on Ella touching me and made repeated visits to the men's room, where I washed with a Howard Hughes–like fanaticism. Sure that she mushed me, I wanted to get her bad luck off.

Finally I put three winning hands together and thought the vibe might be changing when a boisterous group of well-liquored Middle Eastern guys sat down at the table and started laughingly jumping in and out of hands. There isn't worse etiquette at a blackjack table. You expect such behavior at the five dollar tables, but not when the minimum is five hundred dollars a hand. Since the game is about runs, either you jump in at the end of a shoe or if you see someone losing you ask if they want you to come in and mix up the cards. After nearly coming to blows, I got the pit boss to throw them out.

I was still there at 3 AM as the cleaning staff pushed their enormous vacuums through the yawning casino. Except for the industrial hum of machines and the occasional ching-ching-ching of a slot paying off to one of the handful of people still pumping quarters into the machine, the place was deserted. To me, the empty casino had the feel of a haunted house. I could sense the ghosts.

At some point, I looked around, and there was only one other guy nearby: Ben Affleck. He was playing at the table next to mine. He had on a leather jacket and, though coming off the success of *Good Will Hunting*, he appeared more like me, unable to roust himself from the game, than Oscar-bound. But he wasn't like me, which he proved as time went by. One of us responsibly confronted our addictions; the other one ended up headed for prison.

"How's it with you?" the dealer asked.

"Fine," I said. "I'm having my bachelor party."

"Really? Where is everyone?"

"I don't know. Sleeping. Having fun."

"All right. Congratulations."

The next night my brothers planned a dinner at the Palms steakhouse in the Forum Mall at Caesar's Palace. In a private room, my friends did shots and told ribald stories about me. I'd been to dozens of bachelor parties, but no roast was as colorful as mine. My life provided no shortage of material. Everyone seemed to be enjoying themselves but me. I sat at the head of the table, miserable. I was so depressed from my failure at blackjack that I couldn't enjoy the attention or affection. Afterward, everyone but me headed to a strip club. I spent the rest of the night in the casino.

The next afternoon everyone gathered in my room to watch the Super Bowl. It was my favorite game of the year, and this finale of the football season featured my favorite team, the Green Bay Packers, against the Denver Broncos. I couldn't have asked for more. Prior to kickoff, I called Gerry and put $50K on Green Bay and another ten grand on stupid bets like the coin toss, first points, and so on. Because it was the Super Bowl, he took more action than normal.

Then I climbed into bed while my friends ordered up a feast from room service. It was a ridiculous buffet, like the kind you'd find at a wedding. And it was all complimentary. But I passed out as soon as my head touched the pillow. I was spent from the past two days. The next thing I knew, I woke up to the sound of my friends whooping it up in the other room. They were buzzed, loud, and thoroughly enjoying themselves before heading back to the airport for various flights home. I staggered out of bed, bleary-eyed, with a headache, and stared at the TV. The Packers had lost.

"Pathetic," I grumbled.

"What'd you say?" my older brother asked as he wrapped his arm around me.

I'd lost every bet but the coin toss.

"Fucking Packers," I said. "I never should've bet on my own team. You don't do that. Now I hate 'em."

We took the red-eye back to Chicago. I drew the bulkhead and folded my six-foot-two-inch frame into the sardine can–size space. While everyone snored, I stared at the wall, trying unsuccessfully to get comfortable and stewing that I owed Gerry eighty thousand dollars and I didn't have it and didn't know where I was going to get it. The flight seemed to take forever before we arrived in Chicago, and then I met Meredith and we went to the caterer that night and tasted food.

I don't know how I did it, but I kept Meredith from finding out details about the next few harrowing weeks I had with Gerry and Dimitri. Because I owed Gerry money, I played solely with Dimitri. I had a string of bad days with him, but fortunately covered them with winning afternoons at the Empress. I was like a spectator at a tennis match, turning my head from side to side. Was it good, bad, out? Which side was ahead? I was keeping track of a lot, not to mention chiming in on wedding plans.

I also tried to keep Gerry from finding out about Dimitri. I thought I was doing a good job, but I lapsed a couple times when I let Marty tag along while I paid Dimitri. I did it because our meeting place, Papa Milano's, an Italian joint, was a couple blocks from Marty's apartment.

Of course Marty told Gerry, who called one day wanting to go for a ride. It was a cold, gray day in early February when he and Marty picked me up. Another guy was already in the car, a man they introduced as an Illinois state senator. We went to the boat, talking sports and politics on the way. There, the senator and I went to the blackjack table. After a while Gerry tapped me on the shoulder and motioned for me to follow him. We went outside.

"You got my eighty G's?" he asked.

I sighed and shook my head. Gerry's face filled with anger though he managed to keep it in check. There was something else on his mind.

"You had a good thing going with me," he said. "But you've been playing with that greaseball and you gave him my money."

"I'm trying to pay both of you," I said.

"Adam, first off, I like you. You know that. So you shouldn't take business away from me. Second, you're only going to get into trouble with that scumbag."

I didn't have a response.

"I'm your bookie, but I care about you. I got guys with higher limits than you. But I don't want to take you down. That's not who I am."

"I don't plan on going down," I said.

"Yeah, well. I've been around. I'm cutting you off until you're done with that guy. We can still hang out. But no business until you dump him."

"Thanks."

"As for what you owe me, I know you're getting married soon. Give me twenty-five now and the rest after your honeymoon. That's my present to you, kid."

I took a deep breath and exhaled.

"I appreciate that."

After that, as if on cue, I started to get buried by Dimitri. I had my losing streaks with him, but thus far nothing unmanageable. Then I had a weekend that was cataclysmic, a total wipeout, and I woke up on Tuesday morning owing him $105,000. I buckled under the thought of that much money, which I didn't have. I could almost hear Gerry's voice saying I told you so.

Instead I heard Dimitri's voice. He called shortly after I woke up to confirm the amount. We arranged to meet in two days.

I spent those forty-eight hours trying unsuccessfully to raise cash. I sweated every second up till the time we met, worrying about how I was going to tell him. I decided to give him what I had and hope that he didn't count it until he got home. I prepared a grocery bag with about forty-five bundles of cash—fives, tens, and twenties, with hundreds on each side of the bundles. The bag felt heavy enough. And I'd convinced myself it looked right by the time I handed it to Dimitri at Papa Milano's.

He grabbed the bag and looked inside. He took out one bundle and fanned it. He saw the smaller denominations. He checked another and threw it back in the bag. He glared at me.

"Fuck you," he said. "Fuck you. Who the fuck do you think I am?"

"This is everything I could get my hands on," I said, trying to sound a note of both sincerity and surrender.

"Fuck you. We're talking a lot of money that you owe me and aren't giving me. You fuck me, I fuck you. That's how it works."

"I'm not trying to fuck you," I said.

"You're getting married, right?"

I didn't have to answer. He already knew it.

"If you don't find the rest of that cash, I'm going to tell your fiancé. I'm going to barge into your wedding. I'm going to run over your fucking dog."

I believed every word he said. He was evil. Like one big frayed nerve, I stayed up all night, fretting, on guard, and worrying. I was out of options. I had fifty-six hundred dollars in the bank, money that I'd set aside for Meredith's wedding band, and I decided the only thing I could do was to give him what I had and plead for more time to get the rest.

I called Dimitri and arranged to meet at three in front of Papa Milano's. I knew there was a strong possibility that he might hurt me. He could beat the crap out of me, cut me up with a knife, or even shoot me. I didn't rule out anything. In truth, all of those seemed better than seeing him crash my wedding.

But I was betting that he'd probably take whatever amount I had and give me a chance to get the rest. It would be ugly, but how else was he going to get paid?

I parked my car in front and put the bag of cash on my lap. Dimitri came around the corner right on time. He opened the door on the passenger side and slid in without saying a word. I was nearly pissing my pants from nerves as I handed him the bag of cash. Suddenly, without warning, our transaction was interrupted by several police officers. I saw the flash of a badge, the long, dark end of a gun, and then I heard someone say, "Don't fucking move!"

The action lasted seconds. Later, I marveled at how perfectly choreographed it had been: two cops crashing our party, several others backing them up on the sidewalk, and before I'd regained any sense of what was going on, before a word was even said to me, Dimitri was whisked away.

I stood on the sidewalk, next to my car, feeling gratefully like an afterthought while the two main cops, both plainclothed, conferred near their car. Periodically one glanced in my direction. Finally he turned and in a smooth motion tossed me my bag of money. I was astonished.

"We're not interested in you," he said. "We want information on Dimitri. Would you be willing to cooperate?"

"Yes, of course, I'll answer your questions," I said.

The main cop introduced himself as part of the Cook County Sheriff

Department's Organized Crime Division—Gambling Unit. He was a friendly guy, and we discovered a mutual interest in movies and Hollywood in general. We got together the next day for lunch. After I answered his questions about Dimitri, we arranged a golf date. We played numerous times over the next few months. Ironically, although he saved me a hundred thousand dollars, I probably lost thirty thousand dollars to him on the golf course.

After Dimitri's arrest, I still owed Gerry eighty thousand dollars. I arranged to borrow twenty-five thousand dollars from my friend Craig. The terms were one month at 30 percent interest. Craig was excited; he was a gambler himself. But on the morning I was supposed to pay Gerry, he phoned with bad news. From the sound of his voice. I knew what he was going to say before he said it. He'd lost what he called a "fucking unreasonable amount of money" at the boat, and he wasn't able to help me out anymore.

"That's cool," I said.

"I hope it doesn't screw you too badly," he said.

"I'm fucked anyway," I said.

Later that morning, fatigued and overwhelmed by everything from Dimitri to my wedding, I had a panic attack. I didn't bother pretending that I could get my shit together. I went straight to Northwestern Memorial Hospital. A nurse put me in a bed as soon as I mentioned the golden words "heart attack." I was immediately hooked up to various monitors. The ER doc confirmed the rapid heart rate. My performance could've earned me an Academy Award nomination. In reality, I knew it was all a melodramatic charade intended to buy me time because I didn't have the money to pay Gerry.

A nurse hooked me up to an IV. When she finished, I asked her to call my friend Gerry and tell him I was in the hospital. I explained that I was on my way to meet him when fate intervened. I wanted her to deliver that part of the message—that I'd been on my way.

A few minutes later, she returned to tell me that she'd made the call. When she entered the room, I was taking the IV out and getting dressed.

"What the hell? What are you doing?" she said, alarmed.

"I have to go," I said.

Then the phone rang. The nurse and I locked eyes for a long moment before I picked up the receiver. I already knew who it was.

"I'm just verifying that you're there," Gerry said.

"Yeah, I am," I said, dropping my voice back into I'm-sick-and-scared-mode. "Great timing, right?"

"I'm pissed at you, Adam, but take care of your health."

"I'm trying."

"That's the most important thing. Enjoy your wedding."

"I'm glad you understand."

"I want you to understand something, too. You owe me eighty thousand dollars. I want it the day you get back from your honeymoon."

I hung up the phone. The nurse, not even trying to hide her disgust, shoved a clipboard with a release at me and said that I needed to sign it before I left as I was checking out against medical advice. I thought about saying something in my defense but decided against it. I just wanted to be on my way.

18

THE HONEYMOON'S OVER

The rehearsal dinner at Yvette's Wintergarden Restaurant was a gourmet extravaganza straight out of the pages of *In Style* magazine for one hundred ten people, topped by a breathtakingly sweet table of chocolates, cakes, cookies, and candy—a tribute to my fabled sweet tooth.

Early the next day, my wedding day, I took a steam with my friends Aaron and Fish, neither of whom was close to settling down. Both thought I was crazy to get married. I laughed at them. The one thing I did know was that I was marrying the right person.

After the steam, I heard from my father. He didn't have the money to pay for the liquor and the band for the wedding, as he'd promised. I hid my annoyance. I didn't want to ruin this special day for my parents, though I was sure he hadn't told my mother. I knew what I had to do.

"I'll cover it," I said. "Don't worry. Let's just have a good time tonight."

And we did. The wedding was held at the Four Seasons Hotel. From the flowers to the food, Meredith's parents didn't stint on anything. Meredith took my breath away when she walked down the aisle in a simple, elegant, white gown. Our two hundred ten guests, some of whom knew the tricky, secretive waters I'd navigated to get to this place, erupted in applause when we kissed after tearfully exchanging *I dos*. Taking the microphone during the dinner speechmaking, I cried when I spoke about Meredith. Then, after removing my tuxedo jacket, I joked about needing my sweat glands removed; I was on my third shirt of the evening and the serious dancing hadn't even begun.

"The most amazing thing about this wedding is"—I stopped to check my watch—"that it's almost 9:00 and Meredith is still awake!"

The next morning Meredith and I left on our honeymoon. We flew to St. Martin. With a stopover in Puerto Rico, it took almost a full day to get there. Both of us were exhausted from the wedding and the travel. From the billboards in the airport to our hotel when we checked in, it was apparent that gambling was legal on the island. She didn't say anything about it until we were in our room.

"No gambling on the honeymoon," she said, adding a couple of pecks on the cheek that promised more.

"None," I nodded.

"I'm proud of you for going so long without gambling," she added.

What a sick joke. I didn't know if I was that good at hiding it or if Meredith was in denial. I didn't want to think about either one. I had no desire to gamble on our honeymoon anyway. I was disgusted by everything I'd been through lately and at the same time intent on enjoying our honeymoon. But the reality was slightly different. Although I didn't gamble, I spent most of the time on the phone with consulting-related work or figuring out how I could pay Gerry his eighty thousand dollars.

At least Meredith enjoyed herself in the sun. But after six of the ten days we'd planned to stay on the island, we went home. I couldn't sit still any longer. Meredith wasn't ready, but she gave in because she didn't want to spend four more days listening to me carry on about wanting to leave. That was no honeymoon.

We flew to Puerto Rico, where we had a brief layover before the connecting flight to Chicago. As we waited, I looked up and saw Gerry sitting directly across from me, staring. For a moment, I thought that I might be hallucinating the sight of my bookie, but no, he was quite real. I nearly fainted. Meredith turned toward me and saw the color drain from my face.

"Are you all right?" she asked. "You look pale."

Ignoring her, I stood up and walked over to Gerry. I made a preemptive strike by mouthing the words "don't say anything." Meredith was right behind me.

"Honey, I want you to meet a friend of mine," I said. "This is Gerry Greenstein."

Gerry held out his hand.

"I know Gerry from the East Bank Club," I said, referring to my gym.

"I should go more often," he said with a shrug.

Gerry played along. He introduced us to his girlfriend, Sally. She and Meredith exchanged pleasantries long enough for me to engage Gerry in a surreptitious sidebar about the money I owed him. He gave me another full week, until he got back from vacation. Meredith didn't suspect anything when we said good-bye and got on the plane home.

I spent the next few days thinking about ways that I could lay my hands on the eighty thousand dollars I owed Gerry. Sometimes the process was as easy as going to the bank or getting a hold of someone who'd lent me money before and enjoyed the quick profit they made from my desperation. Other times the money was harder to find than shade in the desert. I kept a list of potential sources in my head.

This was one of those difficult times when I had to dig deep into the list. I never gave up until I found someone who was receptive. Need was like being in sales; rejection was part of the business. My father had set the example, and I'd improved on it by offering higher returns on the dollar. Depending on the level of my desperation, I sometimes promised 50 percent interest in two months when I could've offered a fifteen APR and still been considered generous.

Rarely did anyone ask why I needed the money or why so much money. They were distracted as soon as they heard the potential for quick profit. But if they were among the few to ask why I needed the fast cash, I was prepared. I usually said something nebulous, like "it was for business," or I explained that I was about to invest in a startup and needed a bridge.

I was more successful than not. There were times when people on my list called me to see if I needed to borrow money.

I finally hit pay dirt with Leonard, a tall, introverted Russian émigré whose name popped into my head as I feared that I might run out of options. I knew Leonard through one of my health care-related business deals. We'd had a conversation about the stock market and investments the first time we met, and from then on he asked me for advice on how to make money.

He had eighty-five thousand dollars in cash. He claimed that his wife and mother had made the money from babysitting. (I found that funny; cash was the only thing gamblers and babysitters had in common.) I offered him 50 percent interest over two months.

"It's a bridge for you?" Leonard asked, confirming the reason I'd given him for needing the money.

"Yeah," I said.

"Fantastic for both of us."

I paid Gerry at Giordano's. That day First Chicago closed my checking account because I'd bounced too many checks before our honeymoon. I shouldered these prophetic events without a peep to Meredith. She had perfect credit; we used her account for bills. That spring, we talked about starting a family. It seemed like the natural next step since we'd been together longer than most newlyweds. As a measure of the blinding authority of my addiction, I never thought about my gambling in the context of marriage, children, and responsibility.

But that's the destructive power of any addiction. Why else do people drive when they're drunk? They don't think about the consequences. I've fantasized about being able to go back in time and confront myself with what I know now about the pain and hurt that I would inflict on the people I loved. Would I have knowingly put Meredith and myself in jeopardy by driving into a bad neighborhood?

No, never in a million years. But . . . look what happened.

In June we found a cute 1,500-square-foot home with a wraparound deck in Glencoe, a beautiful suburb of multimillion-dollar homes outside Chicago. We signed a twelve-month lease for twenty-four hundred dollars a month. I didn't figure we'd have to stay longer. If I was able to successfully marry Medline and IHS, which I believed would happen, I estimated that I was looking at sizeable percent of $60+ million a year.

I worked my ass off through July. I had Medline's sales force trying to market IHS's various services. I floated the idea of a joint venture in a new home incontinence supply business that everyone agreed would be lucrative for all parties; it was put in development. I nurtured a potential deal between Medline and an IHS-owned business called Symphony Rehabilitation Services. Dr. Elkins asked me to use my relationship with the Gosmans to buy their 10 percent interest in his Indianapolis-based lithotripsy company. Lithotripsy is a medical procedure that uses shock waves to break up stones in the kidney, bladder, ureters, or gallbladder.

I nurtured these relationships. I played golf with the Mills, went to their club, and sat in on poker games. Hard working and conservative, they were amused by my zestful recklessness. (And I toned it down around them.) My IHS contact Charles Murphy was a devoted fan of morning radio talk star Howard Stern. When Stern talked about a life-sized latex sex toy called the Real Doll, I bought Murphy one for sixty-five hundred dollars. The president of Symphony Rehab was a tennis enthusiast. I gave her center court seats costing eight grand for the Wimbledon All-England tennis championships in London. They either loved me or used me.

One weekend, Murphy had Meredith and me to his farmhouse in Maryland. It was a spectacular piece of property. We ate a delicious brunch on his deck and marveled at the rolling landscape and the peacefulness of nature. I dreamed about having my own estate someday. Murphy spoke about new business opportunities for us, and he asked me to meet the next weekend with a businessman whose family owned nursing homes in Kansas City.

"The guy's name is Pete," he said.

"Who is he?" I asked.

"His family owns the business. He works on deals for them."

Murphy excused us from the brunch table and took me into his office. It was a dark wood-paneled room, like a library. He lifted a briefcase onto his desk and flipped the locks. Inside was a phone. It looked like something out of a James Bond movie. Or the old TV series *Get Smart*.

"This is how I communicate with Pete," he said. "It's the same kind of phone government officials use. It can't be traced or tapped."

I never asked why he needed such a phone. I assumed some of their business was extremely sensitive. I didn't want to make waves. Medline and IHS were moving in the direction that I'd orchestrated. If Murphy wanted me to meet this Pete guy in Kansas City, I'd go in order to keep him happy. It might, as he intimated, also lead to new business.

I took a Southwest Airlines flight to Kansas City from Midway the next weekend. I waited outside the baggage claim area as I was told until a pickup truck pulled up in front and a dark-haired man rolled down his window and said, "Adam?"

I opened the passenger side door and saw an enormous shotgun. It looked like it could bring down a plane.

"Come on, get in," the guy said.

I was tentative as I buckled up. Something about the shotgun between us. He never told me his name during the forty-minute drive. I tried to make small talk. I asked questions, but he wouldn't respond or look at me. It was pure intimidation. Our destination was a one-story brick office building with few windows. It reminded me of a bunker when we pulled up.

I was met inside by a woman who said she was leaving but that Pete would be with me in a minute. Indeed, a minute later, a man opened the door and motioned me into his office. Pete was in a swivel chair. He said hello without turning around to look at me and opened a cabinet full of guns.

"Do you like guns?" he asked, finally turning around.

Pete reminded me of a younger version of actor Paul Sorvino. He was built like a side of beef. Everything about him was thick and tough. He looked like his favorite classes in high school had been weight-lifting and beating the crap out of gays. I never liked that type. I couldn't picture him as a businessman either.

"No," I said. "Not really."

He took out a gun from his collection, a .44 Magnum, and played with it while telling me about all the business we were going to do together. He took me into their conference room and introduced me to his cousin, Ron, who was an attorney with a prominent firm. A centerfold-caliber blond brought in lunch, ravioli that was delicious and all the more memorable because Pete made a big deal that his mother had made it herself. We talked business; then Ron led me into a back office filled with files. He had me sit on a sofa.

"I've got a surprise for you," he said.

He left and a moment later a dark-skinned girl entered. Although she was about thirty pounds overweight, she had a pretty face, with eyes like turquoise.

"How are you?" she asked.

"Fine, I guess," I said.

She smiled and got on her knees in front of me. She put her hands on my thighs and let them ride slowly up to my waist. Then she started to undo my pants.

"What are you doing?" I asked.

She didn't say anything. I saw that her upper lip was covered with tiny beads of perspiration.

"You're obviously nervous," I said.

She looked up. Her hands were on my hips.

"This is being taped, isn't it?" I asked.

I shook my head in disgust.

"Get up." I stood up, too. "Give me a hug. This is sad. I don't want this, and you don't have to do it."

I looked around, wondering what was really going on. I saw a miniature camera sticking out from a pile of blankets across from the sofa. What the fuck? I walked out. Pete and his lawyer cousin turned from whatever they'd been doing and grinned, as if we shared a secret. They thought they had their leverage.

"Did you enjoy yourself?" Pete asked.

I knew these weren't the kind of men that I wanted to confront. They'd told me as much with their gun collection.

"Yeah, I had a great time. But I have to get home."

I walked out the door, called a cab, and wandered down the road until I saw the taxi and flagged it down. I flew home and immediately called Murphy. I asked what that had been about. He didn't want to talk on the phone. We agreed to meet a week later at a restaurant a few miles from IHS headquarters in Maryland. It was strange, but even stranger was Murphy's appearance: He arrived for our breakfast disguised in a fisherman's garb.

"What the hell is going on?" I asked.

"I'm being pushed out." He was agitated, not the confident guy who'd had three phones going nonstop the first time we'd met. "There's an investigation into this pharmaceutical company, among others things at IHS. I'm taking the fall."

"Jesus," I said.

"Don't worry. I have to do it or there will really be problems."

"Where does that leave us?" I asked, concerned about my pending deals.

"Your contract is fine," he said.

"Good. Let me ask you a question. What went down in Kansas City?"

"I told them that you're a good, hard-working, honorable kid and that they didn't have to do that to you," he said.

"Yeah, but what the fuck?"

"Pete did that for his own protection. But he said that he liked you."

"What do you mean his own protection?"

"I can't go into it. I'll say only that I don't own me. Pete owns me. You can infer what you like. When you make money, someone will contact you and—"

Oh, so *that* was the reason for the Kansas City trip, the chick trying to blow me, the guns, and so on. I understood. It wasn't about new business as much it was about how business was done. It was about Pete getting a piece of my IHS commission. He had a percentage of Murphy's and he wanted mine, too.

I stared at Murphy in his fishing outfit. Why was he wearing a disguise to a coffee shop? Why was he so fidgety?

"Do you need help," I said.

He drew a breath and let it out with the slow dejection of someone who'd already taken out the white flag.

"Adam, I appreciate everything. There's nowhere I can go."

Murphy made me nervous. I hurried through breakfast and said good-bye. All I wanted to do was get the hell away from him, and the urge got stronger the longer I stayed around him. Even though I hadn't done any-thing wrong I was paranoid that someone might be watching or listening to us. I don't think they were. But within 24 hours, I heard that Murphy's office had been shut down and he was out.

Stressed to capacity, I woke up a few days later with my head in a bad place. I needed relief, but I didn't know how to find it at home. It was the end of July, and between Dimitri and Gerry, the wedding, my business deals, Kansas City, and Murphy's immolation, I had run out of patience for deal-ing with life. I literally ached. A sane person might've gone to a spa for the weekend. But only one place offered the kind of relief I wanted, and that was Las Vegas. I put fifty thousand cash in my backpack and borrowed another hundred thousand dollars from my friend Doug at 30 percent interest because fifty thousand dollars didn't seem like enough. I told Meredith that I had to go on a short business trip, and then blew out of Chicago.

It was July 30, and I arrived in Las Vegas at 6 PM, planning to play through the night and take the 6 AM flight the next morning back to Chicago. Outside the airport, I breathed the desert air as if my doctor had prescribed the change of scenery. It was the last breath of fresh air I took until the next day.

I caught a cab to the Mirage, where the losses I accrued during my bachelor party and another brief trip later had earned me VIP status. Eric Semel, the son of Yahoo! CEO and former Warner Brothers studio chief Terry Semel, introduced himself as my host. In his twenties, Eric, who went on to own UKbetting.com, worked for the Mirage's owner, Steve Wynn. Sharp, directed, he was clearly a product of his brilliant father.

As my host, Eric was responsible for making sure I was comfortable and entertained. All the casinos employed handlers like him to take care of the big players, the high rollers, and at the top of the heap, the whales, those who routinely posted up one million dollars and more. Of course there was a difference between the salmon and the whales. One got dinner and tick-ets to a show. The others got ringside seats and private jets. I was like George Jefferson. I was in the mix and moving on up.

"Everything is great," I said as I settled into a chair at a high-stakes table.

"Let me know if you need *anything*," Eric replied.

I never asked for anything. I wasn't there for the comps.

Eric checked on me more frequently after I got hot. I played standing up, a rarity for me. Normally I hunched over the table; when I was losing, I slumped. But now I was like a break-dancer, busting moves as I asked for hits. The action was physical. It took over my whole being. My bets were averaging five thousand dollars a hand; I was breaking personal records. By 2 AM, I was ahead four hundred fifty thousand dollars. It was the biggest, and longest, run I'd ever had. I was locked into the zone.

Then a loud, excited shout from the neighboring table pierced my concentration. I looked over and saw Tom Cruise playing blackjack. He was with three guys, and they were having a great time. I stared in disbelief—not at Cruise's Hollywood smile but at the startling discovery that he had no clue how to play. He hit on sixteen and seventeen when the dealer had six.

"Wasn't that guy in *Rain Man*?" I said to the dealer. "How insane! He doesn't know how to play."

Maybe it was that he was an exceptional actor or maybe it was that he just didn't care. He was having a blast. Later, I overheard him on his cell phone going, "Nic, don't kill me. I'm still at the casino." Later still, he turned to the three guys with him and said, "She's going to kill me if I lose all the money."

But he left with winnings of roughly thirty-two thousand dollars—and that was after a night of playing like a complete idiot. I was irate at the injustice. In the meantime, I'd gone on a losing streak that was equal in pitch to the run of good luck I'd had earlier in the night. By 4:00, I'd given back the $450K as well as another two hundred fifty thousand dollars. I'd never played that big before. Nor had I ever lost like that at a casino. I let my head drop onto the table and sat there in a relative stupor for I don't know how long.

Cruise's words echoed in my head: "Nic, don't kill me. . . . She's going to kill me if I lose all the money." That struck a chord in me. He had hundreds of millions of dollars, yet I was the one who lost way more than I could afford. I'd even squandered the money I had for the flight home. So who was the real idiot—me or Tom Cruise? Eric brought me some hot tea. I took a sip but it tasted foul and I couldn't relax anyway. Eric got me a room where I could lie down before going to the airport; I was in a panic. There was no flight at 4 AM and I wanted out—now.

"What time is your flight?" he asked.

"It's in a couple hours."

"We'll take care of everything. Lie down. Relax."

The room he got me was one of those palatial Las Vegas suites—endless acreage, seating areas, TVs, and mirrors—but all I felt like was sitting in a corner. I fell face-first on the bed, then quickly turned over when I thought of the millions of germs that had just touched my face. Grossed out, disgusted at myself, I wanted to disappear. Unfortunately, since I was surrounded by mirrors, I saw my pathetic self whenever I opened my eyes.

If that wasn't enough, I soon had company. There was a knock at the door. I opened it and two women, both in their mid-forties—and in the unmistakable garb of hookers—walked right in.

"I'm not looking for a present," I said. "And I'm not in the mood for"—

"We're sorry," one of them interrupted while the other one put her hand on the back of my neck and let her fingers run down my back.

"Have you had a rough night?" the other purred (which annoyed the shit out of me).

"I don't want to go into it," I said. I was surprised that Eric would be involved in something like this, but I soon learned that it wasn't Eric at all. I had another benefactor.

"Let us make you feel better. Vince the casino host told us to relax you."

I looked at myself with these two women, whom I wouldn't have been attracted to under any circumstances. I'd reached a new low, I thought. Broke in a consolation-prize hotel room with two cut-rate hookers. I was on a gambling addict's equivalent of a crippling hangover, a vast and quivering emptiness that was matched exponentially only by the high of betting thirty thousand dollars a hand and feeling like you couldn't lose.

"If the two of you want to massage me, you can give me a massage," I said. "I'll take a massage and *nothing* else."

They would've agreed to anything, and I asked for the least amount of the effort they were willing to expend. Their disappointment was apparent. They were bummed that the lack of friction would lead to a nominal tip. I lay down on the bed and felt my tired bones sink like weights into the firm mattress. The women got on either side of me and started the massage. I wanted a real massage to put me in a better place before the airport. But pretty soon they started making out. Then they started taking off their clothes and going down on each other. I wasn't in the mood.

"Get out," I snapped none too appreciatively or kindly.

I got up, showered, and put on the same clothes. I still felt dirty, and I felt awful about myself. I was mired in the dark, sinking feeling I got after losing. This time, the hole was deeper and darker than ever. I looked at myself in the mirror and realized that no one in my life knew where I was. I was alone, lonely, a speck of dust in the universe. I had the sensation of being entombed. Then I grabbed for the door handle with a sense of relief. And yet I knew for a fact that when I walked out that door I was leaving a different person.

"Have a nice trip home, Mr. R," I told my reflection in a voice dripping with sarcasm. "You fucking H-bag."

19

BOYS ONLY AT THE BELLAGIO

I owed two hundred and fifty thousand dollars.

I didn't tell Meredith, obviously. Nor did I tell her that my new checking account at the North Shore Community Bank in Glencoe was closed the day after I opened it. The closure, as it was explained to me, was due to negative remarks from First Chicago, where I'd bounced numerous checks, as well as credit issues.

"You may open a savings account," the bank officer said, adding a positive note to the call.

"Thank you," I said politely.

Meredith was compulsive about getting pregnant, and I was happy to oblige her as often as she wanted to try. Pregnancy tests were stacked up in our bathroom. At Meredith's urging, I bought several tests each day on my way back from the casino. She matched my compulsiveness with old-fashioned determination. I'd complain about the cost of the pregnancy tests without feeling guilt or responsibility for spending the afternoon betting five thousand dollars per hand.

I wasn't working either. I put together deals here and there, but my concentration had stranded me without a concrete plan. I fell into a routine. Most days I got up early, went to Once Upon a Bagel, and stuffed my fat ass with eggs, cheese, and bacon. Then I wolfed down a sweet roll for no other reason than I couldn't resist. I read the sports section front to back. I stopped at the gas station and bought a hundred dollars in lottery tickets, though I never checked the numbers against the winning tickets. I could've won the Mega Millions and never known it. For money, I was bouncing checks from a still-viable Citibank account. I played golf a couple times a week with my copper friend from the gambling unit, who took me for a hundred dollars to two thousand dollars a round playing skins games. I went to the boat with Gerry and Marty and bet sports at night.

I was biding time until I cycled my way out of this bad period. But nothing happened.

"I need cash," I told my attorney Ross Emmerman.

It was August 1998, and I was eating lunch with Emmerman at my house. He worked for Medline through his firm Neal, Gerber & Eisenberg, which was how we'd met. Then I'd hired him to do some outside work for me. Before the lunch, I debated whether to tell Emmerman about my personal financial situation. It exposed a weakness, and as a deal maker I knew that was the last thing I should do. But Emmerman exuded trustworthiness, and I was getting desperate for money. Andy Mills was his best friend. Emmerman was close to the entire Mills family. He spoke glowingly about them but cautioned that when it came to money Andy and the family were all business.

"They didn't get to be billionaires for nothing," he said.

An idea came to me while listening to him.

"As I said, I'm short on cash," I reiterated. "I probably shouldn't mention any of this to you, but I think of you as a friend even though we've only been working together a week."

"This is a privileged conversation," he said.

"So let me ask you a question. I have this large contract with Medline. I'm working the deals. They're slow, but they look like they'll be profitable. And I have no guarantee that everything will work or whether I'll get paid if it does."

"Have you been getting paid?"

"Sort of. I feel like they've been good-copping and bad-copping me.

But here's a thought I had. Should I stay in my contract? Or should I take a buyout?"

"If I were you, I'd take the sure thing."

"Even knowing this could be worth eight figures?"

"Yes."

That's what I wanted to hear. A short time later, I entered into negotiations with Medline. They were short, and defined by one particularly illuminating surprise that actually occurred at the end. After Jon Mills and I agreed that Medline would buy me out for a high six-figure sum, he added that they'd be deducting the sum of my father's loan from their payment to me.

"My father's loan? What loan?" I asked, caught off guard.

"I cosigned a loan for him at the Johnson Bank, and he hasn't been making the payments," Mills said.

That was the first I'd heard of a loan to my father, and I went apeshit. I excused myself, called my father, and went into a four-letter-word-filled tirade that was profane even for me. No wonder the Mills brothers had been able to sense leverage. They identified my Achilles' heel. My father had sold me out, forcing me to negotiate from a position of weakness, and it cost me millions.

I got immediate salvation in exchange for long-term security. The Mills brothers were smart to make the deal. They theoretically saved their company a fortune. Afterward, despite promises of other businesses I could do with Medline, my contacts disappeared. Phone calls went unreturned. I got the message: I was shut out.

The more I thought about how our relationship ended, the more I felt that they'd taken advantage of me. If they were going to toss me like a piece of garbage, I wanted more in return. I set up a meeting with Jim and Andy Mills at a place down the street from their office. I admitted that I'd initiated the buyout because I was in trouble, but I told them that I thought the deal we'd struck sucked, and that I thought they'd screwed me over. They disagreed, and it got uncomfortable.

"I may have to sue," I said. "I'm going to have to go to court."

"Adam, go ahead and sue me," Jim said as he looked at me intensely then smiled. "But make sure you still come to my house on Thursday for cards. My friends love having you there."

At the time, I had contempt for them. It wasn't until I sobered up years later that I saw us all for what we were. The Mills were always kind to me, but they were tough businessmen. I was the one who blew it. They could've been more generous, knowing what I'd contributed, but it was I who accepted the buyout. I was the weak one in a world where strength determines survival. Who knows if they would've honored the big-money contract for its full term? I'll never know. And that's the point.

In the fall, I got the first installment from my buyout, a large six-figure check. I endorsed two hundred fifty thousand dollars to Gerry, paid off my Vegas debt, and divided the rest between a savings account at North Shore Community Bank, two safety deposit boxes, and gambling. I was solvent, maybe even secure, but definitely not safe. My mail contained letters describing Steve Wynn's new luxurious Bellagio Hotel in Las Vegas. The letters were followed by invitations to the spectacular grand opening.

Luxuries, entertainment, and gee-whiz light shows were the last things people like me cared about at a hotel in Vegas, which the powers behind the Bellagio knew. But they also knew their approach had to be tasteful, given that it would reflect a publicly traded company, and thus the psychology in their letters and invitations was subtle. It was designed around the build, the idea that the Bellagio was newer, bigger, better, and hotter than any casino on the Strip. Though you may have been to other casinos before, even world-class resorts, you'd never experienced anything like Bellagio. It mirrored the idea of tolerance, one of the criteria that determined gambling addiction, which was the idea that you had to increase your bets to get the same high as before.

Well, they had me. I'd already made about a half dozen trips to Las Vegas that year—five more than Meredith knew—and I knew I'd make at least one more. The question was when.

October 15 was the official opening of the Bellagio, whose $1.6 billion price tag was greater than that of any other hotel in history. They offered me a suite. I turned it down because I'd convinced my brothers as well as Fish, Aaron, and some other friends to join me for the fun and parties, and it was impossible with the crowds to get all of us rooms. We went the following weekend instead. I sold Meredith on the idea that it was a boys-only weekend and afterward I'd settle down and raise our family.

"But the gambling," she said.

"I swear I'm not going to gamble," I replied.

I had my brothers assure Meredith that they wouldn't let me gamble. That made her feel more comfortable.

But everyone had to know I was going to gamble. Does a lion pass up meat? Why does a gambler go to Las Vegas? I didn't care about the Dale Chihuly glass flowers, the indoor botanical garden, or Cirque du Soleil's production of "O." I made it seem like I did in my pitch to my friends and family. I sold it to them as the next wonder of the world. Maybe I was lying to myself, too.

Before we left, I bought a brand new CLK 430 Mercedes from Loeber Motors in Lincolnwood. I was driving Gerry back from the boat and he owed me seventy-five thousand dollars. He hated my Acura TL 3.2, which I leased for four hundred fifteen dollars a month. The car sounded like it might come apart every time I hit a pothole. Gerry slapped the side of the door.

"I don't understand you," he said. "You play up to five grand a hand, you bet ten to twenty grand a game, and you drive this jagoff car."

"It's my car," I said. "What do you want me to do?"

"Get a real car!"

After dropping Gerry off, I drove straight to the Mercedes dealer and bought the flashy sports coupe for $59,476. I arranged a pickup on the following Monday, October 26.

I flew to Las Vegas on October 22, a Thursday. It was a day ahead of the other guys. I wanted a day there by myself. I brought all the cash left from my Medline check—about two hundred thousand dollars. The Bellagio was a zoo when I arrived. Hundreds if not thousands of people stood outside gawking at the massive fountains, and more people wandered through the gardens inside. I checked in around 4 PM and left seven hours later—down ninety-seven thousand dollars. The hotel said I averaged $4,409 per hand.

I was at the table again the next day. By the afternoon, I was up two hundred thousand dollars. Fisher and his friends from New York arrived in time to marvel at the piles of chips.

"Dude, let's cash you out right now, charter a jet, and go to Pebble Beach," he said excitedly. "We'll play golf the rest of the weekend."

"What?" I said, looking up at him. "Are you out of your mind?"

I went to dinner that night with the gang. We had a sensational meal at Prime, the fancy steakhouse, where my first taste of Kobe beef cooked medium rare made me pause, for a moment at least, and wonder how many phenomenal meals I'd missed in my life because of gambling.

I went back to the tables after dinner and stayed there through the night while everyone else saw the Cirque show, hit a strip club, and then went to bed. I caught up with them—rather, they caught up with me—the next morning when they played the private Shadow Creek golf course, an immaculate patch of golf heaven set in the desert. I rode in the cart, hungover from gambling. I dozed as they played. I ate my first meal since dinner at the club house on the course and went back to sleep.

There were only two homes on the whole course; one belonged to Mirage board member Mark Shore and the other was Steve Wynn's mansion. I idolized Wynn and knew everything about him. As we passed his home, I woke up from my drowsy daze and stared at his palace. It inspired a self-reflective blast of reality that nearly brought me to tears.

In 1994, when I was trying to find myself after college, I had read a magazine profile on Wynn. The piece inspired me to the point where I wrote him a gushing fan letter. I described my passion and knowledge of casinos and my dream of becoming an entrepreneur—or, as I phrased it, a "visionary" like him. Apparently Wynn saw the letter and was impressed. His assistant called my parents' house and left a message with my father that Mr. Wynn wanted to speak to me.

I don't know where I was at the time, but for some reason I never returned the call. It was a golden opportunity missed.

"And now? Look at you," I said to myself. "What a loser."

Wynn's mansion was across the way. I felt like crap. I'd been up all night at the tables, which I didn't pretend was fun. I moaned and groaned as if I'd been in a street fight. I laid back and let the sun massage my face. If I admitted the truth, gambling hadn't been fun since . . . well, I couldn't remember when I'd enjoyed it. I didn't even know what fun was anymore (and I was someone who took pride in being fun). What did it feel like? What had happened to my Wynn-like dreams?

Among the things addictions destroy is your common sense, and the thing about losing your common sense is that you don't have any when you need it. Consider: I returned to the blackjack table after we got back from golf. I'd forgotten about the verbal lashing I'd given myself on the course. I went on a fantastic run. Around 5:30, Fisher and my brothers checked on me. When they saw the sea of chips in front of me, they went out of their minds.

"How much is there?" Jonathan asked.

"Three-hundred and sixty thousand big ones," I said.

I got high fives and a shoulder rub. They were all smiles. Nothing like winning to make everyone excited, including me.

"We're going upstairs to rest and change before dinner," Fish said.

"Come on up," my little brother Joshua added.

"In a little bit," I said. "What time's our reservation?"

"8:30."

Fast forward through those two hours. All of my trips, whether it was the dog track or the Bellagio, ended the same way. By the time I walked into the suite, I was down more than two hundred thousand dollars. I didn't know the exact amount I was down. All I knew was that I'd been on a downward swing of more than half a million dollars.

It was 7:15, and the guys were sitting in the living room area of the suite waiting for me. They were dressed up and ready to go to a fancy dinner. The last thing on my manic brain was a five-course gourmet meal.

"I need to borrow some money," I said.

"What happened?" Jonathan asked.

"I got fucked," I said.

"How much did you lose?" Fish asked.

"About two hundred." I stared at them. "I need to borrow money from you guys."

"Why don't we go to dinner?" Fish said.

They were used to me losing, but I wasn't in my right mind after such a complete and thorough drubbing and what I saw as Fish's cavalier response set me off. *Didn't he hear me?* I didn't want to sit in a fucking restaurant. I wanted to win back my money, and I needed a loan to make it happen. But no one offered. No one moved. I think they were stunned. I'd sucked the spirit out of the room—a total buzzkill.

"Fuck you guys," I said. "I arranged this trip. I got your rooms comped, your food, the golf—everything. I'm just asking for the money that you would've had to pay if not for me."

They said no. I couldn't believe it.

From that point on, I went off. I lost my mind. I stormed and stomped in front of them and refused to let them to get a word in. I was beyond irrational. I demanded their credit cards and one by one, they succumbed to my abuse and offered them. But even that wasn't good enough. When one of Fisher's friends said his credit line was only twenty-five hundred dollars, I demanded that he get on the phone and extend it.

In the end, I squeezed roughly twenty thousand dollars from them. I also squeezed the fun from the rest of the weekend. None of them wanted to give me the money. They knew I wasn't a good risk. They also knew what was going to happen. Years later, some would confess that they'd hated themselves for making a painful situation worse. But I'd traumatized them to where they felt it was easier to give me the money than continue to fight. Sadly, I understood. It's easier to enable than to intervene.

We went *en masse* back to the casino. I clutched the money I'd wrung from their cards and headed back to my table. Fisher was next to me. He hadn't given up yet.

"What's twenty grand?" he said. "Stop and think."

I didn't stop.

"It's twenty grand," I said.

"What's that going to do for you?" he asked.

I sat down and changed the cash for chips.

"I'm playing ten grand a hand," I said.

"What the fu—" my older brother said, unnerved.

"Why not slow down and work it back?" Fisher added.

My brothers and friends echoed his advice. I ignored all of them. I played two hands. Each hand took about ten seconds to play.

Twenty seconds later, I was finished.

Done.

Busted.

The guys went numb watching me. I was already numb. I went up to my room while they went to dinner. I was still in shock when I boarded the flight the next day. I'd worked for nearly three years to make all that money, and then I'd lost most of it in a weekend. When I called the casino to find out the exact amount I'd lost, their records showed a couple of hundred thousand, but I think it was more, since I didn't put my player card down every time. Also, I didn't believe that most casinos were likely to tell you every dollar you lost. What would be the point?

I'd inquired only to punish myself further. But what was the purpose?

On Monday, I picked up my new Mercedes at Loeber Motors and drove straight to Auto Title Lenders, on Clark Street, where I borrowed against it. I got a three-month note at 20 percent interest. I felt a knot in my stomach as I signed the paper. Ordinarily I didn't think twice about an IOU. But this was different. The Benz was the first asset I'd ever owned, and I was borrowing against it within minutes of taking possession.

Around this time, Gene Kim, the branch manager of my Citibank at 539 North Michigan Avenue, which was near my office in the Equitable building, asked me to come in and talk to him. Kim had always been personable and helpful to me. I benefited from having set up my account at the same time as my friend. His family had a substantial amount of money on deposit and banked through the private bank. I received service by association, I think.

Kim also knew me from the numerous trips I made in and out of the bank to get cash for the boat, for Gerry, or the friendly gin rummy games I played with friends in my office down the street (which weren't so friendly). I always took a moment to chat and ask how he was doing. Today was no different. Kim's office was all glass. He greeted me warmly. After I sat down, he shut the door and got to the point.

"Our security department contacted me and said they were concerned about the activity in your account," he said.

"Really?" I said.

"They said it's highly suspicious," he continued. "I said that I'd look into it. But I know you, Adam."

"I hope you aren't concerned," I said.

Kim leaned forward and gave me a serious look.

"Adam, you aren't into drugs or selling drugs, are you?" he asked.

"No, God no," I said taken aback. "I'd never—"

"Then what's the deal?"

"Honestly?" I waited for him to nod. "I'm a compulsive gambler."

"Seriously?"

"No ifs, ands, or buts."

Kim sat back and ran his hand through his hair. I didn't know what else to say. I felt strange in the wake of it. Other than the GA meeting Meredith took me to on our second date, which we'd walked out of before it started, this was the first time I had made such an explicit and honest admission.

But it wasn't the profound, emotional moment you'd expect. Why? Because the power of the statement was usurped by its purpose. I wasn't asking for help after hitting bottom. On the contrary, I was using the admission as an excuse for the questionable behavior that had caught the bank's attention. Would it work? Could it work? I didn't know, but the blatant honesty seemed as if it might appeal to Kim. He struck me as overly responsible, and I guessed that he might sympathize with someone with a problem that caused him a total lack of self-control.

Kim put his hand over his mouth as he thought how to respond. I could see his brain paging through the official Citibank manual for his job.

"Adam, I want you to write a personal letter to me, stating what you just told me," Kim said. "I want it for my files so I can prove that I looked into it."

"I will do that," I said.

And I did. I went home and wrote the letter:

Dear Gene Kim,

As you know, I am not a drug dealer or a crook. I have a gambling problem and have had one for many years. I take large sums of cash to pay casinos and bookies with. I've never done anything illegal (or intentionally illegal) as I am a good person with a horrible problem. I apologize if this has caused anyone a problem.

UNUSUAL ACTIVITY

In November, Meredith found out she was pregnant.

We were in the bathroom when she tested positive. She took three other tests to make sure. Most people wait three months before telling anyone that they're carrying another life inside them. Meredith waited three minutes.

The news came right before her twenty-sixth birthday, and we treated it as the best present she could've wished for. I threw her a surprise party at Tavern on Rush, sparing no expense and showing total disregard for limits. Our families and five best couple friends enjoyed appetizers in the VIP section, followed by a main course of steaks, chops, lobsters, and gigantic crab claws, all washed down with bottles of Dom Perignon. The pièce de résistance came when Tavern's waiters carried in platters of oversized Macadamia turtle pies—not from the Tavern's kitchen but from Gibson's Famous Steakhouse across the street, where I preferred the desserts. The Empress casino picked up the entire fifty-six-hundred-dollar check; all I had to do was sign a ticket.

As Marty said, stick it to them, they always stick it to you. Indeed, the thirty-seven thousand dollars I lost there earlier in the week more than covered the tab. By the time I finished tipping each waiter, the maître d', and the busboys five hundred dollars each, which I did discreetly, the comp was inconsequential. Dinner still cost me many thousands.

I was thrilled by the prospect of becoming a father and it prompted me to pause—at least for a moment—to ponder the state of my life. I imagined myself with children, and I liked the picture that flashed in my head. I wanted to be a cool dad, young and in shape, fit enough to run up and down the soccer field if we had a boy, or hip enough to know my way through the fashion magazines if we had a girl. I wanted my kids to like me. I wanted to be a good provider and head a stable home.

Wanting and doing were two different things, but I figured there was a reason that God gives us nine months to prepare for a baby. Meredith's pregnancy was a wakeup call to me, no doubt about it. I knew I was a mess and, although my own father would've counseled that what really mattered was having a heart of gold, I considered good intentions just a starting point. Why have kids if you aren't going to love them?

I thought about the huge sum of money I'd lost at the Bellagio and the letter I'd written Citibank. Almost every bank in the city had shut me down: I was having trouble getting credit cards. I saw that I was cultivating the same kind of track record as my father. And the last thing I wanted was my kid growing up with the same financial uncertainty I'd experienced in my house. The cause of my difficulties was clear: it was gambling.

With a mix of nervousness and determination, I told myself that I needed to quit. No more blackjack. No more bookies. I thought about it often, in conversations with myself while I was shaving or driving—times when I could look at myself in the mirror, look myself in the eye, and make sure I was square with myself. And I was. I wanted to quit, and I felt good about the decision.

Meredith's due date was July 22, 1999. I vowed that that would mark my rebirth too, as if I could stop time, start it over again, and be some different person, a new and improved Adam Resnick who didn't gamble. I paid the law firm of Gardner, Carton & Douglas five thousand dollars for a comprehensive estate plan. I also took out a multimillion-dollar life insurance policy (but of course it was term; whole would have been the more responsible decision). That made me feel I was responsible. The next step was to get a job and make money.

Because some of my settlement agreements have noncompete clauses,

I had to reinvent myself, so I decided to go into the lithotripsy business. I knew from my work with IHS that partnering with urologists was a small but incredibly profitable ancillary business.

In my region of the country, the lithotripsy business was dominated by a company named Parkside. But my research suggested that there were opportunities for new business in northern Indiana and Wisconsin. I called the doctor who headed Parkside's competition, American Lithotripsy Group. I'd met Dr. Joel Cornfield when I'd tried to purchase his company for IHS, but he'd turned down the mostly all-stock offer. He remembered me when I approached him again in February 1999.

By this point, American Lithotripsy was in financial trouble. I pitched Cornfield hard. Although American Lithotripsy's market share was considerably less than Parkside's, I believed that I could help engineer significant improvement. I promised Cornfield millions in new business and showed him how we were going to get it. He purported to have some of the same ideas, but I knew his talk was a negotiating ploy. He was salivating at the business I promised. By the end of the meeting, I got the job. He gave me equity based on what I delivered.

The first thing I delivered was a piece of advice: Cornfield's partner had to go. From what I found, the tension between the two of them had stifled the company's decision-making process. Cornfield concurred. With a substantial loan from LaSalle Bank, we bought him out, consolidated the company's debt, and improved efficiencies. Then I went into fever-pitch sales mode. I hit the road and met doctors, spent time with them in surgery, learned their lingo, and sold them on the advantages of American's program.

Going head to head with Parkside, I signed up five of every six doctors whose business we sought. The competition replaced gambling, for the most part, in my life; it was risk, action, and challenge all in one. Except for an occasional ride to the boat, I didn't gamble through the latter part of 1999.

Factors beyond the lithotripsy business also kept my gambling to a minimum. In March, Gerry shut down his operation after some of his politically connected friends warned him about potential heat from an investigation into the fixing of a Northwestern University men's basketball game in 1995. My savings account at North Shore Community Bank was closed as a result of irregular activity (including two wires I'd sent to VIP Sports, an offshore sports book). And Citibank filed suit against me for $147,738, stemming from a cashier's check on which I'd stopped payment at a riverboat casino in Indiana at the end of '98.

Meredith never found out about the Citibank lawsuit because the papers were sent to a post office box that I'd purposely set up, so she never saw anything but water, power, and phone bills. My lawyers negotiated a settlement that kept it from blowing up. The same thing had happened at the Empress casino when I stopped payment on a thirty-thousand-dollar check; the casino's collections department didn't pursue it because my '98 losses with them amounted to three hundred fifty thousand dollars.

In these odd moments, I shuddered at the enormity of the world that I kept from Meredith. But her growing tummy and glowing face reminded me daily to be my best, and my times of crisis were few and far between. I became very attentive. Without the distraction of gambling, I was with her every afternoon and night. We hadn't spent so much time together since college. In what we both considered a last hurrah before parenthood, we had as much fun as we'd had before—if not more.

In June, at a wedding with Meredith's parents, I was introduced to Terry Navarro, an accountant starting his own firm. He handed me his business card almost immediately after we shook hands. I usually recoiled from those types; I didn't like the hard sell in anything, whether business, gambling, or friendship. I never handed out my business cards at parties. When we ended up seated next to each other at the dinner table, I'd assumed he'd arranged it

"I wanted to meet you," Terry said. "I heard you're in various businesses."

"Health care," I replied.

"I was told that you're doing well."

"I'm trying."

He was on me all night, in a polite but overwhelming way, about getting together socially. By the end of the night, I agreed to go golfing with him. He arranged a 6:25 AM tee time at Highland Park Country Club on July 3. As I walked up to the tee box on the first hole, my phone rang. It was Meredith.

"My water broke," she said.

I heard both nervousness and excitement in her voice. I felt the same emotions inside me.

"But it's three weeks early," I said.

"I know."

"Your timing is impeccable," I said. "We're about to tee off."

Navarro was ten yards away from me. He watched as I slid my driver back in my bag.

"My wife's water just broke," I told him. "I have to go."

"Good luck, man," he said.

An hour later I drove Meredith to Lake Forest Hospital; a few hours after arriving, without any complications, she gave birth to a beautiful girl we named Ariel. The nurse brought her into Meredith's room that night for her first feeding. We were officially parents. I'd never been happier or more in love.

For months, I was focused on being a good husband, parent, and provider. Then, in early 2000, Michael S., an old college roommate from New York, asked me to help arrange a bachelor party in Las Vegas for one of his friends. Michael was killing in the hedge fund business. I felt a twinge of yearning for the rush of being in action as he described what he wanted.

"Can you hook it up?" he asked.

I hesitated, and Michael knew it was because I'd cut way down on my gambling.

"Yeah, I can take care of things," I said.

"I feel bad for asking. But I can control you."

"It's not a problem. They love me at the Bellagio."

"That's the one catch," he said. "Sandy"—his friend who was getting married—"wants to stay at the Mandalay."

That was a problem. The Mandalay Bay was *the* hot hotel on the Strip, and the destination du jour for partiers headed to Las Vegas. It was likely booked. The top hotels in Vegas enjoyed a high occupancy rate year round, and I didn't have any play at the Mandalay. Nonetheless, I understood the local dialect. I called the hotel, asked to speak to a casino host, and explained the situation. I even put her on a three-way with the Bellagio to confirm the amounts of play from my last trips.

That did it. She rolled out the red carpet. All she asked for was my credit card.

"In the event you don't play the way you've indicated," she said politely.

"I understand," I said. "It's not a problem."

I told Meredith about the trip. I swore that I could control myself, that I had no desire to play like I used to, and that I'd turned a corner now that we had a child. Responsibility ruled, I said. Or something to that effect. And she reluctantly let me go after relentless assurance by Michael that he would watch me.

But I already knew I was going to gamble. How much was the only question I couldn't answer yet. I struggled with the sense of responsibility I felt to Meredith and my child, my family. But as I talked to myself about maintaining a grip, even as I made a point of telling Michael that I wouldn't gamble heavily, I was secretly packing a hundred thousand dollars of my lithotripsy money. I could've helped myself, I know now, but I didn't want to. Whatever I told myself didn't matter. I'd already made my choice.

We got to Vegas, and I went straight to the table and lost the hundred thousand dollars in the first few hours.

The eighteen guys in the bachelor party had never witnessed someone lose that much money, and their astonishment was compounded by the speed with which I lost it. At dinner, Michael felt guilty. Although he hadn't stopped me from playing, he threw up a serious roadblock when I asked to borrow more money. His "no" was emphatic. I went off. I put down my drink, rather hard, and let him know that I didn't think he was being properly appreciative.

"Listen, you brought me out here," I said. "You wanted me to hook up you and your friends. And I did. I got the suites comped. I got you into every restaurant you wanted. I've done everything you asked. Now I need money. Why is that such a big fucking deal?" It was all so familiar, as though I were reciting a script from memory.

"Adam, you have no control. That's the big deal."

"No, it's not," I said, turning the argument around. "You cheap fucks could've paid for your rooms. You knew this would happen . . ."

We went at it until I basically sanded him into submission. As I'd proven before, people have a hard time saying no. He took one hundred fifty thousand dollars off his Merrill Lynch Visa Card. The cash advance fee alone on that was in the thousands. I stopped to admire his ability to get that much cash. I'd seen people take ten or twenty thousand dollars off their cards, but not a hundred fifty thousand dollars. And Michael could've pulled out more if he wanted. He didn't seem to have any limits; then he explained he didn't, that it was hooked to his brokerage account. But he cautioned me not to expect more.

I didn't care at that point. I was back in action.

The infusion lasted me until the wee hours of the night, when I lost the last five thousand dollars. In the morning, I ran into Michael and told him what had happened in the casino. He turned red, then walked away before he snapped at me. The truth was, he didn't blame me. He was livid at himself. He understood risk, but ruin was another story. I caught up with him a few minutes later.

"I'll pay you back as soon as I get the money," I said.

"Don't worry. I'm the one that screwed up."

"Give me six months," I said.

"Take your time, Adam. I shouldn't have given in to you. I knew what was going to happen."

As I left Vegas, I felt like I was holding my breath. The sky was gray and filled with dust. I didn't like what had happened to me in Vegas—the loss of control—and I wanted to be home.

Once I was back with my family, I was able to regain my footing, writing the Vegas trip off as a bad dream. The farther behind me it was, the better I felt. I liked my life as a husband and father. Ariel was now more than seven months old, and Meredith and I loved to decipher her cute baby noises and chasing her as she crawled through the townhouse.

In June, Meredith got pregnant again. It was excellent news. We had wanted this second child, and now we felt like the gods were smiling on us. I was hoping for a third, and she felt the same way. Everything else appeared to be on track. If the lithotripsy business kept growing the way I'd projected, which appeared likely, I foresaw positioning a merger with Parkside. That would be a nice payday.

I could've done well—if nothing had changed. But one day in June my cell phone rang. I was in my office when I answered it.

"Adam?"

"Yeah."

"David Fisk."

Fisk was my brother Jonathan's fraternity brother. He ran a large commodities business. We'd only met twice, but I knew all about him. He was an excellent golfer and a huge gambler. My brother had talked about him since college. Fisk tales prompted awe, disbelief, and shock in their own right, yet mine dwarfed his. Before he could say anything more, I knew exactly why he'd called.

"How much do you need?" I asked.

I realized that he'd likely called fifty people before my name popped into his head. That was what you did.

"Twenty thousand." He paused for a second. "Can you get it in an hour?"

I didn't flinch or ask questions. I knew what it was like to need the bailout.

"Yes."

I gave him directions to my office. Then I walked across the street to the bank and got Fisk a cashier's check for twenty thousand dollars. He showed up forty minutes later.

"I don't know when I can pay you back," he said.

"No shit."

"I'll pay you interest."

"I won't accept it," I said.

I always paid interest; in fact, I paid high, borderline usurious rates. But I never accepted it when I loaned money. I didn't want to make money from other people's weaknesses. The idea of dining out on somebody's desperation wasn't my idea of a good time.

Fisk was in a hurry. Since we weren't close friends, he didn't stick around to chat. As kindred souls, we already knew the conversation.

"Let me know if there's anything I can do for you," he said.

"I'm good."

"Do you need a bookie?

"No. Nothing. Thanks."

Not an hour later, I called Fisk back. Something about seeing him— and, *who knows?*, maybe what he was going through, maybe the idea of having a bookie again—reawakened my desire to gamble. Once the thought entered my brain, I could feel it spread, and mutate until the powerful urge controlled me like a robotic play toy.

I didn't know how to fight back. I just didn't know I could.

I was in my office, where I'd been working on the computer since early morning. The TV was tuned to CNN, as it had been when I'd begun my day. Nothing had changed, including the news stories being broadcast. So what was different about me that all I could think about was laying some bets?

Fisk picked up on the second ring.

"Hey, it's me," I said. "I think I'll take you up on the offer of that bookie."

"Really?"

"Yeah, why not?" I said, rationalizing my return after a couple months of relative inactivity. "I'll earn some money."

"Let me call the guy and get back to you," he said.

I was still at the office when Fisk called back later that afternoon. The crux of his message was this: the bookie didn't want any new players, but if I wanted I could play through Fisk. It was a no-brainer. I lost sixty-eight thousand dollars the first week and eighty thousand dollars the second. I paid both promptly when Fisk came by to collect for his guy. I won one hundred thirty-five thousand dollars the next week and waited eagerly to get paid.

"Hey, Rez, I'm not coming by today," Fisk said in a message he left on my phone at work. "My book had to go out of town."

I got Fisk on the phone.

"When's your book back in town?" I asked.

"Don't know offhand," he said. "Let me get back to you."

My first clue that something was amiss came when Fisk left his first message on my office phone, not my cell. That was transparent rookie shit. Then I spent two weeks trying to connect with him; he responded with messages on my machine, each one with a different excuse about when the guy would be back in town, each excuse lamer than the last. By then, I had lost patience. I knew what was going on, and I was angry at myself for two things: for being back in gambling mode and for letting Fisk scam me.

"Dude, I don't care where this bookie is," I said into his answering machine. "You're responsible for my one hundred thirty-five G's."

I spoke to friends about the situation. I played them his cockamamie voicemails about the phantom bookie. It became a joke. They were sent all over town, like Jim Florentine's famous phony phone calls, only they were true.

Finally, I convinced David to meet me in my office. I was surprised when he showed up. He may not have realized that I'd figured him out, or perhaps he had no other options but to play out the ruse and deal with the consequences of my wrath. People with low enough self-esteem, like David and me, often think we deserve such harsh treatment.

"David, let me ask you a question about this bookie," I said.

"What?"

"I think I know the guy."

"Really?"

"Does he look like a balding, relatively short guy? And is he a scratch golfer?"

David turned bright red. I saw his slow disintegration before my eyes. He bit his lower lip, exhaled, and hung his head in shame. He literally crumpled in a chair on the opposite side of my desk and cried. Friends of mine who'd heard Fisk's messages and knew the amount of money he owed me suggested that I kill him. I understood the sentiment; people killed other people for a lot less than one hundred thirty-five thousand dollars. But that wasn't even a remote possibility. I felt bad for him.

"You acted like the bookie," I said. "You were taking my money."

"But you lost," he said.

"Yeah, but then I won and the bookie disappeared. I get it. You heard I always lost, and you thought you could get away with it. Not a bad business. But I fucked up your business plan. I won."

Fisk wouldn't look at me. I felt like a parent scolding a child. The bizarre thing was that I cared about his well-being even though he disregarded mine.

"There never was a bookie, was there?" I asked.

He shook his head no and then stood up. He'd had enough.

"I don't know what to tell you," he said as he left my office. "I owe you the money. I'll pay you back."

He walked out after making that promise. But he never did pay me back, and I never went after the money.

NOT FOR NOTHING

Stung by Fisk, I didn't gamble again with a bookie until early 2001.

I didn't have the time. I was pretty thoroughly occupied by Meredith's pregnancy and the merger, finally, between American Lithotripsy Group and Parkside. Unfortunately, Fisk had left me hurting for cash, and I persuaded Cornfield to buy me out of my share of the merger. It was a repeat of the Medline scenario all over again. The settlement was in the seven-figure range; in exchange, I gave up years of long-term security.

But now I was out of work, with cash in the bank (read: bored, lack of direction, absence of passion, low self-esteem), and I invited trouble. In February 2001, my friend Madden, a trader at the Chicago Mercantile Exchange, introduced me to his bookie. I'd been asking around after overhearing some guys laying bets on the NCAA basketball tourney. It triggered a desire for action, and Joey Delgiudice, a short, loud, aggressive pro, was happy to provide whatever I wanted. Roaring back into gambling mode, I took a licking three weeks in a row: $47K, $30K, and $80K.

I lived up to the adage usually applied to alcoholics who fall off the wagon: one drink is too many, and a thousand is not enough. In my case, it was bets. I couldn't make just one, and if there was an end in sight I couldn't see it. I started frequenting the boat and some of the other casinos along the water.

My old business partner Craig also somehow got hooked up with Joey at the same time. The two of us were on the same circuit—the boat and the bookie. We commiserated daily about Joey, who annoyed the crap out of us in countless ways. One week, I lost eighty G's and when I couldn't pay him right away, he turned into a prick and started harassing me nonstop by phone.

"What the fuck?" he said. "You owe me."

"I just don't have the money right now," I replied. "I'll pay."

"You're fucking right you will. Tomorrow."

"But I don't have the money."

"You better get it or you're going to be fucked like you never been fucked."

This back-and-forth was in full swing, when on the last day of February, Meredith thought that she was going into labor. Resting at home, she began to feel contractions. She called me. It was afternoon, and I rushed back from lunch. We'd been through this before, so we knew enough not to panic. But she wasn't due for ten more days, so we called her doctor, who had us come into his office. Meredith was slightly dilated, but not enough to be hospitalized. Her doctor sent us home after stripping her membranes.

"Get some rest," he advised. "Tomorrow's the big day."

Meredith fell asleep that night, as she always did, at nine. I was a human jumping bean. With too much on my mind, I got in and out of bed, changed channels on the TV, checked the computer, fixed myself something to eat, and finally, at some odd hour in the middle of the night, I took the phone outside and called Joey's cell.

"Hey Joey, please stop calling," I said. "My wife's about to give birth. I'll get back to you in a day or two with the money. But right now I'd appreciate some time."

Meredith went into labor the next day, March 1, as predicted. As we drove to the hospital, Joey called my cell.

You fucker, I thought, *how dare you ruin this special time.*

"I'm on my way to Lake Forest Hospital," I said in a clipped tone. "I need a few days to enjoy having a son."

"Fuck off," he said and hung up.

"Who was that?" Meredith asked.

"A business acquaintance," I replied. "He wants to get together. And you heard the rest. I want to spend time with you and our baby."

We settled into a private room. Meredith was just two centimeters dilated, and her doctor indicated that it would be a while before the show started. I went out—as I'd done during Meredith's labor with Ariel—to buy the staff some food. It would provide an edge if we needed special attention. I came back with several boxes of Krispy Kreme donuts.

But on my way back in, I thought I saw Joey's beat-up Jeep in the parking lot. But I was so tired and anxious about having a healthy baby that I blew it off. It couldn't be, I told myself. After a couple of hours, Meredith sent me out to get her a Sprite and a cup of ice. As I walked to the cafeteria and back, I sensed that I was being spied on.

"No way," I told myself. "You're being paranoid."

Finally Meredith went into full labor. As her doctor tended to her, I stepped into the hallway.

There was Joey walking toward me. I quickly turned, went back inside, and shut the door. Meredith was in full cry, and the room filled with the sound. I glanced up, distracted by something I saw out of the corner of my eye. The timing was beyond impeccable. Just as my son's head was beginning to crown, I saw the door to the room open a crack—wide enough for Joey to stick his head in. He looked at me, pointed his fingers like a gun, and pulled the trigger. Then the sicko grinned.

He sent shivers down my spine and killed the joy I should've felt on the arrival of my son, a perfectly shaped little boy we named Sam. I was livid. As soon as I could, I stepped outside and called Joey.

"That's the lowest thing anyone's ever done," I said.

Joey continued to harass me until I brought Meredith and Sam home. I spent the next day scrounging for money until I came up with the eighty thousand dollars from a doctor who loaned me the money at 40 percent over a month. Two days after I paid Joey, I played with him again. It was sick. But I didn't care. I went on a three-day winning streak that put me up sixty-five thousand dollars. It was my turn to get paid.

"I'm not paying you this week," Joey said.

"What the fuck are you talking about?" I screamed into my cell.

"You know your friend Craig? That cocksucker won about four hundred G's from me the past month. Then last week he loses three hundred thousand dollars and he didn't have one fucking penny. So your friend don't pay me, I'm not paying you."

"That's a problem between you and him. You owe me sixty-five thousand dollars."

"As I told you before, fuck you." And he hung up.

I went berserk. This guy had invaded my wife's hospital room while she was giving birth. *Fuck him*, I seethed. *He's crossed a line. Fuck with me, but don't fuck with my family.*

I hunted him down by phone, determined to berate him if he answered. Through my cop friend, I found out that Joey wasn't connected to the mob, as he pretended, but was in fact the front man for some degenerate wannabes. That only made me angrier—and bolder. I drove to his house after paying an attorney to run a Lexis-Nexis search for his address. He lived about fifty-two miles from me, in a crappy little place surrounded by a chain-link fence. The shades were drawn when I walked up the front steps and rang the doorbell. I didn't know exactly what I'd do if Joey answered the door, but I'd do something.

I thought I saw him sneak a quick look at me from behind a shade. I pounded my fist against the door.

"You scumbag! You loser! You pussy! I want my money!"

Suddenly, I saw Joey running toward me from the shadows on the side of the house. He came full speed as if he were going to bowl me over, but at the last moment he slammed on the brakes. He stopped two inches from me and looked up. I was five inches taller and probably seventy-five pounds heavier. But he had his hand in his pocket as if he were holding a weapon.

"I'm going to cut you if you don't get the fuck outta here," he said.

I shook my head, unimpressed. "I don't believe a word you say, little man. You aren't going to do a thing. You threatened me when my child was being born. And now you won't pay me? You are the most pathetic fucking little rat bastard."

He pushed me with his shoulder.

"I'm not going to hit you," I said. "But if you get a step closer—" I pointed my finger in his little prick eye.

He took a step closer and leaned his weight against me, almost a soft body check. It was definitely a challenge. I grabbed him with both hands, trying to decide what to do. Never having been in a fight, I didn't know what to do next. But at the instant I was about to let instinct and adrenaline take over, I looked behind him and saw his wife in the doorway. She was holding a baby and crying.

I didn't want to be the person I was at that moment. I let him go with a push to the side and walked to my car.

"I want my fucking money," I said.

I never got it.

Out of work and bored, I made a handful of gambling trips to Las Vegas over the next few months, giving Meredith the vague excuse that I was on business. One night, following a stint at the blackjack table, a man whom I recognized as a regular on the scene approached me. He was short and wore ripped jeans and a wrinkled dress shirt that wasn't tucked in. He introduced himself as Manny.

"Do you need a bookie?" he asked.

"Absolutely," I said.

"Let me put you on the phone with my boss."

The next thing I knew I was talking long distance to Richard. Richard was a high-stakes bookie out of Baltimore. He operated by phone. My understanding was that he ran a huge business nationwide. Manny fronted for him in Las Vegas. Richard spoke with a thick Baltimore accent.

"I've heard about you," he said. "It's not for nothing that we're talking."

"How do you know about me? We've never met."

"I have people. They know people," he said with a chuckle.

I wasted no time betting with Richard. Then I chatted up Manny, who obviously handled Richard's pay and collect in Vegas. Manny had been in and out of prison for years, and he knew how to make himself a formidable presence or disappear into the background. The few times that I missed payments because I was short, I heard directly from Richard.

"Not for nothing, but we need our money Saturday."

I always managed to get some money to him, and our relationship stayed cordial. My two rules on owing bookies were that calling earned you a grace period, and paying something was better than paying nothing. In May, on a trip to Vegas, I ran out of money. It was one of those times where I ran through the fifty thousand dollars I'd brought but didn't want to stop. Besides wanting back in the action, I needed to come back with more fire-power. I always needed the stakes bigger than before.

I thought about different places I could try for money, but it wasn't easy at 2 AM. So I called Manny.

"Can you guys lend me like two hundred thousand dollars in cash?" I asked.

"Two hundred in cash," he said. There was a pause. "We'll charge you a vig—you know, the juice—but you want it?"

"How soon can you get it to me?"

By the end of May, I was hard up. I had to pay Richard the two hundred thousand dollars, plus the interest. Missing a date isn't usually an immediate problem with bookies. They're accustomed to the procrastination of gamblers. But in a series of tense conversations with Richard, I got the message that he was different from the bookies I'd bet with in the past. He was sharp, controlled, and professional. I didn't know a thing about him, other than that his silence was painful, and that he knew about me—little details he'd drop into conversation. He made me nervous.

"I'm trying to get it together," I said.

"Adam, you know it was not for nothing that we gave you two hundred G's when you asked," he said.

"I know. I'm sorry."

"Sorry isn't two hundred G's, is it?"

Click.

He sent Manny into Chicago on the red-eye. Richard instructed me to pick him up, and that Manny would inform me of our destination. I still didn't have the money when I drove to O'Hare to meet his plane, and I was shitting bricks. Some might've canceled the meeting or not shown up. The masochist in me pulled up to the curb as if I were picking up a relative.

Manny was waiting outside when I arrived, and he got in the Mercedes without revealing anything he might have in store for me. Like Richard, he was a professional. He told me to drive around the airport. After I pulled into the slow-moving traffic circling in front of the terminals, he took out a knife and put the sharp silver blade against my neck. I felt the pointed tip pierce my skin. I tensed.

"I like you," he said. "I think you're a cool kid. But this is business."

For the first time in my life, I was genuinely scared.

"What? Just—I'm trying," I stammered.

"Get the money," he said. "That's all you have to do. You're already late. My boss wants his money."

"I know."

He moved the knife to my side.

"You understand this is business," he said. "Richard is very serious about his money."

"I understand."

Manny motioned me to stop by the curb. We were in front of the terminal where I'd picked him up fifteen minutes earlier. He put the knife back in his coat.

"Look, I'd kill you if Richard told me to. I'd slit your throat and apologize while I was doing it." He opened the door. "Kid, Richard takes games, he doesn't play 'em."

Without another word, Manny left the car and disappeared inside the terminal. I couldn't get away from the airport fast enough. I drove a mile or two before I took a breath, my first real one since Manny got out of the car. My heart thumped inside my chest. I put my hand inside my jacket and pressed against it as if I could calm it down. My shirt was soaking wet.

I arrived home with my brain in a knot. More than two hours passed and I couldn't get beyond the trauma of knowing that I'd fucked up. Meredith had the kids at a play date. I moved through the house slowly, aimlessly, getting up from one chair and moving to another, not knowing how to calm down or what to do next.

I went through the kitchen like a buzz saw, stuffing food in my mouth.

I tried to think of ways that I could come up with two hundred fifty thousand dollars, and I drew a blank. I was still thinking a couple hours later when I picked up the phone and heard Richard's voice on the other end.

"I heard you saw Manny earlier today?" He said the statement as a question. "Not for nothing did I send him out."

"I know."

"I know where you live in Lake Forest," he said. "I don't want to have to send him to your townhouse."

How the fuck did he know where I lived? I started to shake.

"It would be a shame for something to happen at your home. Let's work this out by next week."

He hung up and I sat utterly frozen, as if paralyzed, listening to the hum of the appliances at rest in the silence of our house. This was fucked up. I felt unsafe and vulnerable knowing that Richard had our address, and God only knew what other information about my family and me. I'd never felt as desperate. I'd always had a plan, something I could hang some hope on. But not this time.

I looked around the house. I still hadn't moved. I wrestled with the horror and hopelessness of the situation.

"Fuck!" I said out loud in the empty house. "Fuck, fuck, fuck . . ."

A moment later, I saw my way out. I had one option, I figured, and it was the last one available to me. Once I thought of it, I felt a quickening of my heartbeat; not excitement per se, more like a perverse anticipation. I sensed movement coming back to my arms and legs, clarity to my head.

I got up, went to the computer, and searched for my life insurance policy. It came on the screen like the map in *Indiana Jones*. I read it quickly, looking for one part in particular. It paid out $3 million for suicide once the policy had been in effect for *two years*. I checked and rechecked the date: the policy was almost *three years old*. The policy provided for Meredith, the children, and even my parents.

Well then, I thought matter-of-factly. That's was the plan.

I didn't have to think about what to do next. Somehow I knew. Mentally, I severed my ties to Meredith and the kids, the family photos, my possessions, watching Ariel and Sam grow, getting old with my wife, waking up to laughter, the smell of cooking, the future in general . . . There are only so many strings that bind human beings to life, and one by one I cut them all.

I remember the phone ringing, and I let it ring while I set up my video camera to make a recording for Ariel and Sam. I talked about my life, my thoughts about Meredith, my hopes and dreams for them. I told jokes, shared my passions, and cried as I explained the depth of my love for them.

"Don't let what Daddy did scare you," I said. "It had nothing to do with you. You are the lights in my life. I want you to enjoy your lives. Follow your passions . . ."

At the end, I added a lengthy message to Meredith.

"You deserve to be with someone who doesn't have this problem," I said, wiping tears from my eyes. "Meredith, you have no idea what's gone on with me, which is perhaps a good thing. Let's remember the best and most loving times. You know there is no limit to the depth of my love for you."

"I'm going to stop here. I know everyone is going to talk about this and wonder what was going on and if they could've done anything different. I want to close by saying that I don't think anyone understands the passion I have for life. I really don't want to end my life. I want to live it to the fullest. But I put myself in a position where I'm not able to enjoy it. I think this is best."

"I love you, Meredith. I love you, Ariel. I love you, Sammy. And Harley . . . I love you, too."

I put the video camera away and stuck the tape in an envelope. I got in the car and left the tape at my Mailbox Etc. place. I drove to Milwaukee from Chicago. It was the middle of the day and the traffic was light. I made the trip in less than the usual 90 minutes. Though my eyes were heavy, I wanted one last look at everything, like a life review. I visited different spots in town that had meaning for me. I parked at the end of the cul-de-sac where I'd chased leaves with Tippy as we waited for the school bus. I went to the soccer field. I sat outside my old house, which my parents had sold at the end of the 1990s. I passed the coffee shop where I used to go with Toby.

Finally I pulled up in front of my father's office on the corner of

Wisconsin and Plankinton. I sat there for a while, thinking about my parents. I'd criticized them for screwing up their lives, living in denial, failing to help themselves, and then retreating: my mother into her sadness and my father into a Xanax fog. I'd sworn that I'd be different. But look where I was, what I was about to do.

The irony was the bitter pill I had to swallow. Patterns were hard to break. Was this fated for me? Was life mapped out? Or could you write your own script? I wondered if I'd arrived where I was supposed to be at this point in time, parked in front of my father's building, moments away from committing suicide, or if I'd screwed up things along the way, if I should've taken more responsibility. Why were my brothers on track? I was the child blessed with golden hair, with a quick mind, athletic talent, a warm, outgoing personality, voted most likely to be a millionaire—and I'd accomplished that as well as marrying a beautiful girl and having great children.

Finally, I cut myself off. This was the end. Soon I wouldn't have any worries, and Meredith and the kids would be financially secure. I stared at myself in the rearview mirror. I felt rational, like I was making sense. Taking a deep breath, I looked up at my father's building. He was the last string tethering me to the living, to the here and now, and it was time to cut it.

I called him on my cell.

"I need to talk to you about something important," I said. "I'm in my car, parked outside your office. Will you come down?"

He stepped outside from the building's front doors and glanced up and down the sidewalk until he spotted my car. He got in the passenger's side and turned his head toward me. I stared into him as if I was seeing him for the first time, not the last, and felt time melt away.

"Dad, my gambling is way out of control. I owe people a lot of money. And I've run out of options, except for one. I'm going to kill myself."

My father didn't move, didn't change expression.

"How?" he asked.

"I'm going to drive my car off the freeway overpass in downtown Milwaukee."

He put his hand on my knee and closed his eyes. I couldn't imagine the thoughts going through his mind, though deep down I knew what I wanted them to be. After twenty seconds, he looked me in the eyes, put his hands on my cheeks and kissed me, as if I were a child he was seeing for the first time. Or the last.

"I'm proud of you for being more of a man than I was," he said. "Our family might have been better off if I'd killed myself." That had to be the Xanax talking, I thought, not my father.

He gave me another kiss. "I love you. I will always love you."

"Me too."

"Is there anything I can do?"

"No, I've made my decision."

My father looked away. After a few seconds, he got out of the car. I stared as he went back into his building without turning around. I drove off with a sinking heart. I didn't want to kill myself. I'd wanted my father to take me in his arms as if I was a child and say he loved me too much to think of me committing suicide.

I drove to the overpass where I intended to take my life and kept going. When it came down to it, my will to live was too strong. I revisited the same spots in town that held meaning for me. I didn't know what I was looking for. My cell phone rang several times, including one call from Meredith. At some point I realized I was crying. I pulled over to the side of the road and let myself sob. It was a physical release. When I ran out of tears, I sat in the car feeling empty.

Now what? I thought.

SO MANY ISSUES

On the drive back to Chicago I decided that, rather than stay in a house Richard and Manny already knew, we'd move to an undisclosed location.

I went home and told Meredith I'd had a blowout with our landlord about the rent. Things had spiraled out of control. I told her we were leaving immediately and he could find someone else to move in and screw them instead of us. Since we'd already had an actual dispute with him, she believed me.

"What's the plan?" she asked.

"You're going to take the kids to your parents," I said. "We're going to live there while we look for a house to buy. And I'll put our stuff in storage till then."

"We're leaving just like that?" she asked.

"I don't want to give this jerk another cent of our money. I know it's strange—"

"To say the least," she interjected. "But typical of you."

"But it's going to be worth it."

Meredith called her friend Lorri, and they gathered up a bunch of things and went to her parents' house. I rented a U-Haul and leased space at a storage facility. From 8 PM until 6 AM, I packed everything we owned into the U-Haul and unloaded it at the storage facility. I worked nonstop. I hadn't slept for two days when I showed up at Meredith's folks' place later that morning, dirty, sweaty, and exhausted.

Meredith met me at the door with a Gatorade. After a rest, I went into town and destroyed the videotape I'd made for my family.

Instead of saying, "I'm so glad you're alive" or "I knew you weren't going to do it," my father moved on to the next topic.

We stayed with Meredith's parents from June through September. I changed our phone numbers and made sure our mail went to a P.O. box. I did my best to take us underground, or at least out of plain sight without Meredith or her parents suspecting more dire motives. I still had to deal with the money I owed Richard. I may have moved homes, but I knew he could hunt me down in Las Vegas.

I called Fisher in New York. He'd always been a strong option when I needed twenty or thirty grand, though I'd never been in such a dire jam. I tried to plan my approach, but by then I was so desperate that I broke down as soon as I heard his voice. I just wanted Richard off my back, my family safe.

"I just blew up again," I said. "My wife, my kids . . . they may die. I'm involved with this guy who's really connected, and—"

"How much do you need?" Fisher interrupted.

"How much can you spare?" I replied.

"That's not the right question," he said peevishly. "How much money do you *need*?"

I was unable to give him a straight answer. I was embarrassed. Humiliated and feeling pathetic was actually more like it.

"How much do you need to get yourself out of trouble?"

"Two hundred and fifty thousand dollars."

The money wasn't a net-worth problem. Fisher made a ton in development. But it was four times more than I'd ever asked him to loan me. With the death threats that I'd mentioned, as well as my income, which he knew, he felt the situation was out of control, more so than any time before, and therefore beyond a loan.

"I'm not going to answer you right now," he said. "I'm going to think about this over the weekend."

"Come on, dude," I pleaded. "I've made you money."

"Adam, if you want to put it like that, let me rephrase. I don't consider this a good investment. You know why. Still, I'm going to think about it."

I didn't hear from him until late Monday morning. I was in my car.

"It's over," he said.

"What do you mean?" I asked apprehensively. "You aren't giving me the money?"

"I mean that I'm done codepending you," he said. "I spoke to my father, which I've never done before. I've considered what to do. If I thought giving you two hundred fifty thousand dollars would end this problem today, I'd do it in a second. But it's not going to help. It may help you today, but not tomorrow."

"You don't know that," I argued.

"Here's my proposal—take it or leave it," he continued. "I have lawyers and resources. I will bring them to the table, sit down with your creditors, structure something that gets you out of situations, and do it all on my nickel. That's my gift."

I wiped my brow and took a breath.

"You don't understand," I said. "You can't sit down with these types of creditors. They don't take meetings. There isn't a paper trail."

"This is about helping you," he said.

"You know what will help me? The two hundred fifty thousand dollars!" That's all I cared about. "Fuck you."

I slammed the phone on the seat and drove around town as if I might run into the answer. If only it were that easy. I thumbed through the contacts in my phone. I had about a dozen or so last-resort lenders. I made several calls before finding a guy willing to lend me the quarter million for a month at 20 percent interest in a month. He was around my same age. I'd met him through various connections. He drove a bus after getting a law degree. Different. But he'd made a tidy sum off me in the past.

I used various pay phones and a FedEx delivery to arrange a drop with Manny in Las Vegas. I took extra precautions to maintain a safe distance. After that, I never contacted Manny again. I never heard from Richard either. By June the nightmare was behind me.

You'd think I would've learned a lesson, but no. By August, without any lasting consequences, I was playing with another bookie. Luciano Petrelli, a star high school athlete in his mid-forties, owned a local deli and took bets while he worked. When he answered the phone, you could hear him chopping in the background.

We played back and forth through August and into early September, but I woke up one day owing Lucky, as I called him, thirty-seven thousand dollars. You'd have thought from the change in his tone that it was ten times that amount. He called me three times that morning. I finally answered that afternoon. I hadn't been avoiding Lucky. I'd been consumed by events much greater than my miserable plight or the money I owed him or any other book, and I let him know it when he laid into me for the money.

"Don't you give a shit about what's going on?" I replied. "We've been attacked. Two planes crashed into the World Trade Center. They're gone. Thousands of people have been killed. Two other planes also crashed—one into the Pentagon. I haven't moved from the TV set since this morning. This is the worst day in the history of the U.S. and you're harassing me for thirty-seven grand?"

"I'm sorry. But it's time to pay."

I drove to Bank One in Northfield, where, through a power of attorney, I was able to use an account in Meredith's name. When I asked to make a withdrawal, I was told that the Federal Reserve had shut down and the bank wouldn't have that type of cash on hand. I understood. Lucky didn't.

"What kind of excuse is that?" he said. "Banks have plenty of money."

Nothing I said placated him. Having him speak to a teller didn't work either. I walked outside and erupted in anger.

"What kind of American are you?" I said. My sentiments were genuine. "You clearly aren't understanding the impact of this. Or you just don't care. But Americans are dying. We were attacked. I'm not denying that I owe you money, and in fact because of your sniveling, self-centered rants I am at the bank trying to get it for you. But people are dying. This seems very petty. And you know what else? I'm so offended that I'm not paying you. You can go fuck yourself."

Lucky called me fifteen times a day for three days. I never returned his calls. That breakdown in communication left me with another problem.

I didn't have a bookie. Since I was in full-tilt gambling mode, I needed one. I called Fisk, who owed me a favor, and he set me up with Luke Roberts. But Fisk also told me that he was in trouble—"Big, big trouble," he said.

"I owe money to everyone in town. My credit cards are maxed. I'm defaulting on my mortgage. My marriage is in the toilet. I feel like my life's over."

That confession touched a nerve. I knew the feeling too well. And while I may not have wanted to see that I was in the same trouble, I didn't waste a minute before helping him. I called Fisk's brother, Jeff, a psychologist, whom I'd met once before, and shared with him what Fisk had told me. His brother found a rehab clinic in Baltimore and got him in. Fisk stayed in through Thanksgiving. The irony, if any, was lost on me. If I was the one getting Fisk help, I figured it meant I didn't have a problem.

Except with my new bookie. Roberts was fifty-six years old and lived in an enormous house in Barrington, Illinois. I knew he was a bookie and a businessman, but nothing else.

I started playing with him and lost roughly a hundred twenty thousand dollars, which I paid. Then I won seventy-five thousand dollars a couple weeks later. When I called to collect, Roberts told me he was spending the rest of the fall in Aspen and would pay me when he returned home. Not knowing whether that was true, I called him for days without a response. Either he didn't have the money or he wanted to stiff me.

I found his address, made it to his house using Mapquest, and pounded on the door. No one was inside. I called and staked out his place until I reached one of his relatives. She confirmed that he was in Aspen. I wasn't really mad about being stiffed—my real problem was that I wanted to play and without Roberts I was stuck. I sucked up my pride and called Lucky. He apologized and said he was happy to have me back. I paid him the thirty-seven thousand dollars I owed, but in the course I also told him about Roberts' disappearing act.

"Do you want me to help?" he asked.

"Yeah, I think I do," I said.

I had a thought and briefly put on a detective's hat. I called United Airlines and talked a ticket agent into confirming that a Luke Roberts flew to Aspen, and giving me his return flight information. Luciano then hooked me up with a gigantic specimen of a human being whom he introduced as a "sometime associate of mine." Timmy was six foot five and 280 pounds of rock. I met him again in the baggage-claim area at O'Hare the day Roberts was scheduled to return.

"Just point him out and I'll handle the rest," Timmy said.

We waited about twenty-five minutes before I saw Roberts stroll in among other travelers. I nudged Timmy and motioned to Roberts, who was maybe five foot five and 140 pounds sopping wet. I hid behind a nearby pole as Timmy walked up to him. I was close enough to see Roberts's eyes widen and rise like an elevator as he took in Timmy's towering size.

"Do you owe Adam Resnick money?" Timmy asked.

"No," Roberts said.

Without even a half second of hesitation, Timmy backhanded Roberts across the face. Roberts stumbled backward, fighting to keep his legs from buckling. Roberts was seeing stars. Timmy walked past me, and I turned and caught up to him. We left without saying anything. It was business.

I had no idea that Timmy was going to hit Roberts. I didn't condone violence. I'd had enough of my own narrow escapes from harm's way to sympathize with Roberts. However, I heard from him the next week. He offered twenty-five thousand dollars with the stipulation that he never had to see my friend Timmy again.

Meanwhile, after several months of house shopping, Meredith and I purchased a two-story stone-and-cedar home on three and a half wooded acres in Long Grove. We put down 20 percent on the $765,000 price.

"Can we afford this?" she asked as we signed the closing papers.

It was October 1, 2001, and despite everything I'd been through with bookies and gambling, I assured her that we could. As far as Meredith was concerned, I had a decent income. But she never knew how much I made. We filed separate tax returns. I didn't want her to see the amount I made or where the money went. That was an unnecessary can of worms.

"The one thing I really don't like about this house is the safe room," she said after we took possession and began moving around boxes.

She was referring to a secret room that you entered through the closet in the spare upstairs bedroom. The realtor had called it a safe room. It could've fit four people comfortably. We were the third owners since the home was built in 1987. We heard, but never confirmed, that the first couple had put in the safe room after being attacked. We'd also been told that the owners before us also had problems.

"It is kind of creepy," I said. "I've never seen anything like it."

Meredith paused on the stairs while holding a box and surveyed the downstairs.

"I hope this place isn't cursed," she said.

"Not gonna happen," I said.

"I don't know. There's something about this house. Maybe I'm nervous about how much money it cost. I'd hate to move in and have our lives fall apart."

If anything had fallen apart that fall, it would've been repaired by one of the dozen of men working on the extensive remodel we did upon moving in. The construction was practically nonstop between October and the end of November. I was a freaking nutbag when it came to finishing the work early. Instead of six months, I wanted the jobs completed in two, and I pushed the contractor and his crew into working overtime. They were out before Thanksgiving. I was manic.

One day in early December, as I was leaving the Bank One branch in Deerfield, the manager had me follow him into his office. I knew this drill; I could imagine someone in the background yelling, "Dead man walking." The manager's office was a small room with a desk and two leather-backed chairs. He had several landscape paintings on the walls and family photos arranged behind his desk. I stared at a picture of his children and envied his "normal" life.

"I'm sorry to tell you but we have to close down your account," he said. "There are too many irregularities."

"Irregularities?" I asked.

"Large cash requests," he said earnestly.

He opened a file folder on his desk and tapped a pen on what I supposed was a printout of the account's history.

"The account isn't even in my name, if I'm remembering correctly," I said.

"Mr. Resnick, as both of us know, though the account is in your wife's name, Meredith Resnick, you have power of attorney," he said, emphasizing this reality by raising his eyebrows. "I tried to keep it open. You're very nice and I always enjoy seeing you. However, our security department said that we have to shut it down. I don't have a choice."

I rubbed my chin and sighed.

"Do you know what distresses me?" I said. "Last month I came in and one of your older tellers helped me. I requested a cashier's check for $87,500. When I got home later that night I looked at the check and saw that it had mistakenly been made out for $815,000. Even though it was after hours, I called the bank to report the error. I spoke to the teller, who was still at the bank. He'd realized what he'd done when his drawer was off. He also knew cashier's checks are hard to stop. They're like cash. But when I called, he said that he knew I was honorable and trustworthy."

"I have no disagreement there," the manager said.

"My point is that if I were going to do anything shady, I would've done it with the extra seven hundred fifty thousand that I was given."

"I agree with you. But there are too many things we're uncomfortable with. For instance, we can't meet your demands when you ask for two hundred thousand dollars cash within an hour. We've prepared to give you a check with the balance from your account."

He gave me the check for eighty-five thousand dollars and a receipt showing a zero balance. Later, I'd tell Meredith that my old bankruptcy and other credit issues had found their way into the file and made the bank nervous enough to close the account. My past, with its minefield of red flags, was something she didn't accept but had gotten used to, kind of like an annual flu. If I hadn't been a good provider, she would never have tolerated such annoyances. She thought we'd outlast them.

As it happened, after leaving the bank, I had lunch plans with Terry Navarro and his partner, Larry Elisco. We met at Once Upon a Bagel. Navarro and I had developed a relationship since I'd run off the golf course the morning Ariel was born. My comfort level with them was such that as soon as I sat down I lamented what had happened at the bank.

"There's no way I can open an account anywhere in the city," I said.

"What's the problem?" Larry asked.

I tilted my head back and looked skyward, as if scanning a universe of stars, not sure where in the vastness of millions of galaxies to start. I didn't come off as melodramatic; more like overwhelmed. There was the incident at the bank just a few hours earlier. I tried adding up all the Suspicious Activity Reports that had been filed on my accounts. How many were there? Six? Seven?

"I have so many issues I don't know what to do," I said. "An old bankruptcy . . . I can't get a checking account anyplace . . . the crap is endless."

I looked at them both. Larry just looked concerned for me. He was an honest guy, and from that point on the only role he played was being my friend. But Terry was a different story. To me, Terry was the kind of guy who was determined to penetrate certain social and business circles. To some, he might have seemed like a scammer. He heard I had some money and wanted my business. Furthermore, he wanted me to hook him up with all the successful people I knew. Like a lot of others, he lived vicariously through my adventures as a high roller. I told a good story and left out the harrowing parts. He saw my problem as his entry point, and he seized the moment.

"Adam," he said, leaning over the table, "I have an idea that could help you."

NO LIMITS FOR
MR. R

Normally I hated winter.

Meredith had joked for years that I suffered from Seasonal Affective Disorder. When deprived of sunlight, I lost all energy and initiative. But today was unusually warm for Chicago in mid-December. The temperature was in the high fifties. People outside were in sweaters and shirtsleeves (as if they were in Jamaica). The warmth of the sun bathed my arm through the deli window while Terry spoke. I took both as good signs.

"I have an account that I hardly use," he said. "You could use that account."

"What do you mean?"

"We want to do your taxes anyway," he continued. "If you're using that account, we can sort everything out for you. You can put everything through the account."

I'd been picking at my salad for a few minutes while I politely waited for Terry and Larry to finish their lunch so I could order some cookies for dessert, and then the ramification of Terry's offer sunk in. This meeting was suddenly more interesting than I'd anticipated. Terry, in his early thirties, knew about my gambling. His partner didn't flinch either. I took a moment to stare out the window, marveling at Chicagoans walking around near the holidays in sweaters and shirtsleeves.

"Everything?" I asked. "I can run everything through it?"

"Yes."

"My business? My personal expenses? My gambling?"

Navarro took a sip of water. He was finished with his meal.

"Adam, what do you think accountants do?" he said. "Let us work it out."

I needed someone to work it out for me. Despite my sophistication in so many aspects of business, whether it was analyzing a balance sheet, developing competitive strategies, or offering insights about mergers and acquisitions, I was a disaster when it came to my own finances. I went to H&R Block for my taxes one year when I made seven hundred fifty thousand dollars. I didn't know about balancing a checkbook or saving receipts or even cheating on my taxes. I was my father.

"What bank do you use?" I asked. "There aren't many banks left in the city that I haven't been thrown out of."

"Universal Federal Savings and Loan," Terry said.

"I've never heard of it."

"It's in the Pilsen area," he said.

"Where's that?"

"Just south of the city."

"Hmmm."

"It's a small bank. My mother happens to be the president, and my sister is the COO."

He nodded his head slightly, a subtle sign of confidence. I returned it with a puzzled look. How had I known this guy for more than two years and never heard about these connections? He knew I gambled. He knew about some of my business interests. Why wasn't I better informed?

"Yeah, it's pretty convenient at times," he said, smiling.

After lunch, we went back to their office. Navarro Elisco & Associates was situated in a rehabbed two-story building on Skokie Boulevard. Larry, a gentle giant, shook my hand good-bye and stepped into his office. Terry and I then went into his office. Terry's office was simple; a couple of file cabinets were the most memorable of his design touches. NEA had the look and feel of a start-up. I got the impression that many of their clients were struggling companies.

Terry closed his door and called his sister Toni. Their conversation, after quick small talk, was brief.

"I'm sending a very good client to the bank . . . Adam Resnick. Please add him to my NEA account."

Terry gave me instructions for driving to Universal and his sister's name. I was to see her when I got there. I stood up to go. As we shook hands, I looked Terry in the eye.

"Terry, you know I won't clear check systems," I said.

"Don't worry. I'll talk to my sister."

I went to Universal Federal Savings and Loan that afternoon. Toni had one of three private offices on the first floor of the bank. She looked and sounded very much like a professional banker. Short, with dark hair carefully done, she had me sit. I saw a folder on her desk with my name on it. She took out a signature card.

"Sign this and you'll be on the account," she said.

"I won't clear check systems," I warned. "I have some issues."

"Don't worry," she replied. "Terry told me you were a substantial client."

I stood up momentarily and gave her the eighty-five-thousand-dollar check I fished from my pocket. She stepped out to deposit it and returned with the receipt.

Outside, I called Terry and thanked him.

"It's about time I got your business," he said enthusiastically. "I'm glad I could help."

A short time later I owed Lucky six figures and wrote him a check from my new account, knowing it wouldn't clear. Back in the fall, when I'd lost in the neighborhood of one hundred fifteen thousand dollars to him, I'd charged the large sum at his butcher shop on my American Express card. We'd had to talk to the fraud department, but it worked. It was also convenient. But he didn't want to do it again.

"It took too long to get the cash," he explained.

Hence the check. I immediately warned Toni Navarro that I'd written a rubber check.

"I won't be able to cover it for a few days," I said. "What should I do? Should we stop payment? Can you cover it for a few days? Or should we let it bounce?"

She paused.

"Terry told me to take care of you," she said. "Why don't you take a check from your Navarro Elisco account and write it for the amount that is deficit."

"Okay," I said hesitantly.

"Take that check to the American National/Bank One branch and deposit it into the Universal account. Then call me with the amount of the deposit. I'll enter it into our computer and make sure it clears."

I took a moment to digest the instructions.

"Why deposit it into an American National/Bank One branch?"

"We're a small mutual," Toni explained. "After the savings and loan debacle, the S&Ls have become mutuals. Universal isn't a large institutional bank. We need a large correspondent bank to clear our checks. That's why I'm telling you to make your deposit into American National. It's the same as Universal."

"Really?" I asked, skeptically.

"Yeah, it will be like a float; deposit the money when you get it, tell me, and I'll make that deposit as well."

"Got it," I said. "Thank you."

I went to the Libertyville branch and wrote the NEA check for the deficit, as I'd been told. I realized I was taking a check from Universal and writing it to Universal—effectively using the same account. The government called it check kiting; experts described it as embezzlement or single-account check kiting. In either case, no one had ever seen such an arrangement before.

But it was rather simplistic. I'd deposit an NEA check at American, call Toni with the amount, and she'd credit me for the deposit to the NEA checking account at Universal. She automatically made the funds available. There was no holding period no matter the amount of the check. I was supposed to make good on the funds within the next day or two depending on the time of the deposit. I was religious about calling in the amounts to Toni, and if she wasn't there, she directed Olga Ruiz, a bank employee (who wasn't in on the scam), to make the deposit.

My reaction to getting essentially an open line of credit was joyously sick. I envisioned sticking out my arm and tapping it, like a heroin junkie looking for a good vein. Years later I would literally act that out, as I explained to investigators in graphic detail.

"Use the checks when you need them," she said.

I don't think either of us intended for me to use the NEA checks every day. But that's what happened. I was an addict. I needed them all the time.

From the beginning, I enjoyed a good relationship with Toni. She seemed to be taken by my warm and personal style, and I could tell that she liked the attention and friendship. As a good salesman, I had a sixth sense for how to talk to people, knowing what they needed to hear. When Toni mentioned that she was going away for the holidays, I bought her a DVD player for Christmas.

"I can't believe you're doing this for me," she said.

"It's my pleasure," I said. "You've been making my life so easy."

On January 11, I returned to Las Vegas for the first time since the Richard fiasco. Why not? I had money and Larry Elisco wanted to go with me. I arranged for an amazing three-thousand-square-foot one-bedroom suite at the Rio. I had to wire them four hundred thousand dollars because they wouldn't take my check since I had credit problems with their parent company, Harrah's. But funds from the NEA account (which didn't even have my name on it) didn't seem to bother anyone.

Larry and I played blackjack at the same table, though our differences were quite extreme. He bet twenty-five dollars a hand and couldn't lose; I was playing from two thousand to ten thousand dollars per hand and couldn't win. At a certain point I tired of getting beat up and ran over to the Bellagio, where I won fifty-eight thousand five hundred dollars. Later, following the bank's collapse, Elisco told people that we'd gone to Vegas for a porn convention. But anyone who knew me would've known that wasn't true. Given a choice between porn stars and poker chips, my interest was obvious.

My balance sheet bore that out. The Rio showed my losses for the two-day jaunt at $323,200. At home, Elisco told Navarro, who'd later tell me he wasn't concerned about the size of my loss, as he assumed I could cover it by brokering medical equipment. I wasn't concerned either. I returned to Las Vegas on January 28 through 31, and then again on February 22 through 26. Meredith thought they were business trips, and they were, in the loosest sense. I won thirty thousand three hundred dollars at the Bellagio the first trip and ninety-four thousand dollars the next time. It was pure binge gambling each time, forty-eight hours of nonstop playing, then a sleep-filled flight home to my unsuspecting wife and children.

During that second Vegas trip, I was spotted playing by someone connected to the Empress, since renamed the Horseshoe after its purchase by fabled casino-owner Jack Binion. They remembered that Binion's had a judgment against me from the end of '98 when I'd canceled a cashier's check for thirty-five thousand dollars. They'd never pursued it because I'd lost more than three hundred thousand dollars there that year. Since then, however, I'd drifted away, lessening my value as a customer, and they wanted payment.

They used insider's relationships to find the source of my money—namely, Terry Navarro's NEA account. Legal papers landed on Toni's desk at the beginning of March. She called me, concerned. Her mother was flipping out, she said. I promised to take care of it.

I phoned Marty, whom I hadn't spoken to since my old bookie Gerry shut down. He still hosted at Binion's. He was glad to hear from me.

"What's going on with this garnishment?" I asked.

He looked into it and called back.

"They found out that you were gambling," he said. "This was the first time they had the ability to attach some assets, because you've never been on an account before."

"My name isn't on the account."

"But you can write checks off it."

I took care of the garnishment and Toni was relieved. But something dangerous had happened when I spoke to Marty. His familiarity triggered a warm feeling. When he invited me back to the boat, I felt the urge to go. I missed lunches at the Tavern and rides to the boat.

"I promise they'll take care of you," he said. "It's much better run since Binion took over."

"Can you get me higher limits?" I asked.

"Whatever you want," he said.

That was enough to ignite my mad dash into gambling hell. But there was more—so much more—happening at that instant; it was like a perfect storm of events coming together to set off the greatest binge I had ever experienced. Toni called a few days later with news that the NEA account was deficient by $1.4 million. She explained that her mother and the auditor had caught the short.

"You forgot to make the deposit in February," she said.

Under normal circumstances, I would've panicked upon hearing that I needed to come up with $1.4 million while knowing that I didn't have close to that amount. Honestly, I wouldn't have known what to do. That was a lot of cash even for people with considerable assets. But in the arrangement I had with the Navarros, all I had to do was write a check, and the check, of course, wasn't even real money. It was all from the same account.

"I'm so sorry," I replied calmly. "I'll do it right now."

"Don't worry," Toni said. "I walked the money over because the correspondent bank said there wasn't enough in our account to clear the checks."

"You walked it over?" I asked.

"Yes. We literally have to bring it over."

"In cash?"

"No. With an internal check. But it's not a big deal. We have a $3 million reserve to cover checks so nothing will bounce at the correspondent bank."

That was the moment when I grasped the shocking level of negligence of everyone I associated with at the bank. It took them almost five weeks to discover a million-dollar-plus shortage, and now their COO was telling me not to worry. But what was there to worry about? I made deposits from checks into that same account. It was insane, I told myself.

I'd been trying to stay in relative check, but once I realized that the Navarros didn't appear to know fact from fantasy, I decided to take advantage of the open vault and gamble to the outer limits of my addiction.

With my thirtieth birthday on March 10, I treated myself to a week-long vacation at the Bellagio. I felt like I was back at the University of Arizona, screaming "Gamby!, Gamby! Gamby!" Every synapse in my brain was psyched for the trip. As far as I was concerned, I had no limits. If the bank didn't care, I certainly wasn't going to.

I told Meredith I was going to Los Angeles for business, and I booked a room at the Four Seasons Hotel in Beverly Hills. I left the ticket on the kitchen counter for several days so she'd see it. A part of me got off knowing that for three hundred fifty dollars I could cover my ass. It seemed cheap.

I invited a friend I'll call Dan, and we jetted into Vegas knowing it was going to be a trip of a lifetime. I'd wired five hundred thousand dollars and promptly lost 80 percent. By nighttime, I was loving the cards. Thanks to a run of $700K, I was up about three hundred thousand. The casino was delighted when I stepped away for some dinner with Dan.

Afterward, they sent us up to Light, the hotel's exclusive nightclub. It was up a floor from the casino. You stepped off the elevator and walked through a dark hallway of mirrors lit by candles before entering a dramatic space of dark wood, dim lighting, mirrors, pulsing tunes, and fabulously sexy women. As our host took us past the crowd of people waiting to get in, I overheard a guy say, "It's amazing inside. You get a hard-on just walking in."

My casino host, Jeff, sat us in the best booth. He knew it was my birthday. He sat down and a waiter appeared. He ordered drinks. Another host joined us. We were having fun. The conversation was excellent. Everyone was witty. And God knows, there was plenty to look at.

"The way you roll, Adam, you can have any girl in this club," Jeff said.

"I doubt that," I said, laughingly.

"This is Vegas," Jeff's pal chimed in. "We can show you a side of this city that you've never seen."

"You're probably right," I said. "I've probably made close to seventy-five trips here and I haven't seen much other than the blackjack table and sports book."

"Let's get some girls and have a party in your villa," Jeff said.

"I'd rather go back and play," I said.

Just then, as if on cue, a beautiful dark-haired girl, a cross between Jessica Alba and Penelope Cruz, strolled by the table and stared at me.

"Did you see that?" I said to my friend Dan.

"Yeah."

"I want to play. But I can't believe how gorgeous she is."

"She's the most beautiful chick I've ever seen."

Jeff overheard me and within two minutes Lindsey had joined our table. She was so beautiful that I probably could've introduced her to my wife, asked for a pass, and received permission to have the most incredible one-night stand of my life. If my wife had the opportunity to indulge her fantasy with New England Patriots quarterback Tom Brady for a night and I knew it was nothing more than physical, I'd tell her to go for it. I think problems arise when we try to fight human nature.

But I didn't care about banging Lindsey. I returned to the blackjack table, with Lindsey and Dan tagging along, where I started to lose. Lindsey had called a friend before we left Light and by the time she arrived I had lost five hundred thousand dollars. The karma wasn't good.

"Adam, let's all go back to your room," Lindsey suggested.

She was hard to resist, and so was my villa. The Bellagio had put me up in what a sane person would call a mini-mansion: two bedrooms, four bathrooms, twenty-foot ceilings, a media room, a gym, a fourteen-person dining room, a private swimming pool and hot tub with sculpted rock walls, and a beauty parlor. I led us to this Mediterranean-themed den of luxury. I smoked a joint with Lindsey on the patio. She listened to me talk about my wife and children with a look in her eye that said you can do anything you want with me. I asked about her background and cracked jokes.

After nearly two hours, we went back into the great room. We walked in on Dan and Lindsey's friend having sex. All of us laughed as they covered themselves and sprinted into a bedroom. With the help of the butler assigned to my villa, I sent Lindsey home in the hotel's limousine.

Lindsey found me the next night in the casino. She approached the table as I was collecting from a hand that I'd split and doubled (the Bellagio capped me at two hands of twenty thousand). I admired the sheer fabric of her black silk tank top. You couldn't see through it, but it left nothing to the imagination. I smiled and gave her a five-thousand-dollar chip.

"You don't have to do that," she said.

"I know. It's my pleasure."

The truth is, the chip meant nothing to me at that point. Lindsey hung around for a while, and we chatted until I began to lose. At that point, I politely asked her to leave. Without a word, as if she understood, Lindsey drifted off, leaving me with a smile to remember. I began to win. I gambled for most of the next twenty-four hours. By the morning of the fourteenth, I was up about six hundred fifty thousand dollars. My casino host knew that I was scheduled to leave that morning. He came by several times offering food, a massage in my villa, anything I wanted.

"I'd like to stay and play," I said. "But I have a late-morning flight."

"Let me get right back to you," he said, and then disappeared into the crowd.

A few minutes later, he returned. He waited for me to finish my hand. When I looked up at him, he flashed a smile.

"We can take care of your flight," he said.

"Great. What time does it leave?"

"Whenever you want."

"What?"

"We're going to fly you home on our private Gulfstream. It's a G-4."

I phoned Dan to let him know the change in plans. He hurried to the casino from the room where he'd been packing. He shook his head at the new plan.

"No fucking way," he said. "I know what's going to happen. Let's now and fly commercial."

"Hey, you banged that smokin' hot twenty-one-year-old last night," I said. "That was your pleasure. I want to stay and gamble. That's my pleasure. Is there a problem?"

"Yeah. Both of us know what it is."

"You know what?" I said. "I don't want to argue. Just go."

And he did.

I'd never been on a private plane before. My casino host explained they needed four hours' notice before I was ready to leave. There'd be two pilots on board, a flight attendant, and my favorite foods, which they already knew. (They knew so much about me, they could've filled out doctor forms.) By the time I got on the jet later that afternoon, I had, according to the Bellagio, lost $1,010,500. Averaged over four days, the numbers were staggering, though they'd get more obscene over the next few weeks. But in real everyday context, I could've paid off my mortgage twice; why bother with three-thousand-dollar monthly installments?

The flight home was a nice cushion. I'd been taken by limo to the jet. The two pilots greeted me when I boarded and asked if I was ready to go. I waited for a safety video. Instead the flight attendant, Mary, a cute twenty-five-year-old, poured me a glass of champagne and we were up in the air. I looked at my watch. Four minutes had elapsed since I'd stepped out of the limo. During the flight, I was served a spread of eggs Benedict, filet mignon, peanut butter cookies, and chocolates. I was given a massage, too.

I staggered into the car they had waiting for me in Chicago. I was numb from the four-day jag. Had I really lost over a million dollars? I couldn't think straight as I reached for my phone. I had to call Toni Navarro. I was about to dial her when I heard the beep indicating that I had a message.

THE WHALE

The message on my voicemail was from my casino host, inviting Meredith and me to return to Vegas the following weekend for an Academy Award–themed extravaganza of fun, including Oscar-related activities in Las Vegas topped off by tickets to the actual red-carpet gala in Hollywood.

I punched in his number immediately. This was great news. I had a reason to go back to Vegas and I wouldn't have to lie to Meredith—until we got there. But I'd deal with that later.

"If you give us the same play you did this week, and post up $1 million minimum," he said, "we'll fly you and two other couples to the Bellagio for two nights, then to Los Angeles for the Oscars, and then home from Los Angeles."

I didn't have to think whether I had a million liquid to post. I had an entire bank vault. That was the problem. Even if I wanted to lighten up on the checking account, something like this would come along. I was a deer in the headlights.

"Are you for real?" I asked.

"We can do anything in Las Vegas," he said. "We're owned by MGM. And MGM is MGM."

"I'm in."

A minute later I was in the house, telling Meredith. I made it seem as if I'd met Steve Wynn in Los Angeles. She knew that I'd admired him since I was a college student. He was a titan, someone whose interest demanded attention. When he spoke, you jumped. Hundreds of people tried to get into business with Wynn. I was among the chosen. We were talking about opening a casino in Chicago. The state's governor, George Ryan, might also get involved, I said. This had the potential to be a big deal, one worth millions, maybe billions.

I put all my effort into the sale. Because there were elements of the story that were true, I was able to convince myself. Once I did that, I knew Meredith was next.

"They're flying me out," I said. "They want me to bring you. And they said to bring two other couples."

Meredith was speechless.

"It's crazy," she said. "I can't believe it." She put me in her crosshairs. "Do they know you don't gamble?"

"Of course," I said.

The rest of the week was a blur of activity reflective of my manic state of mind. I wanted everything bigger, better, more outrageous, and NOW.

On March 15, I wired two hundred twenty-five thousand dollars into the Horseshoe so I could play astronomical Vegas-like numbers there. I spoke to Lucky about raising my limits to $50K for the upcoming baseball season and $100K on basketball. He had me post a two hundred thousand dollar bond. Not a problem. I wrote a check. Four days later, I bought Toni Navarro a new BMW for $36,876. I wrote a check from the NEA account. Although she worried about affording the luxury car, I raised the notion of a consulting role in my business as a way of giving her added income. What was money to me?

In the middle of the week, I stood in our still relatively new backyard, imagining a sweeping remodel—make that a re-creation of the luxe tranquility of the pool and spa from my private villa at the Bellagio. I, actually Mr. R, pictured my backyard with the same rock pool, spa, everything but the proximity to the casinos, Bruno, and Lindsey. Within twenty-four hours, I'd signed up an architect, a landscaper, and a construction crew to build my dream pool, tennis court, and patio. They estimated the job would take six months. That was no good.

"Mr. Resnick, we can't do it any faster," the contractor said.

Mr. R knew that wasn't true. I incentivized them by handing out fistfuls of cash. More came later. I got the finish date down to six weeks.

That left the Oscars at the end of the week. On March 21, Meredith and I, along with two other couples, flew on the Bellagio's G4 to Las Vegas. After landing, everyone settled into our three-bedroom villa. They headed to the spa for treatments, where I'd arranged a variety of services from facials to massages, while I disappeared for a "meeting" with Wynn that I estimated would take a couple of hours. I went straight to the high-roller area, of course, and quickly got slaughtered.

I was nearly finished when my casino host delivered bad news. We weren't able to get into the Academy Awards. In the wake of 9/11, security was extremely tight; all attendees had to be screened by the FBI; as it was now Friday night, he said, there wasn't time for us to be cleared by show time on Sunday.

I got very angry. I let him know that I felt used and taken advantage of. How did I know this hadn't been a lie from the beginning to get me back to the Bellagio?

"Mr. R, I will make it up to you," the host promised.

He outlined an itinerary that included two tickets costing five thousand dollars per head to talent manager Norby Walters's annual Oscar party at the Beverly Hills Hotel and a gift for one couple up to ten thousand dollars in value at a store of our choice. Since we totaled three couples, I bought four more tickets to the Oscar party, paying from my own pocket. Then I upped the shopping ante by throwing in an additional twenty thousand dollars and arranging for reps from Gucci, Armani, Fred Leighton, and Hermes to march into our suite and make a presentation to each couple as an apology from the hotel for missing the Oscars. No one had to know that I was actually paying for it.

I wasn't as amused as I was relieved that my ruse worked. Everyone was amazed when salespeople from these high-end stores paraded into our suite with samples and promises of more if the women didn't see anything they liked. As our friends picked out watches, Meredith turned toward me. She looked apprehensive.

"What's this really about?" she asked.

"I'm doing business with Steve," I said.

"I read he doesn't own the Bellagio anymore," she said.

"He's still a major shareholder."

"I can't do this, Adam. I'd rather take the cash."

"I can't do that," I said. "It wouldn't be classy. I'm not even gambling."

Meredith ended up with a diamond necklace from Fred Leighton that cost an extra seven grand. Her girlfriends ogled it enviously. Everyone was in a good mood. That night we ate dinner at Prime and went to Light around midnight. As I walked across the dance floor, I felt a tap on my shoulder. When I turned, Lindsey was smiling at me. I received a warm hug and we exchanged numbers. I brought her by the table and introduced her to everyone at the table, including Meredith, as a nice girl who worked at the Bellagio.

"She's pretty," Meredith said.

"Pretty? She's beyond hot."

"So what does a girl like that do here?" she asked.

"Exactly what you think."

"I don't understand Las Vegas," she said. "You know what, I do understand it. I just don't like what it does to people."

If she only knew . . .

At 3 AM, I guided everyone back to the suite. I knew Meredith was tired. It was six hours past her bedtime. The two of us had a nice moment in our bedroom.

"Thank you for not gambling," she said. "I'm proud of you."

Within minutes Meredith was sleeping comfortably under a light blanket and Frette sheets. I went into the great room. The other couples had turned in as well. Everything was as I'd expected. I called our butler, Bruno, whom I knew, liked—and had tipped generously—the previous weekend. I'd prearranged this plan that would allow me to gamble without Meredith knowing. The hotel had even typed up a fake phone message from Wynn and left it in our room. Bruno tip-toed in and sat outside the door of my bedroom.

"Remember, if you hear anything, even the slightest stir," I said, "call me and I'll shoot right up from the casino."

"Got it, Mr. R," Bruno said. "Anything else?"

"Yeah. Call me Adam. Do I act like a Mr. R?"

I gambled into the morning, knowing everyone would sleep till nine or ten. I lost more than seven hundred thousand dollars. I'd lost almost as much with Lucky. As I went back to the bedroom, I thought, hell, if you tacked on the forty G's that I'd shelled out for incidentals, I could've produced an indie film and, who knows, maybe won an Oscar.

Then again, I was living a disaster flick. Our private jet to L.A. was canceled for mechanical reasons. (That's what they told us. I knew a bigger roller wanted it.) The hotel packed a stretch limo with enough food to stock a mini-mart and sent us to L.A. Everyone slept most of the way. We had rooms at the Beverly Hills Hotel. We changed into our formal clothes and went to Norby Walters's Oscar party; Anna Nicole Smith and Lou Ferrigno were the biggest celebrities there. We had a late-night supper at Mr. Chow's in Beverly Hills, then took a G3 back to Chicago.

An army of workmen and heavy machinery greeted us at home. They were ripping up the backyard. Meredith stopped and shook her head.

"What's going on here?" she asked me.

"We're building a pool, a tennis court, a basketball court—the ultimate party yard!" I said. "Look"—I pointed to a pole on the patio—"that's where we're putting the soft drink and beer dispenser."

"You're kidding?"

"This is going to be the ultimate party place. Maybe we'll kick it off with a bash on July 4."

Five days after getting home, I returned to the Bellagio for a four-day blackjack binge. I couldn't think of anything else until I got back there. I told Meredith that I needed to make a follow-up business trip to L.A. I actually booked another room at the Four Seasons and checked the message machine every hour (one more compulsion) in case Meredith called. I lost one hundred fifty-nine thousand dollars. I traveled to another "business meeting" on April 11, staying five days and this time winning almost eight hundred thousand dollars.

I put most of that money into the bank. A legit deposit. That was the irony of my actions. If I'd wanted to get rich, I would've withdrawn millions, set up an account in Switzerland, and left the country. But I was honest. Deluded. Sick. Out of control. Capitalizing on other people's stupidity, greed, and laxness. All true. But I also put money back (millions in cash and casino checks). I felt like a businessman, and why not? I was treated like one.

In many ways, I was still chasing leaves. Even when I missed the bus there were no consequences.

In April, following nice payment from Lucky, I met Toni for lunch. By this time, any pretense of business had become just that, a pretense. She confessed to having concerns about money. She wanted a certain lifestyle that she couldn't afford. She saw the way I was living; it was intoxicating. I didn't want her worries to be a problem. I hired her for eighty thousand dollars a year as a consultant for my company, Synergy Network Group. I also bought her tickets to Las Vegas, set up the hotel, and paid for her friend and other brother and his wife to go. I gave her cash for the tables and a little extra to play for me, too.

"Are you sure you'll be good for all this?" she asked, as she always did.

Believing I was, I replied, "Of course."

Money attacks everyone's weaknesses. At lunch, I handed Toni fifty thousand dollars in cash to deposit in the bank. Large sums of money flowed in and out of Terry's NEA account. In April, Universal's board of directors became suspicious. Someone spotted the unusual activity. The bank averaged transactions of a couple hundred thousand aggregate dollars per day. Terry's account alone handled between $2 million and $5 million daily.

I didn't worry because this was life as I knew it, but just on a different monetary level. I also had the Navarros' endorsement. Without my knowledge, Terry created a false financial balance sheet purportedly from my company, which he gave to his sister, who submitted it to the board of directors.

"Is it going to be a problem?" I asked Terry when he finally told me about it.

"No," he replied. "The auditor loves me. I used to work for him."

Toni developed her own system that had nothing to do with ignoring procedures for Non-Sufficient Funds (NSF) checks (138 in all). On May 2,

I gave her twenty-seven thousand dollars in cash to deposit. According to FDIC investigators, she "engaged in money laundering" by putting it through three accounts, including her own checking account and an LLC belonging to her brother Terry, before transferring it back into the NEA account.

At her request, I sent her back to Vegas the first weekend in May. She went with family and friends, and I set them up with golf, dinner, and activities at the Bellagio. It was Kentucky Derby weekend, and, for shits and giggles, I gave her three thousand dollars to pick a horse. She bet War Emblem and played one thousand dollars across the board—win, place, and show. That winner paid thirty-nine thousand dollars. She brought me the ticket so I could see it.

Hoping Toni would have beginner's luck, I'd laid out twenty thousand dollars across the board on War Emblem with Lucky. It paid nearly eight hundred thousand dollars. I didn't see a dime, though, as I lost nearly $1 million that weekend betting my usual array of games.

I was barely able to keep track of all the action. It was everything I'd dreamed of, and I was drowning in it.

Lucky was using an offshore affiliate to handle my action. My numbers were too large for him to deal with in cash. In one ten-day arc, I wired $2.4 million. Between March 15 and June 26, I made thirty-two trips to the Horseshoe. I never went on the weekends; that was family time. But the icing was Las Vegas. That's where I really escaped. Between January 11, 2002, and my final trip on June 11, 2002, I spent forty-three nights there.

No two nights were as memorable as a particular weekend in May. Along with two friends, I flew into the desert with $1.2 million in checks from the Horseshoe and another one hundred fifty thousand dollars in cash. Upon landing, I checked Sports Phone and added up my losses to Lucky from baseball and basketball—$1.1 million. A guy affiliated with the offshore sports book that Lucky used met me moments after I sat down at the blackjack table. He ID'd himself as Drew.

"Lucky sent me," he said.

Without looking up, I gave him two hundred fifty thousand dollars in chips, assuring myself of playing the rest of the weekend. But it pissed me off. Interestingly, I'd developed a temper as the stakes had grown. On my previous trip to Vegas, I had been playing in the baccarat room (where the high stakes blackjack games were held for people who didn't want to be seen) and after losing a big hand I'd thrown a chair. After paying Drew, I went on another losing streak, which culminated in an ugly and uncharacteristic display of anger. I picked up a chair and smashed it on the floor. No one said anything.

Later that night I was back in the baccarat room. I was getting annihilated. Then, at one point, I had a chance to come back. The dealer showed a six. I was playing two hands. In the first, I doubled on eleven and pulled a seven. Decent. In the other, I had two eights and split them. I pulled two face cards. Eighteen across the board.

I looked at the dealer and smiled. I felt like it was my turn.

"Go ahead," I said. "The only thing we're wasting is time."

I had a moment of positive karma I tried to infuse. Without reacting, the dealer pulled a nine, a one, and a three. That gave him nineteen. He beat me on all three hands. I lost a hundred thousand dollars.

I leapt up and whipped a twenty-five-thousand-dollar chip against the wall in anger. The chip hit an old Asian tapestry, one of the Bellagio's museum pieces. Within ten minutes, an executive in a charcoal suit entered the room and asked if we could talk. We'd never met, but he knew me.

"Adam, those chairs are a couple of G's, and we could've lived with you breaking one or two of them," he said. "But you just put a hole in a four-hundred-year-old tapestry."

"I'm very sorry," I said.

"We love your business," he continued. "We value you as one of our biggest and most consistent players at this time. But destroying our property is not going to work. Please stop."

"I understand," I said. "Maybe this is a good time for a break."

Having lost my marker, I stepped out of the casino and called the two friends whom I'd brought with me. They made me go to Light. We were having a drink when my friendly villa girl drifted into view. Lindsey was happy to see me. The three of them convinced me to shake off my bad mood. Soon I was ready to play again. Lindsey asked if she could tag along.

The four of us were in a booth. I cocked my head to the side and looked at her. I couldn't imagine a more beautiful girl. But I had no desire.

"Let me play a little by myself," I said. "Come down in about thirty minutes."

I got blistering hot. When Lindsey came down, I slipped her five thousand dollars in chips. Her smile was music. But it was all smoke and mirrors. She was a karma killer. How could someone who looked like her be so unlucky? (Life is full of warning signs.) The cards turned ugly. After one hand, I stood up and kicked my chair in disgust at myself and frustration at the dealer. Almost immediately the pit boss walked over and set a container of yellow pencils on the table in front of me.

"Mr. R, we've solved the chair problem," he said. "Every time you get angry, crack one of these pencils. We'll never run out. It's much more cost effective than breaking these chairs."

Even in my crazed state, I laughed. Lindsey leaned into me. I could feel the warmth of her face near mine and then her breath in my ear.

"Adam, you've given me so much," she whispered. "You are such a gentleman. Why can't I ever do anything for you?"

I didn't say anything.

"Let's just slip in the bathroom," she whispered. "I'll go down on you. You'll relax. You'll feel better."

I turned and gave her a grave and serious look.

"Lindsey, if you can give me head while you deal me blackjack, you have a deal."

If she'd said yes, I would've cheated on Meredith.

A tear rolled down her cheek.

"You really do have a problem," she said.

She hugged me and walked away. I watched her leave. What was wrong with me that I didn't want that girl?

Ten minutes later, I'd forgotten all about her. I was back at the table. I went on a run from the gambling gods. I got up huge, over eight hundred thousand dollars overall, including the quarter million I'd paid Drew. Maybe I was being rewarded for having some morals, I thought. For one of the few times in my life, I left the table before I ruined it.

The next night I went to Light with my friends who were having the time of their lives. They were flying high on all the comps the hotel gave them before they were rolling with me. I didn't know some of the people stopping by my table and ordering, but I didn't care either. Legend had it that the liquor tab alone was sixty-five thousand dollars (the owners of the club themselves were ordering drinks, since they knew the casino would pay). But that was merely the start. Lindsey was there with several girlfriends. One of my buddies began making out with one of her friends. Soon everyone wanted to have a party in the villa. I had no interest, but I wasn't going to be a loser.

I called Bruno and let him take care of everything. He stocked the villa with all of the favorites from the restaurant Prime, plus every dessert imaginable, and bottles of Cristal. After the guys and girls left to round up hot women, I sat by myself in the booth. I had the feeling of catching my breath. Amid the lights and hip-hop music, it was an odd place to take a time-out. When I looked up, though, I noticed a dark-haired guy staring at me with an unusual intensity.

I tried to ignore him. The club was crowded. Fat Joe's song "What's Luv" was blasting over the sound system. There was a lot of eye candy nearby. But that guy continued to stare. I waved over the red coat security, but even as I screamed "what the fuck's going on with that guy," they couldn't hear me above the music.

I was about to approach the guy on my own when someone else put his hand on my shoulder. I looked up. The man sat down beside me and put his card on the table.

"I'm a casino host at the Hilton," he said. "I could get eighty-sixed for giving you my card here. But I really want your business. Also, my friend David Copperfield wants to meet you."

"Who wants to meet me?" I asked.

"David Copperfield," he repeated while gesturing toward the man that had been staring at me.

"I'm happy to say hello," I said. "I'd be happier if he could make my money reappear."

After my meeting with Copperfield, I was corralled by the troops. They were all smiles. They were satisfied by their effort and ready to party.

"I think we have enough talent," one of the guys from the club said. "Let's go set off your pad."

I let them go ahead while I went back to the casino. I said that I'd be an hour. It was more like two hours when I staggered back to the villa after perhaps the most ferocious beating I'd taken in a casino. Not only did I lose the eight hundred thousand dollars that I was up, but I ended up, according to the Bellagio, minus $1,134,600. That didn't include the $250K that I'd paid Drew. Nor the fortune, whatever that was, that I'd lost to Lucky. All in all, the swing was more than $2 million.

If someone had stopped me on my way to the villa and asked what had happened to me, I wouldn't have known what to say. I was out of it. I pushed open the door, having forgotten about the party going on inside. I walked into a mélange of naked bodies, drugs, and music. I saw Bruno the butler, naked, snorting lines of coke on the bar. Behind him, I saw a guy I thought I recognized from the club, in his boxers; he and a chick wearing only a thong were feeding each other jumbo shrimps.

I stopped about three steps inside the door. Actually, I was stopped. One of my friends gave me a drunken hug (I hated drunken hugs). He didn't want to hear any bad news.

"I don't care how much you lost, you have to enjoy this," he said. "It's fucking awesome."

I picked up a bottle of Fiji water and went on a tour. Every room was filled with naked guys and women engaged in some form of recreational sex. I even spotted a young, hard-partying celebrity girl half-undressed and out of her mind. It was like the club, except everyone was naked. I saw bodies entangled in one bedroom. I counted six hot blonds and three brunettes skinny-dipping in the pool. I recognized a casino host screwing a stripper at the edge of the spa. People were fucking in the workout room. I walked in on three girls massaging one of my friends in the spa room. One of my friends was reclining in the salon chair getting head. I went into the kitchen and saw a naked girl step out from behind the open refrigerator door.

"Hi." She winked.

I checked my bedroom. Before getting wasted, Bruno had taken care of business and stationed a security guard outside the door. He knew about my neuroses.

I sat down on a leather chair and heard my name. Lindsey, her eyes red, was on the sofa with another girl. She was in her bra and panties. She looked obliterated.

"Tell me you're not going to enjoy this," she said.

"Truthfully, I'm going to bed," I said.

I got up and walked to my bedroom. Lindsey threw a bottle of champagne at me. It fell short, rolling across the carpet.

"You're going to regret this one day," she said.

I shook my head. I had no doubt there'd be regrets, but not this. I turned to the guard by my door and told him to stand there until I came out in the morning. Inside, I went into the bathroom, took three milligrams of Xanax, and then laid down in bed and welcomed the emptiness of a drug-induced sleep.

CASH COUNTING MACHINE

I arrived home Sunday night, and within fifteen hours I was on my way to the boat.

After spending the morning with Meredith and the kids, I picked up Marty on a corner near his apartment. I waited briefly in line at Universal's drive-thru teller window and picked up a cashier's check for six hundred thousand dollars. With Marty's help, I'd persuaded the Horseshoe to up my limit to two hands of thirty thousand dollars. The Bellagio only allowed me to play up to twenty thousand dollars.

We pulled up to the boat at ten. The valet took my keys and inched my car to the curb in front where it stayed until I came out later that afternoon.

"There's no reason to go to Vegas, kid," Marty said as we walked to the blackjack tables in the back.

"I don't know about that," I said. "But maybe you're right. I just want to play where I can get the highest limits."

Then we were inside the casino. I'd learned to call ten minutes before arriving so the dealer was waiting for me with fresh cards and chips at a private table in the back of the casino. I posted my six hundred thousand dollars. As Marty went off to do his thing, one of the Horseshoe's executives greeted me. They were emphasizing service since changing from the Empress, and I was without question the biggest whale, if there were whales, in Hammond, Indiana. Someone mentioned they should give me tickets to the Mike Tyson–Lennox Lewis fight in Memphis on June 8.

"I'll do you one better," the exec said. "If you post up six hundred thousand dollars two times this week, we'll fly you down on a private jet and give you ten tickets, ringside."

That was a no-brainer. I already planned to be at the Horseshoe every day. Before leaving the casino that day to attend Ariel's end-of-the-year performance at school, I confirmed the arrangement. On June 4, I spent a few early morning hours at the Horseshoe before taking over kid duty at home so Meredith could make some appointments. In the ninety minutes I played, I won $212,500. I handed out more than twenty-five thousand dollars in tips as I hustled out of the casino, knowing I couldn't be late. Two days later, I won $205,000. Mr. R doled out more than fifty grand in tips.

I have to say, Adam was always generous with everyone. But not like Mr. R. Mr. R was the biggest tipper anyone had seen.

Anyway, that action earned me the Tyson-Lewis tickets. The Horseshoe rented a G2, an older jet that still lifted off for Memphis around 2 PM from the private airport near Midway. I had ten tickets, but in my confusion invited eleven guys. I shelled out twenty thousand dollars of my own money for two other tickets. I lost fifteen thousand dollars at cards on the plane ride there.

On the ground, Binion's arranged for a BBQ dinner at Rendezvous, a downtown restaurant famous for the world's best dry rub. Before we were limoed to the Pyramid arena, I dealt with the ticket situation. Ten of them were ringside; two were six rows back. I didn't know how to choose who got the two lesser seats. I stuck twenty-five hundred dollars in two envelopes, explaining the casino had thrown it in as an apology. I stood up at the table as if it was an auction and asked who wanted them.

One guy snatched an envelope. He wanted the money, he admitted. No one else wanted the cash; they all held out for the better seats. Finally my dear friend Brad acquiesced. We teased him for having to sit in the sixth row as if that was like watching it from home. But the energy inside the arena was nothing like anyone's home. There was nothing like the atmosphere of a heavyweight fight. I'd never been to one before. I'd had tickets, but hadn't been able to tear myself away from the tables. Right away I regretted the missed opportunities. The air was thick with excitement and tension. This was fun and the fight hadn't started.

I led the way to our ringside seats. I stood and took in the scene. Celebrities. Politicians. Groupies. Reporters. Assorted riff-raff. They were all there, the whole bunch of humanity that gets off on watching two giant men beat the living shit out of each other. As I looked around, I felt a tap on my shoulder. A short, nicely dressed man introduced himself as my casino host.

"Jack Binion," he said, extending his hand.

We had a nice conversation. He was humble. He pointed to his seats. They were about forty rows up. Even amid the hubbub of the heavyweight bout, that gave me pause. What was going on here? What was wrong with this picture? If nothing was wrong, what did it mean? The guy with all the money was sitting in modest seats. The big loser, namely me, was ringside. I was embarrassed, but didn't show it.

Binion knew about the sixth-row seats. He apologized that some of my friends had to sit elsewhere. But as we looked at those seats, they didn't seem bad. Tobey Maguire and Leonardo DiCaprio were two rows behind them! Finally, Binion slapped me on the back.

"Enjoy yourself," he said.

I lost more than money on the fight. That night, my friend Michael called from New York. I was at the airport.

"We're through," he said.

"Why? What do you mean?" I asked.

"You're gambling again and you said you wouldn't."

"I'm not," I lied.

"Oh, really? You aren't gambling? Liz"—his wife—"was watching the Tyson fight and saw you ringside."

"I was at the fight. I don't deny that."

"But you're ringside and you aren't gambling? Please. I know how these things work."

I kicked the brick wall outside the private jet terminal.

"Who gives a fuck?" I snapped. "I paid you back. You had your bachelor party. You got what you wanted from me. You're probably just pissed you didn't make the cut."

I hung up angry and ranted at no one in particular about the world being fucked up and cold. It made no sense whatsoever.

The flight home cooled me off. I spent Sunday at home with my wife and kids like a normal guy. Construction on the pool and tennis court was virtually complete after extraordinary, near round-the-clock efforts. On Monday, June 10, I rewarded myself with six hours of volatile play up and down at the Horseshoe interrupted only by a barrage of phone calls from Meredith.

The only place I could make calls without background noise from the casino was the top deck, where the captain operated the boat. Civilians were prohibited from going there, but exceptions are made when you're playing thirty thousand dollars per hand. I probably sprinted up and down there a dozen times that day. Finally, irritated by the interruptions, I walked out of the boat, carrying a check for three hundred seventy thousand dollars.

I called Lucky. This was going to be a fun conversation, I thought. My past three trips to Binion's had netted me a cool $750K, and now, as of June 9, I was up $2.2 million with Lucky. I'd won so much that I couldn't even figure out what my net-net was. How much was mine? How much did I owe Universal? I hadn't a clue at this point.

"Can I get the money?" I asked.

He laughed.

"Not from me. For some reason, the guys in Antigua won't wire it into your Universal bank either."

"How the fuck am I going to get it?"

"The only way is to pick it up in cash is in Vegas," he said. "We'll get it from my guy there, Drew the poker player."

For me, that was an invitation to get the Bellagio's private jet. They were happy to send it when they heard I wanted to visit. It was my seventh ride on the G4 in three months. I took Lucky and Marty. Instead of riding to the boat, we flew to Las Vegas. We touched down early on Tuesday night.

By then, Lucky and I knew that Monday and Tuesday baseball action had murdered me. I was down $1.7 million. I stepped off the plane complaining about the lack of games left that night.

"Shut your pie hole," he said. "Just pick up the net five hundred G's from Drew and start fresh in the morning."

"No way," I said. "I want the entire $2.2 million. Why not? I don't have to pay until next Tuesday."

"That's a lot of money to carry around."

"I'll manage."

I was hyped up as we checked into my favorite villa at the Bellagio, villa number one. Marty and Lucky were trading barbs about the food business. They were debating whose Italian sausage recipe was better when we called Drew to the room. He arrived with a large duffel bag, the kind you'd take to the gym, and hoisted it on the coffee table between the two couches. It landed with a thud that seemed like it might crack the glass top. I looked in and saw a rare sight. It was filled with cash. Twenty-two bricks of a hundred thousand per.

I reached in, grabbed a handful of bundles, and started to count.

"You must count it," Marty said insistently.

"But that's going to take forever," Lucky said.

"Count it," Marty repeated.

"I'm disgusted by the filth," I said. "Money is the dirtiest thing on the planet. I don't know how many people have touched this shit. But what do you suggest?"

Not a second later, I jumped up and called my butler, Bruno. "Can you get me a cash-counting machine?"

"Hmmm," he said, momentarily taken aback. "I've never been asked that one. I don't know. Let me check."

He called back a few minutes later.

"Mr. R, the machines on the floor are all tied up."

"What about buying one?" I asked. "Will you look into where we can buy one now?"

Bruno found one, brand-new, for four thousand dollars. He delivered it to the villa less than an hour later. Even though I knew they probably padded the cost, I gave Bruno five thousand dollars. Then Lucky, Marty, Drew and I sat on the couches, running hundreds through the cash machine. We were like kids, watching a washing machine bubble over with suds. We laughed; we freaked out; we counted out the bills—one-point-three . . . one-point-five . . . one-point-eight . . . At the end, the total was $10K off.

"Who the fuck cares," I said, figuring Drew had skimmed the cash thinking that I wouldn't notice or care.

"I don't know what happened," Drew said.

"Don't worry about it," I said.

I had another issue. The safes in the room weren't large enough to hold the cash in or out of the duffel bag. I grabbed the bag and faced the guys.

"Follow me," I said.

I led a march into the gift shop and bought a black leather Bellagio bag. Like an idiot, I paid cash rather than sign it over to the room, which was comped. Then we transferred the cash. The bag was heavy. I carried it through the lobby, even dragging it across the floor at one point, as we hit the tables. I wrapped the strap around my leg while I played. While we planned dinner, Marty got wasted on vodka and Vicodin, and Lucky smartly cleaned up at the twenty-five-dollar table. I got shelled before we finally got up.

"Why don't you play at Caesar's?" Marty asked. "If you're going to lose all your money, lose some there. My girlfriend, Marsha, is a host. She'll get credit."

I missed the poignancy of his remark. First that I didn't recall playing at Caesar's since my first trips to Vegas; so at my worst, it was like going back to the beginning. And second, he'd said *if I was going to lose all my money* . . . Did I miss that? Or did I accept it, consciously or not, as inevitable?

The three of us went there, me carrying my leather bag containing $2.2 million. I posted $250K with a check. After sitting down at the table, I was struck by a single memory of having played at Caesar's in the past six years, one time when I was just turned into mince meat. I felt nothing but bad karma.

I stayed eight minutes. Caesar's showed me losing two hundred fifty thousand dollars.

I wanted to strangle Marty.

"Are you happy now?" I sneered as we traipsed back to the Bellagio.

As soon as we entered the hotel, the head of security approached me. He said that I'd caused a scene earlier in the gift shop by transferring so much cash in the open and the Bellagio was concerned for my safety *and* my money as word had spread like wildfire that there was a bald sweaty guy carrying around millions in cash.

"We're going to assign a guard," he explained.

"I appreciate that," I said. "But would you please keep a discreet distance."

"Of course."

We sat in one of the lounges while I assessed the situation. It had nothing to do with a fear of being held up. Going into Wednesday, I was down $500K to the Bellagio, $1.8 million to the book, and I'd just tossed two hundred fifty thousand dollars down the drain at Caesar's. But I had $2.2 million in my bag. I took a breath. Marty was stirring a cocktail. Lucky snapped shut his cell.

"You lost the Lakers tonight," he said.

"Fuck!" I said.

I had three bets on that game—the first half, the second, and the game itself. Lucky had got his offshore guys to up my limit to $600K per game, which meant if I got swept, as I did, my juice was $60K. I didn't care who you were, even if you had access like mine, you couldn't afford that kind of hit.

That brought my total with the book to $2,360,000. But as we sat there I added in another million one in baseball losses. I was down $3,460,000.

"They're getting nervous in Antigua," he said. "Please let me hold the bag. I can't have you lose the cash."

"Forget it," I said.

"Let me call Drew and have him pick it up."

"No fucking way," I said emphatically. "Payday is next Tuesday. They'll get their money then."

"Fine," he said. "They're capping you at $4 million for the week. You can play tomorrow." Suddenly he grabbed the bag of money. "But I'm holding this."

We wrestled for it for a moment. Lucky was tough. I didn't have the strength to fight. I let go.

"I'm going to play," I said.

After they left for the room, I went into the casino, deposited a five-hundred-thousand-dollar check from the Horseshoe, and took my place at a table in the baccarat room. It wasn't my usual table in the back; this one was in the front, visible from the cocktail lounge, and soon I noticed a small crowd of people watching me. They had reason to. I was snapping No. 2 pencils and screaming F bombs like some kind of strange lounge act.

I was oblivious to my crude outbursts until I noticed a heavyset woman's worried expression. She was craning her neck from her seat at the table, straining to see me. I thought I saw panic in her eyes. Other people were pointing at me, too. The attention frightened me into a weird head space. I had the sense of floating above myself. From that vantage, I saw that my wrist was bleeding on the table.

"Can you play faster?" I asked the dealer.

"Mr. R"—he said.

"Just play faster," I interrupted.

The pit boss stepped to the table and leaned between us, breaking the plane of vision. He set a box of tissues next to me.

"Mr. R, take some tissues for the blood," he said.

Apparently I'd cut my hand breaking one of the pencils without noticing until the pit boss brought it to my attention. But he didn't suggest that I stop even while he or someone else got a Band-Aid. I didn't think of stopping either. I played until I ran out of money forty-five minutes later. As I wobbled out of the casino, my bloody hand wrapped and my head battle-scarred, I saw maintenance workers carrying in a new tabletop to replace the one stained with my blood.

We didn't have to wait the requisite four hours for the plane after I railed to Bruno that I wanted to leave immediately. There was no arguing with my tone. It wasn't demanding or angry as much as it was despairing and urgent. In what turned out to be the last time we spoke, the friendly butler came through. He whisked us through the private underground passageway used only by celebrities, whales, and degenerate losers like me and put us in a limo for the airport.

Lucky, Marty, and I were in the air, heading at over 500 mph to Chicago, in less than an hour. Marty passed out immediately from exhaustion. Lucky and I, facing each other with a small table between us, played blackjack for the next three hours and twenty minutes. We worked our way up to $10K from $1K per hand and ran the cash through the machine after every hand.

"This is without a doubt the funniest thing I've ever seen," Marty said when he woke up.

I thought of the classic scene with Joe Pesci in *Goodfellas* when he asks, "What do you mean funny, funny how? How am I funny?" There was nothing humorous in the situation. By the time we landed, I'd lost eighty-five thousand dollars. It was salt in the wound. I owed Lucky and his offshore partners four thousand dollars. Before deplaning, I clamped my hand around the leather bag full of cash before Lucky could reach it. I was determined to hold that sucker till the very last minute.

"I earned the right," I told Lucky.

"Don't fucking lose it in the next six days," he said.

I needed warning of another kind. Unbeknownst to me, sometime in early June, Universal's board chairman, Robert McKinlay, had asked Toni Navarro for copies of statements and checks from the NEA account. Alarmed by the activity, he asked to see the front and back of the checks. He wanted to see where the money was going. Hearing this, I assumed we were fucked. Honestly, despite all my unorthodox relationships with bankers and irregular financial arrangements, in my delusional mind this was the first time I felt I'd compromised my moral compass and done something criminal. I had a pit in my stomach. It wasn't just a banker covering my checks. It wasn't just playing the float. It wasn't rolling over a personal loan. This was a line I'd never imagine I cross—and there was no turning back.

Terry altered, cut, pasted the checks, and I helped him at the copier. Toni submitted them to McKinlay.

It remained business as usual. On Thursday, June 13, I withdrew a check for $1.4 million from Universal. Olga Ruiz innocently credited the NEA account without any corresponding deposit.

I took my check and went to the Horseshoe. I was at the blackjack table for fourteen hours and forty-eight minutes. I averaged $55,608.11 per hand. I lost $387,500.

I was at Tavern on Rush the next day. I needed a breather from the boat. Marty headed the usual cast of lunchtime characters. We were digging into shrimp cocktails when Marty described how I'd dragged that leather bag full of money around Vegas. He physically acted out how heavy it had been.

"The kid even had the words Bellagio branded into his shoulder," he said.

"What the fuck did you do with all that cash," another guy at the table asked. "You put it in a safety deposit box, right?"

I laughed.

"Nah, it's in my car," I said.

Three of my friends sprang up and darted outside. Marty turned to me.

"You fucking lunatic," he said. "What the hell's the matter with you? Leaving $2 million cash in your fucking car?"

"It's in the trunk," I said. "The car's right out front."

Both of us watched as the guys brought the leather bag into the restaurant. Marty put his hands on the table, leaned in, and got in my face.

"You've completely lost your mind," he said.

I was about to lose much more than that.

BUST

People who've come close to drowning often report experiencing a sense of euphoria as they teeter on the edge of life and death, and that's how I explain winning a million dollars at the Horseshoe on June 17 and following that up with another five hundred seventy thousand dollars on Monday, June 24.

It was the gasp before the end.

On June 25, I left the house and pointed my Mercedes toward downtown, I was picking up my friend Freddy in front of the Merc, then heading to Binion's. I turned the radio from news to hip-hop. I'd left the family behind; it was time to psych up. Change one life for another. I took a swig from a water bottle and drummed my fingers on the steering wheel. Even in light traffic, I couldn't go fast enough to satisfy the yearning I had to get there. I fantasized about having a helicopter. I pictured it taking off and landing on my tennis court.

I didn't hear my phone until the third ring. I looked down and didn't recognize the number on the caller ID. What the fuck, I thought, and answered.

"Mr. Resnick?" said the man on the other end.

"Yeah," I replied.

He identified himself as an attorney for Universal. His voice was calm, serious, steady. His may as well have been the voice of God.

"Adam, we know there's a problem with you and the bank account at Universal Federal Savings and Loan," the attorney said.

I stared straight ahead and didn't respond. I didn't have to. I knew what he was talking about it, and he knew that I knew.

"We need you to deposit $3 million within the next day," he said.

I tightened my grip on the wheel and hit the accelerator. I had received so many calls like this over the years that I didn't immediately panic. But I knew this one was different. Freddy was waiting for me in front of the Merc. He traded pesos for a living. He was also a compulsive gambler. Normally I would've cracked a few jokes, but I was distracted to say the least. I couldn't think of anything to say. I focused on getting back onto the highway.

"You look like you're on a mission," he said.

"I need to win a shit load of money today," I said as the speedometer hit eighty-five.

I pulled into Binion's and walked inside with Freddy trailing behind. I reached into my pocket and found three checks totaling $2.3 million. I wonder if things might've played differently if I still had the $2.2 million cash that I'd given Lucky to send offshore. I would've had more than the $3 million the attorney said that I needed to put in the bank. I couldn't think like that, though. And I didn't.

I sat down at my usual table in the back and saw security rope it off. The chair felt harder than normal. I was unable to get comfortable. The dealer gave me a look, asking if I was okay, as he dealt the opening hands. I hadn't even said hello or anything else yet. I guess it was my look. My whole body was filled with adrenaline. My heart was pounding. I'd never played where I felt like I had to win. This was a first, and I didn't like it. Freddy sat quietly at first base (the first spot at the table), watching stoically as I monopolized the rest of the table. He left me alone and in less than an hour I burned through most of the $2.3 million.

I played according to vibe. I needed to feel the cards. But there was too much static in my head. All I heard was that attorney's voice on the phone.

Adam, we know there's a problem . . .

We need you to deposit $3 million . . .

By eleven, I was down to my last couple of hundred thousand dollars. I had pains in my head and my side. I was scared. I hadn't felt like that for a long time. And why would I have felt that way when I had a bottomless well of money at Universal? I knew this was bad, worse than all the physical threats, the desperate scavenging for loans, everything combined. This might be the end. At the same time another drama was playing out at Universal, where American National Bank was terminating its correspondent banking relationship with Universal. Investigators from the FDIC and Office of Thrift Supervision were put on the case.

I kept playing and for whatever reason I went on a run for the record books. The change was barely perceptible at first; I really had no sense the climate had changed. I traded wins and losses. Time stopped, and I entered a bubble. I had no idea of the minutes speeding or dragging. By twelve, I had more than $3.3 million. Freddy came to the table and said he had to go back to work.

I had no intention of leaving. I had to restrain myself from snapping at him for talking to me in the midst of my run. I didn't even look at him.

"Get out of here," I said, flipping him a five-thousand-dollar chip.

"Come on, Adam, you've got to go, too," he said. "You're up a million. Get out of here."

I brushed him off.

"You drove me," he said. "You're coming with me."

"Get the fuck out of here," I said.

I looked past the dealer to the pit boss, who'd stationed himself near the deal but not in my field of vision after I went up a couple million.

The pit boss stepped forward.

"Don't worry, Mr. R," he said. "We already ordered him a limo."

The roll continued after Freddy left. I played two hands, both showing a pair of twos. I split them, giving me four hands on the table. Astonishingly, I pulled two more twos, which gave me six hands. I felt like I was back at the Golden Nickel, except this time the cards were in my favor. The dealer was unable to resist a comment; he'd said he'd never seen a march of deuces like that in all his years.

I had one hundred eighty thousand dollars on the table. Of those six hands, I double downed four times. That made the wager three hundred thousand dollars.

The dealer showed a four.

"Monkey," he blurted, which was gambling slang for a face card. He flipped his down card. It was a ten. Then he pulled a one, another one, and a six.

Twenty-two!

He busted. That made my take three thundred thousand dollars. A six hundred thousand dollar swing.

"Fuck, yeah!"

I could've broken bricks with my concentration.

By 2:15, I was up another $5 million. I had chips in front of me totaling $8.6 million. The bank had asked me for $3 million. I had that and more, plenty more—and that was after tipping the dealers roughly three hundred fifty thousand dollars over the course of the day; yes, three hundred fifty thousand dollars. I stared at the chips truly amazed. I'd never seen chips cover that much landscape on a table.

I tried to put the past few hours into perspective, but I couldn't do it. Mine was a run that only God or the gambling gods sent down. I rarely won, but on those occasions when I did it had never been like this. I knew this was unique, beyond the norm, maybe supernatural. There had to be a point. And realizing that, I slammed on the brakes.

This was the first time in my life as a gambler that I remembered exercising self-control. I knew what was happening. This was God giving me the chance to stop. I shook my head at what a lucky bastard I was. The future presented itself with razor-sharp clarity. I was going to cash out, deposit the $3 million in the bank, walk away with the money I had left over, and never gamble again.

I almost wanted to laugh. I was safe. I pictured myself with Meredith and the kids. Against all odds, it was all working out.

I checked my watch again. It was 2:17. I knew I'd be able to wire transfer cash to the bank until 3:00 central time.

I called the pit boss over.

"Please get Melissa," I said, referring to someone I knew in accounting. "I have to send a wire."

At 2:21 PM, Melissa showed up. She was a tall blond in a business suit.

She handed me a transfer form and a pen. I filled it out quickly. She took the form and disappeared. It was a few minutes past 2:30 when she returned and put the wire transfer form in front of me. I'd turned my chair so that I faced away from the table. I stood up so she wasn't looking down at me.

"We can't do it," she said. "It's too late in the day to send the wire."

I checked my watch and stared at her in disbelief. In my frenzied state of mind, I was convinced I was being stonewalled. *This place knows my history,* I thought. *If I stay, they know they might get their money back.* The calm from a moment ago being replaced by the old anxiety that had ruled my life forever.

"Please don't do this," I said.

"What do you mean?" she asked. "Just get your money and go."

I pounded my fist against the table again and again as if I had no control.

"You know I'm not going to go," I said.

"It's your choice," she said. "Deposit the money here at the casino. Put the chips away. Do whatever."

"You cannot do this to me," I said. "You know very well if you don't wire this money, that $3 million and everything else on the table is gone."

"Adam, it's your choice," she said. "You can do whatever you want to do, but I can't wire that money now."

"Please," I said.

I stood in front of her, my arms stretched to full effect. I got in her face. I began to twitch and shake.

"I will come back at 8:00 tomorrow morning," she said. "I live a few minutes from here. We can do the wire first thing. The money will be there by the time the banks open at ten."

"Don't do this," I said.

She put the wire transfer forms on the table.

"I'm sorry," she said.

She turned and left. I watched her walk back into the cashier's cage. I froze and didn't move for a full minute, and maybe longer. I rubbed my eyes and opened them again, hoping I'd see a different reality. Nothing. There I was, standing in a casino with $8.6 million, and do you know what I did? I cursed my rotten luck. Feelings of rejection and abandonment barreled into me until I stumbled backward, at least figuratively, and fell into my chair at the table.

In reality, I kicked my toe into the floor, turned, and sat back down to play again. The dealer looked ill.

"Mr. R, I think you should go," he said quietly. "You've had an incredible day. Just get up, walk out, and go home."

You'd think the dealer would've encouraged me to keep playing. I was hot. But for some reason I think he and everyone else who'd ever seen me play in that room sensed a tragic end looming ahead, despite or maybe because of the run that I'd had. No one had ever seen such a run. No one wanted to witness the crash.

I got up from the table thirteen and a half hours later, and then only because the casino wasn't licensed to stay open twenty-four hours and had to close at 4:45 AM I hadn't eaten or drunk anything. I hadn't got up to pee. I'd just played blackjack and when goodnight was said I was down to $2.1 million.

The employees knew what had happened, and no one said a word. They seemed to share in the profound sadness I felt as I deposited the chips with the casino. But the employees were merely witnessing the tragedy. I was the one experiencing it. They didn't know the pressure I felt. I had less than the $3 million I was supposed to deposit. Water was lapping over the desk. It was that kind of sadness. No one was yelling I'm king of the world. I was going under, slowly, steadily, and inevitably.

I drove to the Sofitel Hotel and handed the valet a couple hundred bucks to keep my car in front. I got a room, sat down on the edge of the bed, and stared at the wall above the desk. Eventually I swung my legs up and laid down in my clothes. I continued to stare blankly at the ceiling. I never shut my eyes.

At one point, I had a sick feeling that I was at my autopsy, except I'd shown up early. I moved my leg. I was still alive. But barely.

At 7:25, I got up from the bed like a zombie and went to the bathroom. I felt like I had to pee. Dehydrated and sleep deprived, I lifted the toilet seat and watched two drops of blood land in the water. I splashed water on my face without any feeling. Everything hurt. I was in pain from head to toe. I wished that I had Xanax or a vial of something stronger.

I thought about getting help, and indeed knew that I needed help, but at the same time I saw what was going to happen before it did. Maybe if Melissa had showed up on time things would've played differently. But when I got to Binion's at a few minutes before eight, her office was dark. I sat down and stared at my watch.

8:14 . . . 8:15 . . . 8:16 . . .

I sat down at the empty blackjack table where I'd waited for her the day before. I hadn't asked to play, but a dealer appeared and she began to shuffle a deck.

I asked them to get Melissa on the phone. They handed me a phone a minute or two later. Melissa said she was stuck in traffic. I flipped out. What kind of bullshit was that? I hung up while Melissa was still making excuses. I handed the phone back as if I barely had the strength to hold it and looked at the pit boss. I didn't know what to do.

"Fuck it," I said. "Just fuck it. Fuck all of you." I turned to the dealer. "Just deal. I'm going to play."

I was at the table when Melissa finally showed up at 9:15. I acknowledged her with a slight turn of my head, but I couldn't bring myself to make eye contact.

"I'm sorry," she said. "Can I help you now?"

I didn't know how she was able to stand there.

My $2.1 million was down to forty thousand dollars.

I was beyond help.

"I'm so sorry," the dealer said softly, and she repeated it four more times until her voiced faded out.

"Do you know you're going to be the last dealer to ever deal blackjack to me?" I muttered.

"Sorry?"

"It's over."

"I'm sorry," she said again.

The pit boss overheard that remark and frowned at the dealer. He looked at me and nodded encouragingly.

"You can win it back," he said.

Really? Eight point six million dollars? I didn't know whether to laugh or cry. I was aware of everything about my life in minute detail. I felt as if my heart were beating its last beats and in that slowing motion of time, just as they say you will, I relived the most crucial moments and conversations from my past. I saw my relationships with loved ones in painful but gratifying clarity. And I realized that my version of hell was having to confront my lies and mistakes and relive all the wasted opportunities, lost time, stupidity, and hurt I'd inflicted on others to service my addiction.

Thus was my epiphany. Whereas many gambling addicts describe chasing their losses, I realized that wasn't me. I was chasing a lifetime.

"Mr. R?" The dealer wanted my attention. "Mr. R?"

She'd dealt the cards. It was my play, and I was staring at the cards, seemingly in a trance. The dealer gave me a total of ten. She showed a six. I would ordinarily have doubled down, but even after having lowered my bets to prolong the inevitable, I didn't have a dollar left on me. I pulled a seven. The dealer turned a three and then very slowly, as if she already knew, she pulled a ten. I shuddered slightly. It was as if I'd been disconnected from life support. Except I wasn't dead. I just felt like it.

Calmly, I rose from the table. I made eye contact with each of the four people in the room: the dealer, the pit boss, the casino executive, and a waitress who'd stopped by and been unable to leave. None of them said a word. I offered them a gentle smile and in a soft voice I said, "I wish you all the best."

Later, I'd find out the casino recorded me playing twenty hours and fifty-five minutes. They were open twenty-one hours. My hands had averaged $50,916.33. The total back-and-forth handled amounted to *$63.9 million.*

I was unsure which direction to go, literally and figuratively.

I'M A DEGENERATE, PATHOLOGICAL GAMBLER

I didn't know it yet, but as I left the casino Terry Navarro and her mother, Maureen, the bank's president, were being fired from Universal.

I trudged through the casino, my feet like cement. The valet had my car in front and opened the door. I apologized that I didn't have anything to give him. He understood and gently patted my back as if he already knew. I don't remember pulling out, but my first call was to Marty. He knew every major attorney in the city. He gave me Eddie Genson's number. Genson was the Chicago power lawyer the rich, famous, and connected called when they got in trouble, including Lord Conrad Black, R. Kelly, and a slew of politicians and lobbyists.

I gave his secretary my name and waited a moment until Genson came on the line.

"I was wondering when you were going to call, kid," he said.

"Excuse me," I said. "I'm not sure if I heard you."

"I said, I was wondering when you were going to call," he repeated.

"I don't know what you mean."

"Listen, I'm an old man, and I've represented the biggest politicians, celebrities, and gangsters in this town. I've seen and heard it all. But every week I sit at the steakhouse with the boys and they tell stories about this Resnick kid and his gambling. I've been hearing about you since '98, I think. And I've always said nobody, and I mean nobody, could gamble that much and not be doing something illegal."

"I don't know what to say."

"I also understand you're a great kid with a bad problem," he added. "I have a kid your age. I'm going to help you. It sounds like someone should've helped you a long time ago."

I looked out the window. I was sitting in traffic heading into the city.

"I need to see you," I said.

"Come on in," he said.

Genson's office was across from the Federal Courthouse in downtown Chicago, a fitting location for a lawyer who learned the legal system by tagging along with his bail-bondsman father through the courthouse hallways. Genson was old school, and his office reflected that sensibility. We met for two hours. I sat on his couch and talked, though I was in shock.

"What profession are you in?" he asked.

"I'm a degenerate pathological gambler, if that's considered a profession," I said. "Historically, I worked in the health care industry. I built up ancillary health care companies."

"Married?"

"Yes."

"Children?"

"Two."

"Do you own a home?"

"It's in my wife's name. I couldn't get credit to buy the home."

Genson called the bank's attorney that had originally contacted me. He received word that federal regulators were involved in the investigation. He phoned the U.S. Attorney's office to find out who'd been assigned the case. In addition to letting them know he represented me, he also left word that I wanted to fully cooperate. A few days lapsed before anyone returned his call.

"How long have you been married, kid?" he asked.

"Four years."

"Does your wife know about any of this?"

"Not yet."

"Tell her. I can help you legally, but she's going to be your best ally through everything else."

I called Meredith from my car and said that we needed to talk and I was on my way home. She picked up on the gravity in the tone of my voice and the conversation ended there. When I pulled into our circular driveway, she was standing outside, watching as Ariel rode her bike and Sam ran around with a ball. I walked up to her from the car, looking, I suppose, like I was going to a funeral. I knew if I waited or tried to think through anything, I wouldn't say what needed to be said. With about three feet between us, I stopped, and looked directly into Meredith's eyes, which were filling with fear as quickly as mine filled with tears.

"I love you very much," I said. "But I've lied to you. I want to assure you that there's not another woman. It's gambling. I'm sick. I'm a compulsive, pathological gambling addict, and it's gotten me into a lot of serious trouble . . ."

Meredith was shocked. We sat down on the front steps and then moved inside. I told her as much as I knew to that point. Our conversation lasted a long time, hours, though it changed from me talking to Meredith asking questions as she tried to regain her sense of balance and perspective.

"I don't understand, Terry Navarro's an accountant," she said at one point. "How could this happen? I trusted you were working with a professional."

"I can't speak for Terry," I replied. "I can only tell you about me."

And that was hard enough. Meredith was aghast as she listened to me spill my guts. There was so much to tell, and I was so scared and uncertain what would happen. I couldn't answer all of her questions because I didn't have the answers. It was the only time I'd ever seen her not composed. After putting the children to sleep, we moved to our bedroom. We sat in the chairs across from our bed, facing each other, talking and crying. At times, we stared at each other in a painfully uncomfortable silence.

"It's like I don't even know you," she said.

"No, I disagree," I argued. "You didn't know me. But now I'm telling you about everything that you didn't know."

"How do I know it's everything?"

"Maybe there are thoughts and insights that I'll have in the future that I can't tell you right now. But as far as the facts, there's only so much." I got frustrated. "You know what, Mere? Maybe part of the problem was that you didn't want to see what was going on. Maybe you didn't want to know."

She stood up and turned her back to me. I could still see her, at least partly, in the mirror on the wall. She had fire in her eyes when she looked at me again.

"Stop. I know you're scared and freaked out. But you have no right to attack or accuse me of anything right now. You're the one that lied. You're the one that manipulated me. You're the one that did something wrong. You're the one that's in trouble. And you put all of us—me, Ariel, Sam, and Harley—in this position? Is that love?"

That remark went straight to the core of my being. If someone had ever attacked my wife or children, I would've killed them. But Meredith had just forced me to see what I'd failed for years to acknowledge. I was the biggest threat to my family's health and well-being. The reality was crippling.

We lay on the bed, beat and talked out. Meredith changed into pajamas and drifted into sleep from mental exhaustion. I went onto the computer and instead of logging onto gambling sites, as I had always before, I checked for news about Universal. Reports didn't surface until Thursday, June 27, when local TV news stations and the papers reported that the Pilsen institution for more than eighty years had closed because of internal irregularities resulting in losses in excess of $10 million. There was also mention of the Navarros' firings. The FDIC was covering all accounts.

I got a call from Lucky saying that the last check I'd written his offshore people had bounced. It was for close to four hundred thousand dollars. But he'd heard the news.

"Don't worry about it," he says. "They made so much off you, who gives a shit? Take care of yourself and your family."

Meredith continued trying to piece the mystery together. She kept returning to the dinner we'd had in early June at Tavern on Rush when both the governor's and the mayor's sons had come to the table to introduce themselves. She knew that Gerry was a bookie and Marty's social and entertainment life revolved around gambling. None of them felt right to her.

"If you remember," she said, "I made it known that I was uncomfortable and you shut me down. And then came that whole Academy Award scam."

I nodded.

"I hated that weekend," she continued. "Don't you remember the necklace? I didn't want it. I said, let's get the cash."

We told our families. Our parents were shocked but supportive. My mother and father came to the house and hugged me. Meredith's parents also hurried over and said that they'd be in my corner as long as I got help. My brother Jonathan arrived that night with our friend Fisk. I hadn't seen Fisk since he'd gone into rehab. He hugged me before saying a word, as if he wanted to infuse me with his strength. It was amazing how the circle had come around.

"You were there for me when you should've been there for yourself and your family," he said. "Now I'm here for you. And you have to take care of *you*."

"But I have to take care of my family," I said.

"No, Adam. You can't take care of anyone until you take care of yourself."

From our family room, Fisk called the rehab facility where he'd gone and put me on the phone with the director. There was too much to be said on the phone, but I willingly agreed to start treatment as soon as they could take me, which fortunately was right after the Fourth of July. Meredith and I scaled down our plans for a big holiday party. Instead of the blowout we'd planned to inaugurate our redone backyard, we had a few close friends and our families.

Given the circumstances, it was a nicer time than anyone anticipated. I watched kids splash in the pool and barbecued dinner. I stole glances at Meredith, who was receiving lots of hugs and shoulders to cry on. I even saw her smile in the sun. She was as beautiful as ever. Everyone cared about us, and that buoyed us through the rough waters of our unspoken fears. I absolutely believe in God, but I'm not a deeply religious person. To me faith was knowing that people would be there to pick you up when you're down. Our family and friends gave us faith.

I assured everyone that life would continue even though I was scared to death of what the future might be like for all of us. At the same time, I was strangely relieved to have discarded my double life and started to get rid of the crippling secrets that I'd lugged around for years. I didn't realize what a burden that had been until I didn't have to deal with it every day, and this was merely the start of a long process.

Meredith felt the same way and mentioned that she could be around me for the first time in years without having the feeling that I was hiding something.

On July 7, I left for rehab. I was sad and nervous. I didn't want to leave Ariel and Sam. I hadn't left my property for nearly two weeks. I'd grown comfortable in the safety and anonymity of life behind the front door. I was in a holding pattern. I tried to argue my way out of going to rehab. Meredith and several friends much smarter than I wouldn't give me an inch on that proposal. As a friend said, I'd told what had happened, but I hadn't dealt with the why.

The rehab facility was in Baltimore. I wanted to drive there by myself. So I got in my 1999 Lexus truck, a second car that I rarely used except on weekends when I drove Ariel and Sam, and headed out of the city. I was in a mental fog until I got to Ohio. I literally didn't remember any of the drive till then, which was scary. There, with nothing but open highway ahead of me, I set the cruise control to 76 mph.

"I promise," I'd said. "No more fast lane for me."

But what happened? From out of nowhere I saw a cop car behind me. I heard a siren and saw lights when I looked in my rearview mirror. I pulled to the side of the highway. The Ohio state trooper who stepped slowly out of his car, adjusting his belt and hat, couldn't have been better cast. He was six foot five, with perfect posture.

"Do you know how fast you were going?" he asked.

"I do," I said. "Seventy-six miles per hour. Do I have a light out, sir? What's the problem?

"Do you know what the speed limit is?"

"Sixty-five."

"Do you know why I pulled you over?"

"No."

"Don't you think you were speeding?"

"No. My copper friends told me that I can go about ten over the speed limit and no one pays attention."

"So you don't think you were speeding?"

I regressed into my old ways. I didn't get it yet.

"Listen, here's the deal. I'm a pathological gambler. My life is coming to an end. I've just inadvertently taken down a bank as a result of my addiction, and now I'm headed to rehab."

"Okay. You've told me everything you've done. But I'm going to ask you again. What is the speed limit?"

"Sixty-five."

"How fast were you going?"

"Seventy-six."

"Do you know why I pulled you over?"

"Because I was speeding."

"Correct."

"Can't you let me off?" I asked.

He pursed his lips slightly and stared intently. He was processing the obvious: the type of guy I was, where I came from, all the advantages I had, and here I was, headed to rehab and trying to talk my way out of a speeding ticket by using my addiction as an excuse.

"You're right, we don't ordinarily pull people over for going ten over the speed limit," he said. "But I pulled you over and I'm giving you a ticket. And I got a feeling that I might be the first person in your life to not let you off."

I arrived at the Baltimore rehab later that afternoon. It was a four-story brick building that needed updating. The inside was no better. I looked around the reception area. The chairs and sofa were filthy, and the magazines on the tables were out of date. The walls were decorated with posters offering slogans and statistics about gambling. I was wary enough about treatment, filled with mixed feelings, and from the looks of things as I walked in I didn't want to make this place my residence for the next four to six weeks.

A woman sat behind the admissions counter and checked me in. I filled out long and thorough questionnaires: diagnostic, psychological, and basic information. It took two hours to complete the forms. I hadn't finished that much paperwork since the fifth grade. But I had one problem, which I told the woman helping me.

"I'm not sleeping here," I said.

"The requirement is that you sleep here," she said.

"No, I'll check into a nearby hotel."

"Not if you're going to be a patient here."

"I'm not comfortable here. It's unsanitary. There doesn't appear to be a cleaning service."

"Well, gamblers don't generally have a lot of money left."

"True." I smiled. "Okay, I'm in."

By deciding to stay, I was starting down a path of making the right choices. My gut told me that I'd run out of options; old chairs and small cots were the least of my problems. I ate dinner by myself that night. I chatted with a few people. My room was minute with a bed that wasn't long enough for my six-foot-two body and a dresser with two drawers. It was cramped, but at least I had it to myself. I slept that night for five hours. It felt like fifteen.

"How'd you sleep?" Meredith asked when I called her on my cell that morning.

I felt guilty telling her the truth.

"I slept great," I said. "It might've been the best sleep in my entire life. I felt safe."

"What does that mean?" she asked.

"I don't know."

I stayed for six weeks. Although I was too much of a neurotic clean-freak to adjust to the physical environment, particularly after I heard about rats in the kitchen, I rose at 8 AM with everyone else and started the day. The routine began with thirty minutes of yoga and breathing. I'd had hypertension since 1999, requiring a daily dose of fifty milligrams of Toprol XL. I had panic attacks as we did breathing exercises. I didn't know how to relax. But I persevered for once in my life and became a convert. It helped get me through the thing I didn't expect, withdrawal.

For the first week, I was a physical wreck. I had headaches. I was up and down like a yo-yo. The different groups helped keep me focused. Each day was broken into three or four different sessions. These ranged from group therapy, which often got extremely intense, with either the doctor or participants getting in someone's face if they seemed to be saying anything but the truth; to lighter chat sessions led by a graduate student; to deep one-on-one, forensic-like therapy that explored your family history, your relationships, and your life in general, and how it related to gambling and, most important, to not gambling. The one-on-ones were shepherded by Dr. Val, a woman who reminded me of Kathy Bates, but softer, and with light hair.

Meredith also came up two times and worked with me and Dr. Val. Each time I was grateful to see her. Relieved. I was crippled at times by bouts of anxiety from missing Meredith and the kids. I couldn't stop thinking about them. My need to belong and feel loved was transparent. I needed a safe harbor, as she put it. We looked at my parents. Pushed by Dr. Val, I spent days dealing with my anger and disappointment with them. She let me call out my family, but then she called out me.

"You can pinpoint reasons for the way you feel and certain behaviors," she said. "But you can't blame anyone but yourself."

I exhaled.

"It's not that simple," I said. "I hate platitudes. Life is too complex."

"In many ways you're right. It's not that simple. Every day you must navigate difficult situations. But at the core, it is simple. You listen to your inner voice. Is this good? Does it make you happy? Is it healthy? Are you hurting other people? The people you love? Those are simple questions."

Dr. Val helped Meredith and me through valuable sessions. Dr. Val became confident that I was learning and could not only be okay but a better person than before. I came clean with her as much as I could. However, I realized that it might take me years to remember all the lies.

I spent three weekends at home. The first day back I had a horrifying vision. I was watching TV and looked up at Sam as he toddled into the room. I saw bright white rice spilling out of every pore on his entire body, including his eyes. I screamed for Meredith and told her that I was losing my mind. I thought that I might be dreaming, but it kept happening. I literally dry heaved over the toilet.

"I couldn't look at him anymore the rest of the weekend," I told Dr. Val back at the facility.

"It was part of your withdrawal," she explained with a calmness that soothed my concern I needed to be committed.

"He's one and a half," I said. "He looks just like me."

"You're seeing yourself. As you're going through detox, you want him to purify as well. It's your mind at work."

The next weekend presented a different challenge. My mother called on Sunday morning, a few hours before I was scheduled to fly back to Baltimore.

"I have something to tell you, but you have to promise not to get upset," she said.

I was annoyed by that precondition. I was supersensitive to everything said to me. I'd spent several weeks learning how to use words better. For instance, I had a habit of saying to Meredith, "I love you but I'm mad because . . ." Dr. Val pointed out that "but" negated the first part of that statement. My mother was doing the same thing, and it ticked me off. But something about her didn't sound right.

"Okay, Mom, I won't get upset," I said.

I heard her take a deep breath.

"Jamie died," she said.

"What?"

"Jamie, your old girlfriend—"

"I know who she is," I snapped. "She died?"

"Don't be upset."

"Why? How'd she die?"

"I don't know."

"Anything else?"

"You promised not to be upset."

I hung up. The hell with my promise. I was working too hard to not suppress my emotions. If my mother couldn't feel, or wouldn't let herself feel, that was her problem. Jamie had been my first love. She owned a piece of my heart. She was an important part of me. I cared deeply about her and her family. I was going to get upset.

I turned to Meredith. She saw the color drain from my face.

"What?" she asked.

"Jamie died."

Meredith hugged me, but after a minute I pulled away. I was crying. We hadn't spoken again since parting on unquestionably bad terms. I hated that, and the more profound reality that we'd never speak again, time, the most precious commodity in life, had run out.

I put on my sneakers and went for a run and cried until I ran out of energy and tears. Jamie's death was, and has remained, a mystery to me. I heard that she got sick and died suddenly and unexpectedly. I assumed it was a virulent streptococcus infection or something like that. What mattered was that she was gone.

I went to her funeral by myself on July 30. I stayed in the back and didn't speak to anyone. I heard about a remembrance at her parents' home following the funeral. But rather than go back to their house, which had once felt like my own home, I stayed at Jamie's gravesite until all the dirt had been shoveled in. Then I approached the site and knelt down on one knee and patted the moist ground. I remembered kissing her for the first time, her perfume, the videos she loved, and her laugh.

I couldn't believe she was dead. So much life, so much love. Why her?

I said good-bye, and I followed that with something I should've said a long time ago: "I'm sorry."

BREAKING THE PATTERN

A week after I returned from Baltimore, government investigators wanted to speak to me.

Their investigation into the collapse of Universal Federal Savings and Loan was two months old, and they were talking to me for the first time. It sounds almost perverse, but I arrived at the government's offices on August 28, 2002, looking forward to answering their questions. I didn't see myself as a criminal. I was eager to help.

In my mind, the meeting was part of the healing process. For me, the toughest part of the whole ordeal had been deceiving my family. Since I'd already talked thoroughly about that in rehab, the other stuff, the numbers and my relationship with the Navarros, was easy. In fact I was bored by it. What was interesting about that? So I spilled my guts when the first question was asked and essentially never stopped talking until the investigators were exhausted.

It was comical. They were forensic accountants with coplike attitude. They wanted facts. After six weeks of treatment, I gave them psycho-babble.

"If Charlotte had turned me in for what was clearly fraud back then—"

"Who's Charlotte?"

"Charlotte was a banker who helped me when I was going to college at the University of Arizona. I was bouncing checks and in trouble with a bookie, and she suggested I go to this restaurant in the hills and make money by having sex with hard up old ladies. . . . "

"What does she have to do with the Navarros or Universal?"

"I've been a moving target all my life," I said.

I kept going until they warned me to stop rambling. They wanted specifics; I wanted to tell them *everything*. To me, it was all connected.

One of the agents from the FDIC bristled with annoyance after we finally arrived at the end of the session. They had put away their papers and notes.

"Okay, now tell us how it really happened," he said.

I threw up my hands.

"I told you everything," I said. "More than you wanted to know."

They believed wholeheartedly that I was a sophisticated con man. Nothing else made sense to them. It didn't matter how many times I kept returning to the truth or layering my explanations with wild anecdotes, they didn't want to believe that I'd siphoned millions of dollars and caused a bank to go under in order to play blackjack and bet sports. I wasn't a mastermind criminal. I was a pathetic addict.

"You're saying that's it?"

"I wish I could tell you there was more, but that's it."

I didn't go to traditional GA twelve-step meetings after I got out of rehab. My experiences made me feel that there was an inherent weakness in a program that advocated strict disassociation from gambling and gamblers. How could you avoid scratch-offs at gas stations? Friends who went to Vegas? School lotteries? It wasn't realistic. However, I have friends who have found the twelve-step program very beneficial, so I always encourage people to go there or anywhere else that can assist in bettering their lives.

To me, the solution rested in dealing with issues that cause the behavior, finding a balance, and accepting responsibility. Las Vegas didn't make me gamble. The Horseshoe didn't put a gun to my head. Maybe the casino industry would embrace help programs much more if the approach was different. No bookie ever forced me to bet parlays and round-robins. The industry can't be blamed. I feel the same way about liquor companies and cigarette makers. Sure they enable, but the world is full of enablers, and that's why at the end of the day I saw that I had to be accountable for my own behavior.

My thoughts on recovery stemmed from my first day in rehab when I saw posters about gambling on the walls. I brought them up later in treatment.

"Are they a joke?" I'd asked Dr. Val. "You have pictures of slot machines and blackjack here?

"Why not?" she'd replied. "You can't hide from the world. You'll see reminders and temptations every day. You have to decide not to do it."

That made sense to me. *You have to decide.* It was simple and obvious. It boiled down to choice. When I had the urge to gamble, I was the one who had the choice of saying yes or no. It was my decision. Yes or no. When in doubt, all I had to do was ask my gut. My gut was right at least 95 percent of the time. I hated to hear addiction described as a disease. Cancer was a disease; buying a ticket to Vegas or taking a ride to the boat was a choice.

I had every character trait on the diagnostic chart (and then some) predisposing me to gambling, but I still had them after rehab. They didn't go away. I taught myself that it was my choice. I learned to listen to my gut. I thought about the consequences. I made better choices.

To me, the key to making the right choices was breaking the patterns of behavior from my old life and all the lives that came before me, people like my grandfather and father who sometimes didn't make the right choices and left as their legacy the fallout and wounds of their poor choices.

I didn't confine the work I did to myself. That fall, I found out my friend Freddy was in serious debt from his gambling. In light of my mistakes, I was disturbed by the news. We'd known each other for years. He was an amazing father and husband. He'd gone with me to the Horseshoe on my fateful last day. Although he'd always been a heavy gambler, he sounded as if he'd reached a new low. I wasn't going to stand by and let him self-destruct as others had done with me.

I planned an intervention and got our mutual friend Darren to help. Emotional from the aftermath of my episode, Darren didn't want to see another one of our gang suffer a similarly tragic turn. We'd been friends since college. We'd always had a sarcastic, belligerent approach to life's limitations, but we wondered if this was our version of adulthood: the so-called fun from our overindulged teens haunting those of us who hadn't given it up by our thirties.

"I've been sixteen for the past twenty years," I said.

"You're only thirty," Darren replied.

"My point. I was sixteen even when I was ten. But it didn't *have* to be that way."

"Is that an indictment against your friends?"

"It just means that we don't have to accept it. We don't have to ignore these things. Or accept them. It's why we're doing something for Freddy."

We met Freddy for breakfast Sunday morning at Denny's. He came in on time, wearing jeans and a T-shirt. He looked nervous as hell as he sat down.

"Who do you have on the bowl games?" I asked.

"Too many games to count," he said, shaking his head. "And I need every one of them to hit."

Freddy picked up his spoon and tapped the end on the table. I remembered that feeling of overwhelming anxiety. I glanced quickly at Darren, then back to Freddy.

"Those are the last bets you are going to make," I said.

"I can't stop," Freddy said. "I need help."

"That's why you're here." I waved off the waitress. "Do you understand the power in acknowledging you need help?"

Freddy shook his head. He took a drink of water.

"We have to involve your wife," I said.

"No," he said, slamming down his water glass. "I'll get help, if that's what this is all about. But Monica can't know."

"We have to break down the walls," I said. "If you don't tell your wife, you're going to continue perpetuating the lie."

"No. She doesn't know. I can't tell her. I don't want to tell her."

"I will tell her," I said.

"She's pregnant with our fourth child," he said, pulling nervously at the hair on the back of his head.

"I know. It's okay. I will be sensitive."

"No. That's a deal-breaker."

"Freddy, that's not the right decision. Trust me. We're doing this anyway. Let's go. Darren will drive with you and I'll follow."

We caravanned to his house. Freddy lived two miles away. It was 8:30 when we walked in the front door. Freddy and Darren went downstairs into the basement. I followed the sound of running water and clattered dishes into the kitchen where Freddy's wife was cleaning up breakfast from her three boys. She was surprised to see me. Her surprise was quickly overtaken by concern. As far as she knew, I was having breakfast at Denny's with her husband.

"What's going on?" she asked. "Adam, where's Freddy? Is he okay? Did something happen?"

"No, nothing happened—not yet." I was standing next to their kitchen table and pulled out two chairs. "Will you turn off the water and sit down?"

She turned off the water but didn't want to sit. Instead she leaned the small of her back against the sink and looked at me. As soon as I began to talk, she turned away.

"I don't want to hear it," she said. "I can't deal with it right now."

For a moment, I had the sense that I was talking to my mother or rather hearing her. I'd always thought of her as the queen of not wanting to hear bad news, not wanting to deal. I'd grown up with her refusal to confront either my father or me. She didn't want to deal. All of a sudden I felt guilty for the anger I had toward her. She wasn't, as I'd just observed, an isolated case. Like Monica and others, she was too vulnerable, frightened, and secure in her denial to face reality.

"I know you don't want to hear this, but you have to," I said. "You're stronger than you think you are."

"I'm not," she said, pulling at the dish towel in her hands. "Adam, I'm eight months pregnant. I have three children. I can't handle anything else."

"You know what? Think about your life if Freddy wasn't around permanently. What if something happened to him? To your security?"

"What are you saying?"

"You know that he's gambling and has a problem."

Monica had been holding back the tears, but at the mention of his gambling she let herself go and sobbed openly.

"I know about the gambling. But I don't want to know."

"He's in trouble. He has debts. It's not good. But it's not too late. We're going to help."

I felt terrible for upsetting Monica. At the same time I knew without a doubt that I was doing the right thing. Darren brought Freddy upstairs. The four of us talked for about an hour. After the initial conversation, I answered their questions about rehab and gave Freddy the number of the facility where I'd gone. Darren had his arms around Monica as Freddy called and bravely uttered the three words that didn't just save his life but made it better: "I need help."

Most addicts say it. I'd said it and thought it a million times. But there's a leap from saying it to actually getting help and following through.

Freddy ended up in counseling. He stopped gambling and, like me, he quit lying to everyone, including himself. He changed his life. He broke his previous patterns of behavior. Within a year, his income had increased 200 percent, and he became the kind of husband and father he'd always envisioned.

His success confirmed my own experiences as an addict and as the friend who fought to get him help. I turned my thought into a phrase. It's inherently more natural, and easier, to be an enabler then an intervener. If the opposite were true, society would be better off.

Putting that to practice, I decided to confront the worst addict I knew, my father.

It was the spring of 2003, and my parents came over to our house to visit with our children. My parents, despite all the problems I had with them, were terrific, loving grandparents. Ariel and Sam adored them and vice versa. But my father, in his sixties, was a shell of the man that I remembered from growing up, and back then he was addled by problems and prescription medication. I'd been thinking about the toll taken by his longtime reliance on Xanax. I was tired of witnessing his steady decline. But more, I was bothered exposing my children to him.

What were the ramifications? My grandfather had influenced me. *You got the cards, kiddo?*

I was working too hard on my own life to ignore the issue any longer. I felt like I had to confront my father as part of my own healing. That process had become about breaking the pattern, and I didn't want to continue carrying around the baggage that had motivated so much of my behavior since boyhood. My question was when to do it—and how.

Well, I knew the time had come that day after my parents arrived and I heard my father talking gibberish to the kids. The children were still too young to say anything to Meredith or me, but I saw the puzzled look on Ariel's face as my father chattered away in a nonsensical slur. I didn't like it.

I told Meredith, and she was supportive. She took the kids to play elsewhere in the house, and I got my parents alone. We were in the family room off the kitchen. I turned off the TV and sat down. A mood of seriousness consumed the room as the afternoon sunlight streamed through the large windows. My mother, fidgeting, stared at her feet. My father looked at me.

I began with a preamble about my own situation. I acknowledged being scared shitless by the still-unknown consequences we faced as the legal process continued. But I'd gone almost ten months without gambling. Every day I chose not to give in to impulses that aimed for the high of being in action. That urge was hot-wired into my DNA. I dealt with it constantly. I thought about Meredith, the kids, and the consequences—something I never did before. If I ever had any doubts about the right decision, I listened to my gut.

"Dad, I don't blame you solely for where your life has gone," I said. "I blame the drugs. The Xanax. But you're the one choosing to take them. How long have you been taking them?"

He turned his head away from me and looked toward the wall. He made a noise, what I assumed was the sound of disgust or frustration.

"Twenty years?" I asked.

"He's fine," my mother interjected.

"Mom, he's not fine. Those drugs have taken an absolutely brilliant man and broken him down to a tenth of what he was."

"He's older, Adam. Give him a break."

"Mom, this isn't me attacking you guys out of anything but love. I want to help you. How does it affect me if he's taking Xanax? It doesn't. But it affects Dad. It affects his decision-making process. It affects the way he interacts with you. It affects everything he does."

Eventually my father admitted he was an addict. It had taken twenty years for any of us to acknowledge a travesty that we all recognized and left unspoken. He was scared and unsure as he spoke the words, but I sensed a slight tinge of relief as he began to feel the liberating nature of shedding his lies. My mother was silent. My father was unsure around her. He looked at me, bravely exposing his fragility and vulnerability as a father and a man. It was the thing he'd tried to hide since his business failed.

I wanted to tell him that it was okay. That would come later. For now, I wanted to simply be present for him. I could be his strength. It would help both of us.

"I can't afford treatment," he said.

"I'll help," I said. "I'll figure it out. I'll talk to your doctor."

After more questions and discussion, I learned that my father was getting his pills from two different doctors and pharmacies. His insurance covered one and he paid for the other with cash. I confronted his primary doctor the next day. Although the doctor admitted that Xanax had most likely exacerbated my father's decline, he blamed my father for twenty years' worth of prescriptions.

"He's very persuasive," the doctor said.

"He's taking three milligrams a day! That's like eight times the average someone with a prescription would take on a weekly basis!"

Though livid, I worked out a deal with the doctor to wean my father off the pills. Going cold turkey would've put his body into shock and probably given him a heart attack. He got into an outpatient program and made it part of his routine for more than a year. I also tracked down the other doctor and the pharmacy that had been selling my father a prescription for cash. I put them on notice not to deal with my father again.

Despite my intentions to right the wrongs in my life and break the patterns so that my children would have a better chance at avoiding generations of mistakes, I couldn't avoid the consequences of my past actions. On August 5, 2003, investigators still gathering evidence in the Universal case interviewed me again. Two months later, suffering financially, we sold our house for $1.1 million. It didn't cover the fortune that I'd spent on overhauling the backyard and other improvements.

But the real cost was human—something that couldn't be quantified. In the late spring of 2004, Meredith got pregnant. We hadn't planned the pregnancy, but I had always wanted three children, and she enjoyed both the experience of growing another life inside her and raising children. Yet we were shouldering myriad issues ranging from financial to personal, including the looming likelihood that I would be incarcerated some time in the future. They detracted from the confidence Meredith and I would've had about expanding our family under different circumstances.

Instead of excitement, we shared uncertainty. We debated the hardest questions without reaching a decision. Then, unbeknownst to me, Meredith got her doctor to prescribe medication that would induce a miscarriage. She did it while I was in California on a business trip. I returned and went to a lunch meeting with two guys at an Italian restaurant called Tuscany in Oakbrook when Meredith called my cell.

"I need you to come home," she said.

She sounded calm.

"Why?"

"I just went to the doctor. I wasn't feeling well. I didn't want to tell you, but—"

"But what?" I interrupted.

" "I'm bleeding. I have an aneurysm in my uterus."

I went nuts and excused myself from the table.

Then what struck me was that I was screaming at Meredith, blaming her for doing something, when in reality she had terminated her pregnancy and put her own life in jeopardy because of me, because of the bad decisions I'd made servicing my addiction. It took the wind out of me. I thought, look what *you've* done.

"I'm sorry," I said. "I'm coming right now."

I clicked off and became overwhelmed by grief and guilt. I didn't care if

other people in the restaurant stared. I broke down and cried. This was reality, one more consequence of my gambling, and it hit me hard. The love of
my life could potentially die. She'd taken a drug to abort a child, something
neither of us would have ever considered in other circumstances. It was
another tragedy, one more to add to our list. And it was all because of me.

"I hate myself," I said.

I returned to the table and excused myself because of an emergency at
home. I drove 100 mph up the highway and met Meredith at Lake Forest
Hospital. It was a stark realization: we had lost a baby at the same hospital
where our two wonderful children had been ushered into this world. I held
myself together somehow as Meredith was taken into surgery and put
under anesthesia. The procedure took about thirty minutes and she was
fine afterward.

I wasn't. I knew that I'd go to my grave haunted in some way by the life
that I'd never get to know.

Recovery for both of us was an emotional challenge. In the past I
would've dealt with such problems by not dealing, by taking a ride to the
boat or getting on the phone with one of my bookies, but I was two years
into recovery and had tools that helped me through the difficult moments
when the urges hit.

I took a deep breath. I didn't allow myself the easy escape, the quick fix.
I kept my head in the present. I used my intellect and handled my emotions. I thought about my life as it was in the present. I stepped outside
myself and asked, "Do you want to go back there? Is it worth it?"

It was my choice.

Addiction was the easy route. The hard work was what I chose to do for
the rest of my life.

TRUTH AND CONSEQUENCES

Do you love anyone? Do you love anything?

I would've asked myself those questions if I'd been able to step into the picture and talk to myself at any point throughout my addiction. Because those are the things that I gave up in order to gamble. With the same determination, I set out to reclaim them before it was too late.

In August 2004, I gave up the health care business. I was in a position to make a nice amount of money, but it put me in a hazardous mental place. I wasn't happy and decided to pursue endeavors that satisfied my soul. I might not find prosperity, but inner peace was my priority.

On January 5, 2005, I was indicted by federal prosecutors on two counts of aiding and abetting misapplication of bank funds and one count each of conspiracy to misapply funds, making false entries in bank records, and wire fraud. Each conspiracy charge carried a maximum five-year sentence and a two-hundred-fifty-thousand-dollar fine. I faced a maximum of thirty years in prison and a $1 million fine on the other charges.

Following the indictment, I went home and sat in my closet, which now doubled as my new office. Scared, confused, sad, ashamed, guilty, and appreciative, I poured my thoughts into an e-mail that I sent to my family and closest friends. It was dated January 5, 2005.

Dear Family,

I wanted to share with all of you my thoughts that are racing in my mind. This letter by no means is intended to be chronological or have any theme per se. So please bear with me and in the event you choose not to read it, I understand. I feel I owe it to everybody to try at least on some level explain myself.

I want you all to know that I am cognizant of the impact my current situation has on all of you. I can understand if you are having the entire gamut of emotions including but not limited to embarrassment, disappointment, sadness, guilt by association (that's absurd, don't), and anger. I will do my best to mitigate the preceding in any way possible. I take 100 percent responsibility for my syndrome and the actions I took to enable my gambling addiction.

I have been a pathological gambler way before I knew most of you (probably started around when Joshua was born, truthfully). Although I have had some limited successes in my life, I was never honestly happy with myself. Probably because there was always this compulsion controlling my thought process. It impeded better judgment the majority of my life.

Again, I am solely responsible for what inevitably occurred and where I am today. I still do not have all the answers but I have learned an incredible amount over the past thirty months. Sometimes, I look in the mirror and I cannot understand the hypocrisy of my life.

I know I am (and I hope you all do as well) a very generous soul. I also know that I would do anything in this world and have for my family. The difference going forward is I will make cognitive decisions while factoring in the emotional aspects and their ramifications. Rather than the latter, which doesn't benefit anybody in the long run.

Furthermore, when I self-evaluate I am astonished by what kind of father I was prior to June 26, 2002. I was there, but as you all know that was in a physical sense. I was always so preoccupied with gambling that I never could just enjoy spending time with my children. I want you to know there are some memories I have that now are leaving a profound impact on my continuing recovery process.

One very poignant example is the day my son was born (March 1, 2001 also our anniversary). Reflecting back on that day is extremely painful in a way. I was hiding from a bookie and couldn't focus on the ecstasy of having a son. (If I elaborate anymore I couldn't finish this letter from all of the tears.)

Arguably, I lament those emotions that day like no other. Even through it all my love for Meredith, Ariel, Sam, and Harley was there, but none of us were able to feel the true passion coming through. I cannot tell you how depressed I get when I reflect on those feelings. That is the only time I feel sorry for myself. When I realize how sick I was that I just couldn't *be*.

I am blessed with the most beautiful, understanding, compassionate, and narcoleptic (it wouldn't be a note from me without some humor) wife on this earth. I am not a perfect husband either, but I am proud of the unconditional love and passion I have always had for Meredith. Nevertheless, as I did with everything in my life I took her for granted. I do attribute most of this to my gambling. Yet, I assure you I will not let my guard down in continuing to explore whatever other underlying issues took me down this path.

My life isn't over (although at times it's hard to be positive) because I have an incredible family that I love with more heart than anyone could have. Personally, though, I still need to find inner happiness so that the past does not repeat itself. Professionally, that means doing something I enjoy even if the monetary payoff is less than it would be otherwise. Moreover, not following my dreams and aspirations did on some level contribute to my downfall.

I made a lot of money at times, but that apparently wasn't the impetus to happiness. If it was I would have pressed hard and been a greedier, shrewder businessman. As some of you know I could have easily retired comfortably at thirty if I had lived by new "testament" (if you will). I have always challenged everyone else to follow their passion and dreams. Meanwhile I was, as I did most of the time, neglecting myself.

I now know that neglecting my own happiness will be contagious and have a derogatory effect on my loved ones. I do believe sometimes (otherwise I probably would have been dead) this was meant to happen so that Meredith and I would be able to reminisce fifty years from now on how good our life was together. We all have issues, and most people don't address their issues and continue their one life with some degree of unhappiness.

I am not ignorant enough to think that I, we, will never have trying times, but I do believe long term we will be better off than most because of this trauma. That doesn't mitigate at all what faces us in the near and even distant future. I have destroyed us financially and of course emotionally somewhat as well. All I can do is try my best to incorporate all I have learned to make everyone proud of me. Each day I remind myself of this.

If I could I would take back everything I have done that caused all of this pain. I cannot, so the only way to rectify that sorrow is to make everyone proud of what I become. I cannot put into words the powerful emotions that I am feeling.

All I can say, and to me it's everything and so very deep, is that I love you and I am still here for all of you. I ask one thing: please don't take away my ability to help and share in your lives no matter where I am.

Adam

The next day I got up early to make turkey meatballs for dinner. My compulsions hadn't gone away, but I channeled them in healthier ways, including cleaning, cooking, and baking. While Meredith was at work, I made meals as if I was feeding not a family of four but a first sitting at a hot restaurant. The year during the Universal debacle, my weight had soared past two hundred fifty pounds. I got it down to two hundred two and kept it there, making sure it never fluctuated more than five pounds. My weight became my barometer for my mental health.

Anyway, the meatball recipe included a can of beer, which I didn't have. I drove to Dominick's grocery store nearby. I also wanted to buy all the local newspapers. I knew my indictment was going to hit the press, and it did, with stories in every paper. I got to the checkout counter with a six-pack of beer and three newspapers. The checkout lady rang up the papers but pointed to the beer and shook her head.

"I'm sorry, you can't buy the beer yet," she said. "It's 7:30. I'm not allowed to sell it to you until 8 AM."

She had to be kidding, I thought. I looked at my watch. I wanted those papers, but I also wanted the beer. I didn't want to have to come back. My instinct was to unleash my temper and give this woman a dose of bomb-laden reality. In my head, I heard myself saying: *Listen to me, you fucking moron. I'm the same guy in these newspapers. I was indicted for taking down a bank. If I want a beer, don't think for a minute I can't persuade you to sell it to me.*

But then something happened before I exploded in a rage. I paused, took a breath, and asked myself if it was worth it. I changed the dialogue. I made it a choice, or in reality I stopped and recognized that I had a choice. I could go ballistic, make a scene, and perhaps do something that got me what I wanted at that moment while also breaking the law. Or I could do what was right, what was in my best interests though maybe a little incon-venient, which was to buy the papers and get the beer later. I nodded, pleased by the decision I made.

"Thank you, ma'am," I said, calmly. "I'll come back."

At that moment, I knew I got it. I wanted to hug the checker for putting me to a test, which I'd passed. I'd calmed down. I'd proved to myself that I'd learned self-control and choice. I was smarter and wiser, and though I was the same guy, I was also a different person. I'd changed. I was changing. . . .

Toni Navarro was charged with two counts of misapplying bank funds and one count each of conspiracy, bank fraud, and making false entries in bank records. She was given thirty-eight months in prison starting in January 2007.

Terry Navarro was charged with a single count of making false entries into bank records. He was sentenced to one day in jail, time served.

I have improved my relationship with my parents. I understand them better and love them very much. I also know that they are just like every-one else, very very human. Everyone has issues and problems. My father, as far as I know, has stopped taking Xanax.

Freddy no longer gambles. He is an amazing father to his four boys and a devoted and loving husband. I am proud to be his friend.

Luciano is still doing his thing and running his restaurant. He has a good heart.

Marty still owns the Tavern and reps the Horseshoe. He's a great honorable guy, one in a million, and I find him more entertaining now than ever.

Gerry died three years ago. I heard his girlfriend, M.A., wanted to continue to run his book.

I don't know what happened to Richard and Manny. Not for nothing, I don't want to know either.

Jake the Snake is a partner in a nationwide law firm and lives in Los Angeles.

Bruno was murdered several months after the bank collapsed.

My friends are still my friends.

My children are my life. Ariel and Sam are my hope for a better, kinder, and more loving world.

I still confide in my dog Harley.

My wife is a saint. I don't always understand why she's stayed with me, but I'm grateful. She has been my light in the darkness. I love her to pieces. One day we were walking, the four of us, hand in hand, near the water. Meredith turned to me, smiling, and said, "I love being a family." She took my breath away. I fell in love all over again. I love being a family, too.

I haven't gambled since walking out of the Horseshoe on June 26, 2002.

Our financial life has been a disaster, to say the least. Meredith has handled the relief work heroically.

My past has haunted me as tirelessly as any bookie. The reality hurts, as I rarely spent money for anything other than to service my gambling addiction. Aside from my house, clothes for my wife and children, and my damn Mercedes, I never owned anything. I even leased my hairpiece—called Cyber Hair—with an option to buy. *An option to buy my hair!* I'm laughing bitterly. To this day, I get collection notices from a law firm alleging that I owe money on my hair.

I'll never live down my double life, nor will anyone else who makes poor choices the way I did. Even that fucking rat's nest that I called my hair, which wasn't really hair, or really mine, is stalking me. But hey, that's nothing compared to where I came from. I've learned to appreciate a naked cranium—and a life without cover-ups, lies, or excuses.

I spent 2005 and 2006 speaking to groups about gambling addiction and addiction in general. I enjoyed connecting with them. Mine is a simple message: It doesn't matter if you play thirty thousand dollars a hand, blow ten lines of coke, shove a box of cookies in your mouth, pound a bottle of tequila, or smoke three packs of cigarettes a day—it's all relative, and I'm no different from anyone else. The escape routes may be different, but the behaviors lead to the same destructive place. There's only one way to avoid it. If you aren't sure, listen early on to the little voice inside your head. It knows the right answer, but if you don't listen, it may ultimately fade.

I enjoyed connecting with people as I told my story. I believe I helped others.

I waited anxiously through the second half of 2006 for my sentencing hearing. I wanted to know how long I would have to serve and when I would start. I was very frightened. I had nightmares as the pages came off the calendar. The prosecutors had recommended a sentence of forty-two months. Finally, on December 6, I went in front of Judge Wayne R. Andersen. He asked prosecutors for more information explaining their recommended sentence. Some speculated that he might impose a harsher and longer sentence.

I returned to Judge Andersen's courtroom on January 16, 2007. I went there with Meredith, our families, and our closest friends. The proceeding began at 1:30. After some preliminary comments, Judge Andersen went back and forth with the prosecutor and my attorney. Then he asked if I wanted to speak.

"Absolutely, Your Honor," I said. "As you know, I wrote you a long letter articulating how I feel about this, as I knew it would be hard if not impossible for me to get through this sentencing without cracking from emotion. Yet I have something to share, namely there isn't an hour that goes by that I'm not dealing with ramifications of the choices I made to service my addiction.

"I have no idea where or when or even if it will end," I continued. "My greatest fear since getting sober has been the ripple effect of my actions on Meredith and my children. I fear that I altered fate when I committed my crime. I worry that I may have changed it catastrophically.

"On February 7 of 2006, I read an AP story on my computer about a suburban Chicago girl who died from injuries suffered in a car accident. She was driving with her family to Waseca, Minnesota, to visit her father, who was in federal prison. Her father was in prison for conspiracy to distribute narcotics."

I paused to wipe tears and my voice cracked.

"She was on life support for nine days while her family petitioned the prison to let her father visit one final time. Her father didn't get out.

"I feared I had read our own future. The similarities were so close it was like seeing the future in a crystal ball. We were a suburban Chicago family. There was a chance I might be sent to that same federal prison. My family could have been the ones in that car. If that isn't a cautionary tale, I don't know what is . . ."

The proceeding lasted about an hour. Judge Andersen accepted the plea of forty-two months recommended by the prosecution. He gave me a choice. I could surrender immediately or in two weeks. I chose the latter.

Outside the courthouse, Meredith hugged me.

"You're going to be okay," she said. "We're going to be okay."

I fought back the tears and hugged my wife. I didn't want to let go. Ever.

"We still have to tell the kids," I said.

I wished I could've gone back in time and told myself what I know now. Instead I wrote this book as a way of warning others and especially children about the cost of servicing their addictions. It all boils down to this: Before indulging your addiction, ask yourself these questions: Do you love anyone? Do you love anything? Are you willing to give them up for your addiction?

The choice is yours.

LETTERS

Honorable U.S. District Judge Wayne Andersen
Everett McKinley Dirksen United States Courthouse
219 South Dearborn Street, 20th Floor
Chicago, IL 60604

Your Honor:

I am writing to you on behalf of Adam Resnick. By way of background, I have known Adam for almost twenty-five years. He and I grew up together in Milwaukee, Wisconsin, where both of our families lived during our childhood years. Given my history with Adam, I hope I can provide some perspective on his situation.

As a law school and business school graduate of Columbia University, I am aware of the goals of the penal system in the United States. Let me make clear that I believe it is necessary for Adam to be punished. Not only do I believe that society needs the deterrence effects of a punishment, but I believe that behavior needs consequences. Many people "cry for help" through very poorly thought-out actions, and society needs to provide consequences for these acts.

Ever since Adam was a young boy, it was obvious to us that he had incredible talents. He was and is one of the more charismatic individuals I have ever met. This gift, I believe, was not necessarily something Adam understood; I believe he used it in a way that athletes use their abilities. Such people can't explain how or why they are able to run fast or jump high, they simply do these things without any conscious effort. This was always the case with Adam.

I understand that in this case's fact pattern, one of the salient issues was the seeming ability to control some of the people at the bank. While I think these situations can result from an individual's intent to defraud, I can honestly say that Adam never needed to play the "heavy," so to speak. One thing that was always true about Adam, even with a crazy gambling addiction to handle, was that he had an innate desire to be liked and not to harm people. In a way he has always been repressed, constantly focused on others and how they view him. The gambling, even when we were growing up, was his release. It was a way for him to lose himself in his own being and to get away from being a pleaser. I am not sure that anyone of sound mind would end up using such an addiction as a tool to avoid others, but it became Adam's tool.

One can say that but for his efforts to get his coconspirators to do his bidding, none of this would have happened. But I think that that oversimplifies matters, and may imply a level of intent that is not really present within him. It is true that Adam could and should never have gotten in this position, that he should have stopped this situation before it ever got out of hand. That being said, he is one of a number of actors who misbehaved here, and he was not able to achieve any of this without significant help. Adam is certainly an easy target. He is the guy with the big gambling problem, which provided for drama. But the drama was a mechanism for Adam to self-destruct. Adam himself never benefited from the events in this case financially. He only lost money, as was his pattern for years. Where others might have been putting money in their pockets, Adam was simply trying to get out of a never-ending hole.

I want to tell a story about Adam and our relationship. He and I were very close growing up, and I take such friendships seriously; there is something special about a childhood friend that makes walking away from these people difficult. More than six years ago, when Adam was having money troubles because of his gambling, he called me looking for a loan to bridge his liquidity problems. I had provided Adam with loans in the past under similar circumstances, but it had become increasingly clear to me that the problems he was having were endemic, and giving him money was only going to make this worse. Now, turning him down was difficult, not only because of the fear of losing a friend, but also because it isn't easy to say no to Adam, given his charisma. He is the type of person one wants to help. In looking to the future, however, it seemed to me that there was no way this was going to end well. This moment of self-destructive behavior was not an aberration; his pattern was not something he would simply outgrow. If anything, the issue was getting much worse and the stakes were going up significantly.

I told Adam in this instance that I would not provide him money, but instead I would arrange for legal counsel at my own expense, and that I would offer him my time to help negotiate with his creditors. This was not acceptable to Adam, and until last month this was our last conversation. I was not going to be part of the problem anymore, but I did know that it was a virtual certainty that he would continue down this path until he reached the bottom of the proverbial rabbit hole. As painful as it was for me to watch and walk away from Adam at such a troubled time, I knew it would be wrong for me to enable him any more. By this point there was no way to reason with him, because he either did not see or did not want to see his failures. This denial was probably a survival mechanism that helped him to deal with his problems, but it was preventing him from facing the real issues in his life. In combination with a compulsion or addiction, he was bound to face rock bottom.

Nothing that has happened to Adam surprises me. One thing I did know was that Adam would stop eventually, and it would probably occur under the circumstances we are all in now. The question is whether Adam can contribute to society going forward. To that, the answer has to be yes. We all have demons we fight, some more than others. It is the process of dealing with life's challenges that defines our character. Adam has had many of his own making, but his experiences will be of use to society. He can and has been able to become introspective. It shouldn't surprise anyone that through this type of trauma that Adam has become more self-aware, but it's through this awareness that he will be able to be of real value to his family, friends, and others. Adam now has the level of maturity to be a real contributor to society, and in the end the system should try and balance this with the need to punish. We as a society need to hold out people who overcome and show the way because it provides us with a road map. Without the denial, Adam can now shine a light on the road for so many others who have similar problems.

In all the years I've spent watching Adam go through the drama he created for himself, I can say he never once tried to hurt anyone else. Regardless of what has happened, no one who knows Adam would consider him a "con man." He was a deeply disturbed person who spent too much time trying to please other people regardless of their motives. The gambling was a poor release that consumed his energies and ultimately lead to his self-destruction. Adam in many ways is an example of what is possible. We all have things we deeply want to change about ourselves but do not have the courage to confront. Adam is one of the few who has taken this challenge and succeeded in doing the thing we all want to do but will not or cannot. Surely this is something we need to encourage in our society as well. I hope that there is some balance struck in this process that allows us to benefit from Adam's growth.

I appreciate the opportunity to be heard.

Best,
Adam Fisher

March 11, 2005
In Re: Adam B. Resnick

Dear Mr. B.:

The following information may be helpful in your representation of your client and our patient, Adam B. Resnick. He learned of our treatment program through a former patient of ours who also suffered from a severe gambling addiction.

Mr. Resnick was admitted into our intensive residential treatment program on July 7, 2002. The intensive program consists of several individual therapy sessions per day, augmented with small psychotherapy and psychoeducational groups, adjunctive therapies, relapse prevention, and family therapy. He attended all sessions, actively participated, and was highly motivated for recovery from his long-term gambling addiction. He was discharged from the residential program on August 16, 2003, and has continued his outpatient aftercare with a Chicago compulsive gambling therapist and through telephonic sessions with me.

I have specialized in the field of compulsive gambling for over thirty years and can say unequivocally that Adam Resnick was by far one of the worst gambling addicts in terms of monies gambled and lost and time spent during his many gambling episodes over the years. He evidenced years of "living in the zone" or in a dissociative state in which gambling was the norm and other-life activities and interpersonal interactions were secondary to his gambling-induced psychological confusion. Although he was capable of earning a substantial income, especially for someone of his young age, this intellectual functioning was offset by his under-developed psychological and emotional development.

Most compulsive gamblers who start gambling in their childhood or early teens typically do not develop a full-fledged gambling addiction until later in life, in their thirties, forties, or fifties. Adam has been a gambling addict since childhood and basically did not know of a life without gambling. Thus his early-onset pathological gambling and remarkable recovery are virtually unique.

The impact of his many years of gambling addiction has been felt not just on him, but also on his family of origin and his marital family, in addition to the obvious financial devastation and legal complications.

Noteworthy are his many years of "chasing" his losses, which led to increasingly exorbitant bets and debts, which eventually he could not meet. This "chasing" of losses is a significant indicator in the loss of control and impulsivity of gambling, and the definition of gambling addiction. This kind of out-of-control gambling is marked by increasingly unrealistic, "magical" beliefs, and a conviction that the next bet will be the winning one that will replace all losses. The competitive nature of compulsive gamblers, and especially Adam Resnick's, will not permit the admission of being a "loser."

With respect to the Universal account, this served as a means to continue his "chasing" in the desperate effort and magical belief that he would have the Big Win to overcome losses and debts. Although he may have known the difference between right and wrong, his thinking had become so muddled and unrealistic that consequences, not just with Universal but with all aspects of his life, were considered only very fleetingly and just as quickly disregarded. He was unable to stop or control his gambling.

It is a truism of addiction that addicts do not learn from experience; while emotionally healthy individuals have the ability of rational and realistic thinking, the addicted person does not. Judgment is substantially impaired.

Thus Adam's recovery can only be described as extraordinary. When he was admitted into our program he was strong in his intentions to forever abstain from gambling and he was highly motivated to identify and repair the damage that he had created over these many years. He has worked hard at recovery and continues to do so.

By "recovery" we mean all aspects of his life, not just abstinence from gambling. His self-image and belief in himself are noteworthy. His marital relationship is solid, better than ever. He has friends and is developing a lifestyle that includes social and recreational activities, physical fitness, and a general balance in his life. He has cut down on financial obligations and has moved into a smaller house.

In speaking with his wife, Meredith, it is apparent that she is fully supportive of his efforts. She speaks with joy and pride of the changes in their lives.

The remaining hurdles Adam has to resolve due to his many years of gambling addiction are financial obligations and legal complications. He has been in continuous telephone contact with me regarding his needs and progress in these areas, moving between anxiety, optimism, and determination to confront these challenges, make amends, and become a productive, healthy man. I sincerely believe that he will accomplish his goals.

In summation, let me reiterate that Adam Resnick's recovery has been remarkable, superior to that of many other compulsive gamblers, especially in view of his lifetime and severity of gambling. His prognosis is Excellent.

I realize this has been a rather lengthy letter, but will justify it with the knowledge that mental illness, and particularly compulsive gambling, are very difficult to understand. How can anyone so intelligent, capable of hard work and good income, turn around and do something as destructive as Adam's gambling has been? How could he be such a Dr. Jekyll/Mr. Hyde, and for so many years?

The answers become obvious: addicts are not capable of self-diagnosis and addictions cannot survive without active enablers. In Adam's case it is evident that bankers and banks played a major role in this enabling. Without their assistance, there simply would not have been any money available to perpetuate his irrational behaviors.

Additionally, private individuals contributed to his ongoing addiction, such as the sheriff who befriended him in a gambling raid and subsequently won thirty thousand dollars from Adam betting on golf. Adam revealed many such events in the course of his treatment with us.

In summation, Adam's recovery is truly remarkable, and he is in the process of repairing the damage created over these many years.

Please do contact me with any additional information you might need.

Sincerely yours,
Dr. Valerie Lorenz

★ ★ ★

October 17, 2006

Honorable U.S. District Judge Wayne Andersen
Everett McKinley Dirksen United States Courthouse
219 South Dearborn Street, 20th Floor
Chicago, IL 60604

Dear Honorable Judge Andersen,

I am writing today in regard to Adam Resnick. I first met Adam about one and a half years ago when he contacted the Wisconsin Council on Problem Gambling. He was interested in providing outreach to students and to educate them on the compulsive gambling addiction.

Over the past year and a half, Adam has done many middle and high school presentations with me throughout the state of Wisconsin. He is an excellent presenter and tells the students "the way it is." They relate well to him, and because of this his message gets through to them. We have talked at a few schools where the students have led difficult lives and are pretty hardened already in the eighth grade. Adam has been able to reach out to these kids and get through to them.

Adam has worked hard and continues to work on his recovery. It is rare for someone to be as addicted as he was to be doing so well in his recovery. Compulsive gamblers have a high relapse rate, but Adam has had several years of recovery with no relapses. In my opinion, Adam takes his recovery very seriously and wants to share his story with others so that hopefully they may be spared the pain of this devastating addiction. He is not afraid to share all the painful details of the addiction so that others may learn.

As of result of Adam's great connection with students, I referred him to a contact of mine in Washington State. He has recently provided a workshop for them. Adam has a true talent in being able to reach out to others by sharing the story of his gambling addiction.

As you may know, compulsive gambling is an addictive illness in which the person is driven by an overwhelming uncontrollable impulse to gamble. The impulse progresses in intensity and urgency, consuming more and more of the individual's time, energy, and emotional and material resources. Ultimately, it invades, undermines, and often destroys everything that is meaningful in one's life.

I strongly believe that Adam can continue to be an asset to any community by reaching out to teens and young adults about the devastating effects of pathological gambling. I would urge you to strongly consider sentencing Adam to community service so that he can continue to educate students. Adam can provide prevention now to students so that intervention may not be necessary in the future. Instead of Adam being a burden to society through the high cost of prison, he could be an asset to any community by continuing to provide a positive message through outreach and education. Adam has the ability through his continuing recovery and outreach to "save" lives. I hope he will be given the opportunity to do so. The outreach I do will not be nearly as affective without Adam and his ability to touch the lives of our youth.

Thank you for your time and consideration. Please feel free to contact me if you have any questions or need further information.

Sincerely,
Rose Gruber
WCPG Executive Director

Honorable Wayne R. Andersen
U.S. District Court
Everett McKinley Building
219 South Dearborn Street, 20th floor
Chicago, IL 60604

October 25, 2006

Dear Judge Andersen,

Thank you so much for taking the time to review this letter on behalf of my husband, Adam Resnick. As I'm typing, tears are streaming down my face. It's not only what may happen today in this courtroom that has me overcome with emotion, but it's thinking of the fourteen wonderful years Adam and I have shared since meeting at the University of Wisconsin–Madison when we were both just twenty years old.

When I was little, I dreamed of meeting my soul mate. I pictured him to be caring, charming, loving, and smart. A great father, a rock to lean on in hard times, and a fun, easy-going companion to grow old with. Adam is all of those things to me, and more. He truly is a beautiful person inside and out. He has always been there for me and others, from helping to ensure my dying grandfather had the best medical care possible to caring for his older brother Jon, who was fighting kidney cancer. No matter what Adam has on his plate, he is always the first person to help his family, friends, and neighbors.

Watching Adam with our two children, seven-year-old Ariel and five-year-old Sam, is amazing. I can see their eyes instantly light up the minute Daddy walks into the room. I love watching him teach Ariel to play the guitar and play sports with Sammy. He also has learned to be able to focus and engage with them for countless hours (something he couldn't do while he gambled). It is in large part Adam's positive reinforcement, discipline, and love that have made Ariel and Sam the wonderful kids they are today.

I know how sorry Adam is that he let his addiction get the best of him. But Adam is doing what he does best. He's using his experiences to help others and make a difference. As part of his rehabilitation, Adam has been traveling across the country speaking to children about the dangers of addiction. He is so determined to get his message across loud and clear. He doesn't want any child to go through what he did. I believe that, even more important for him, he realizes the ramifications this has had upon every person who has been a part of his life.

Ariel and Sam mean the world to him. Even Adam, who is usually so articulate, is at a loss for words when he tries to describe the passion and love he has for us. He always says, "I wish there were words to express how much I love you." I know that many things, including making restitution as fast as possible, are giving Adam tremendous anxiety. What I know troubles him the most is telling our children that he will not be present for some time. He has told them for the last few years that he had a gambling problem (he won't let them use the word bet as part of their vocabulary). What we haven't done is tell them of his impending incarceration. I know that all children of felons must experience this trauma. Unfortunately, knowing my children, I believe that this will impact them tremendously. Once we have clarity about his date of surrender and location, we plan to go through extensive family therapy sessions in the next few months to give our children the support they need.

Your Honor, I know that many people are trying to attack Adam's character because of what he has done. It's understandable. People ask me all the time, "Why do you stay with him? You should move on." The answer, Judge Andersen, is so easy for me. I always reply, "He is the most generous, caring, loving person I know." That doesn't mean that I would stay with him based on that feeling alone. That is not enough at this point. What has given me a true sense of security is how he has proven that he can conquer something so debilitating as his gambling addiction. That along with his true character is why I am still here.

I know that Adam has come a long way and has made significant progress, and that he will continue to help others despite what lies ahead for him. In the meantime, I truly appreciate your caring consideration.

Sincerely,
Meredith Resnick

ACKNOWLEDGMENTS

Because I sleep only three hours a night, I've had the opportunity to meet more people than most, and I've bonded with nearly all of them. Therefore, I cannot possibly include everyone here. So please don't be offended if you're not included. If we've bonded, you know in your heart and mind what that means to me.

Thanks to my agents at Endeavor, Brian Lipson and Julie Weitz, for convincing me that I had to write a book if I wanted to tell my story and keep control of it. They were right. They were also right, but very unagent-like, when they advised me to sell not to the highest bidder but to the publisher that cared the most. They gave me confidence and made me feel comfortable (and they put up with my phone calls). Thanks for becoming my friends.

Dan Strone, my literary agent by association at Trident Media Group, for his integrity, advice, and general excellence. I'm fortunate to have worked with the best on my first book. Thanks also to Dan's assistant, Alison Masciovecchio.

Carolyn Gurland, for being a friend and my ongoing confidante for so many second opinions (I wish you were a doctor sometimes—you're so comforting). You have an amazing heart. Thank you, Eddie Genson, for your brilliant mind and unbelievable stories (can I write your book?).

Josh Buchman for being such a good friend to Meredith and me after you no longer represented me. You absolutely are the antithesis of the lawyer stereotype, and you are such a great human being. I care about you and your family. Thank you, Jocelyn Francoeur.

Marty Kohler, for making me feel comfortable, safe, and reassured at a time when I needed it most.

Janet Goldstein, for your incredible support and legal opinions.

Leslie Ann Gerardo, for your time, dedication, caring, and brilliant lawyering. Words can't express the gratitude I feel toward you for believing in me enough to take this case with no quid pro quo. I grant you immunity from all pro bono cases in the future. This certainly was a lifetime of "charity" work. I apologize for being the reason you returned to work as a federal prosecutor.

My new and dear friend Mary Louise Cohen. You are the classiest woman I have ever met. You have a heart that is unparalleled. My family is eternally grateful.

Christa Brown (Mrs. Brown), my pretrial service "guardian." For nonfelons, she's the person I report to while I'm out on bond. My kids will be thrilled when they are old enough to read this that you aren't my girlfriend. On a serious note, some defendants may hate reporting in to you. But I looked forward to my Wednesday calls. You assisted in keeping me straight while showing compassion and incredible integrity in the job. I wish there was an award for your job class, because you would run away with it.

Koi, for the spicy tuna on crispy rice (and the bowl of mayo I dunk it into). Your baked crab rolls are insane as well! Thanks to Eris, Randy, Andrea, and all the hostesses.

Thanks Chaz Reinhold, for the greatest comedic montage in the history of film, "Mom! The meatloaf! Fuck!"

Chris Miller, for all your amazing insight into the business, but more important, for attempting to get me over to your team. It's not in my DNA, but if it was, it would be with you!!

Wyclef and Jerry, my friends who in my darkest hours inspire me with their incomparable talents and positive vibes. You're the most brilliant musicians in the world, and I'm honored that you include me in your lives.

Charmont and Beast, you are my friends and I always have your backs.

Sanjay, for your nonstop energy and dedication to helping others.

My future prison roommates, just because I want to buy some goodwill and make friends on the inside.

Ethan Smith (Ethieeeee to my children), I trust you with my story more then anyone else. You "get it." You gave up a part of your life to work with me, and I'll be forever grateful to you. You're one of my best friends, and I can't thank you enough for everything you have done. You should be proud of this book. You're a part of it.

Bino, you have a heart like no other man on this planet. I just wish you would go in the ocean with me, but as you say, "It's disgusting, fish fuck in there." Thank you, Jill, Larry, and Marilyn.

I want to apologize to the U.S. attorneys, FBI agents, FDIC agents, IRS agents, and anyone else from the government who has to deal with the issues stemming from my poor choices. There are serious problems in the world today, and it's just not right that you had to spend your time and resources pursuing me. I should never have been a problem to anyone. I have abilities and had opportunities. There's no excuse. You all work so hard and are underappreciated. I am so very truly sorry. I assure you I will pay my taxes on time, make restitution, and do everything else a responsible citizen would.

Seth Kanegis, you're one of my dearest friends. We have had such incredible bonding over the last few years. I do wish we could go back in time for one brief night to see what would have happened (oh my). Thank you for everything you do for me! I love ya, brother!

Adam Fisher, you're my dear childhood friend. I've come to respect you more each day for your guidance, brilliant mind, and OCD like me. You have the greatest work ethic I've ever known, and inside that perfect exterior (tan, fit, healthy eating, no drinking—a tad boring, some might think), you have such a wonderful heart. Thank you for coming back when it was such a generous and unwarranted thing to do. We thank you and love you! Hi, Haley, thank you for your kindness.

To my friends on the soccer team, thank you for allowing me to play. Thank you for letting me have my passion back. Thank you for being so compassionate to me when I blindsided you when *Dateline* showed up. You don't know how much it has meant to my recovery to be a **part** of the team. I hope to learn to drink beer like you after dehydrating after a ninety-minute match.

Rich Greenberg and Keith Morrison, thank you for keeping your word and producing and conducting my interview with such class. I still wish you would have showed my kick-ass goal rather than that pathetic fall at the end!

Darren, thanks for everything you and your family have done for me over the years. I appreciate the "tickets" and the tickets. I sincerely care about you and your entire family. What about The League?

Jodie from The Griddle at Sunset and Fairfax, for the eighth and ninth wonders of the world, your "Peanut Bubba" French Toast and your Banana Chocolate Chip Pancakes. Thank you for letting us spend so many days on the "porn couch" writing this book.

I'd like to thank the word "fuck" for bringing such good color to this book and to my bedroom over the years.

Barbara Peck, even though I am not an avid twelve-stepper, I still love you and keep cheering you on!

Thank you to everyone who has ever been in therapy with me.

Dr. Sam Krengel, thank you for being a fan. (It's mutual.) Thank you for appreciating all the hard work I did when others around you did not. Thank you for allowing me to use your beautiful home to host the greatest function to ever set off Chicago. You're such a well-rounded man, and I admire you.

Thank you, Schwartzy, Linda Graves, Jenny and Frank DeMaio, Francine and Jason Brodsky, the Shapiros, Wendy and Gary Polisner, Roz Lichter, Lisa Baron, Sherry Shrallow, Marty Gutilla, Art and Bernice, Ellory Zamler, Scott Sorin, my holy bread girls, the Kasofs, Michael, Erica, Jack, and Sydney, all the people who worked tirelessly at the October 1, 2005, Katrina relief event, Cheryl, Eugene, Kim, and Sam, B.P. Hutson, Eric Usinger Schnetzky, Brett Tucker, Clarence Ray Hill Jr., Chris Marlier, David Pelz, Allison Fells, Todd Lansky, Andy Kimelman, Aunt Annie, Uncle Steve, Kathy Kaperman, Peter

Eisenberg, Jason Fabric, Lowell Kraff, the Teplins, the Kaplan-Neufeld-Bushes, the Millers, the Birnbaums, Lisa and Ari Mintzer, Moshe, Eric Semel, Marklen Kennedy, J. M., A. S., C. C., J. S., M. S., J. W., A. K., B. R., and last but not least, The Dom.

Gayle and Cliff Stein, you're family to us. We love you and thank you!

Lorri and Barry Hammer, for your friendship and concern.

John Varvatos, thanks for the hoodies.

Adam Moschin, for being such a good-hearted soul.

Declan McManus, thanks for the lyrics.

To Howard Stern (not K.) for writing *Private Parts,* the only book I had read from cover to cover until 2004.

Thank you, M.J, for giving me credibility. "Ride the train, Mr. James."

Todd Anixter, you are a good friend, and I didn't break your stereo.

Wildfish, for allowing me to teach you how to make spicy tuna on crispy rice.

Las Vegas, I truly believe you are a great place. What happens there doesn't and shouldn't necessarily have to stay there.

Dr. Val, my guardian angel. *I got it.* I attribute so much of the knowledge I have and the tools I have acquired to you. If everyone had the pleasure of spending time with you, the world would be a better place.

Dr. Ken, thank you for being the first one to teach me how to breathe.

David F., thank you for your recovery. Thank you for not becoming me.

Toni Navarro, you are a good person as well who made bad choices.

Larry Elisco, you're a victim of three people's horrible choices. You're a victim of your own kindness and good heart. You're a sweet kid in a man's body. (Please tell me the mustache is still gone. At least I did something positive for you.) I'm so sorry for all the pain this has caused you. I hope you can find something positive out of the experience and grow from it.

I'd like to sincerely apologize to all of the people who feel they have been adversely affected by my choices over the years, including but not limited to Kevin Casey, Dan O'Connell, Al Hubbard, Aaron Wernick, Jeff Schneiss, Ross Emmerman, Angel Angelov, and Mike Schenk.

To all of those who have hurt me, I forgive you.

Terry Coffman, for allowing me to share our pain so others can benefit.

My editor, Cal Morgan. I chose to go to HarperCollins after I met you. You really get it, and I've felt comfortable with you from the moment we first spoke. I'm so glad you care about this book. I hope I'm worthy enough to do book number two (quite presumptuous) with you. It would be an honor. Thanks for your accessibility, your bedside manner, and the amazing editorial skills you brought to make this book the best it could be.

Cassie Jones, without question the wittiest person I know. Your utility skills in publishing are frickin' cool. Thanks for all your work and dedication. You're so very tenacious and smart, and I know you'll always have a good prison joke to lighten up the situation. Thank you to you and your husband for genuinely becoming my friends.

I'd like to thank all the other brilliant and hardworking people at HarperCollins who've worked on my book: Sabrina Faludi, Matt Cacciola, Courtney Kohl, Donna Lee Lurker, Larry Pekarek, Gregg Sullivan, Suzanne Wickham, and Mark Jackson.

Betsy Schenk, you have such a forgiving heart. You are a very special person, and I hope you feel like this in some way, shape, or form was meant to be, so that we could experience this journey together. Okay, maybe not, but surely we have a great friendship, and I really care about your welfare! Thanks for supporting me.

David Rubenstein, my business attorney (well, technically, not anymore, since I can't pay your firm). Beyond that, my dear friend and confidant. I owe you much more than some very good "tickets." You've been a rock for us. Your level head and street smarts would have served me very well had I listened to you more than the cards. Thank you for your unconditional support. I know, as you say, I'm a bit like ShlepRock, but I know our relationship doesn't have a cloud over it. Thanks, Susie (do I still scare you?).

Devo, wherever you are in the Middle East, I love you. Please tell me you still aren't dry-humping couches after all these years.

Goody, you are the nicest person I know who can bench four hundred pounds. As a matter of fact, you're one of the nicest people I know, period. Thanks for sharing all these experiences together. I wish you continued recovery.

"Kid," I know you want me on your sheet (we need it) just so you can brag about it! Thanks for the good laughs. You're a great guy with a big heart and a wonderful family.

Jack Binion, you're a very classy gentleman!

Brad and Andie Zamler, you're such wonderful, loving people, and I appreciate how much you care. Thank you for your support in so many ways. I love you and would do anything for your family.

I want to thank Jon Mills for teaching me about perspective, as you did when we looked out your office window. You were right! I believe I have found some. I apologize to your entire family.

Dr. Marc Kern, for your unwavering dedication to your craft. For enlightening so many people about other options for treatment. For being the brightest in your field. Your message will soon become worldwide, and I'm honored that you're part of the show *Addict* that I have created. And Michael Goldstein, for being my producing partner and following through with my vision for *Addict*.

Rose Gruber, for a professional relationship that has turned into a personal one. Thank you for believing in me and giving me the first chance to relay my message to children. That opportunity enabled me to do so much more. You're such a wonderful woman, and I wish you nothing but happiness. Thank you, Sherrie.

Matt Rudnick, maybe I should have kept your checks and then I wouldn't have ever bounced one. We have had one of the most amazing arcs as friends. When friends say they have been through everything together, it sounds so clichéd, but the fact is that we have. I love you like another brother. Thank you for coming "out of the hills" and following your heart. Thank you for supporting me and my family in more ways than either of us can remember. Thank you for listening to your father. Thank you for growing into a responsible, successful adult. I know you are hurting because of my situation, and I love you.

Ellen, thank you for your dear friendship (and food!), and more important to me, your amazing generosity and friendship with Meredith. It means a lot. I love you, Lucy and Danny.

My brother in-law Aaron, Gail, and Chloe, I love you guys, and thanks for being such a close family. We love the time you spend with us!

Thanks to my in-laws for screwing thirty-four years ago creating the world's first angel. Thank you for standing by me when many parents would have put down the hammer. Thank you for your compulsive shopping, as I now appreciate the fact that you clothe my children. Thank you for being such great grandparents. I'm sorry for the inconvenience and embarrassment this has caused you. Bubbie, I love you too.

Thanks to the L'Ermitage Hotel (Christine and Sean) for memories that can't be memorialized! Sincerely, Mr. T.Y.G. (trust your gut)

Marty Siegel, thank you (and the rest of your family) for being the most underappreciated friend in the world. Hopefully this serves as notice that you are the best. Your care for Meredith, Ariel, Sam, and me is so pure that I can't do it justice. You are a best friend, and I've always said if I had a sister I would want her to marry you.

Karen, you're the sister I never had, and that is why I introduced you to Marty. That should be enough said, but it clearly isn't. You're one of my biggest supporters. You are the Cajun spice when vanilla extract isn't enough. You are my best girlfriend in the entire world. I love Vaughn, and I love Elly (mini you). You three are our family.

Steve Wynn, I hope to finally make your acquaintance—still a fan.

Hillary, thank you for always being my friend. Thank you most importantly for being the best sister to Meredith than anyone can possibly hope for. You are her boulder. You are so very cool, and I am glad you, Greg, and Camryn are such a huge part of our lives. I love you all.

Oh, yes, thank you to every chocolate and peanut butter company that's made a product I can put into my tapeworm. Rest assured, I have.

Special thanks to Todd Gold. You started out as a ghostwriter, and it was clear after twenty-four hours that that description doesn't begin to cover it. How can someone be merely a ghostwriter when they help you interpret everything you ever wanted to say? You took a chance on me after working with celebrities. I was no one but an infamous convicted felon. But your instincts told you there was so much more to it. Our first meeting at L'Ermitage was a connection that felt right. Our guts told us this would be an amazing journey and collaboration. You wanted to help people as much as I did, and understood we could do it in a subtle way. I'm confident we've done that. I thank you for going back in time, reliving my life—not always a pleasant task—and helping me tell my story so artfully. I can tell you unequivocally that nobody else could have gone through such an emotionally and physically challenging endeavor. I hope we can do it again sometime. I thank your family for lending you on such important occasions as birthdays, anniversaries, and so on. You aren't just my co-writer, you're my good friend!

To my brothers—I know it's not easy being my brother. I want to thank you for your support, as I know how much this has affected your lives in so many ways. You shouldn't feel guilt by association; you are your own honorable men. You're both extremely successful and have tremendous moral compasses. You're much stronger than I because you didn't succumb to "environmental issues" and end up with a catastrophic debacle like me. I love you both very much. I know neither of you has any interest in the publicity that surrounds this kind of thing, but I hope you know I've tried as hard as possible to respect your privacy (we both know I could have included some very graphic and classic stories). I care greatly for my sister-in-law and of course my adorable nieces. I love that our generation is finally building a family. Watching our kids together is one of my biggest pleasures in life.

Mom and Dad, I sincerely hope you've made it all the way through this book. I hope you cried, laughed, and learned. You have caring souls. You were misguided, like many others in the world. You didn't break patterns. This book is about using the forgiving, healing power of love to summon the courage to confront scary truths. We have such an incredible opportunity to share our lives, including poor choices, so that others can learn and not travel our troubled road. I'm so much part of your being. Not just DNA, but personalities as well—some I hate and so many I love. I'm proud of who I am at my core, and I can attribute that to you. I also know that I'm responsible for my failures and disgusting choices. Most important, I am responsible for the changes I've made and the patterns I've broken. That, besides my wife and children, is the proudest thing in my life. It feels so good that I wish it upon anyone struggling in a cyclical nightmare. I'm always here for you, and I pray that you take a moment and despite everything understand how blessed we all are!

To Ariel Samantha Resnick, Daddy's (my favorite two syllables) princess. I always dreamed of having a little girl first, and that blessing came true on July 3, 1999. You're everything I dreamed of, and so much more. You're not just that little beautiful angel that I thought would dress up, sing, and dance. You're cool beyond your years, with an amazing sense of humor. You're so brilliant, and can with confidence and proper direction be anything you want to be. Most important, you're sweet and love us all so much. Since you know how to read, I highly doubt we'll be able to keep this from you for very long. Since you're so much like me, I'm sure if we don't let you read this book you'll find a way to make it to the bookstore yourself to get a copy. (You better not take the car like I did, although your mother has a Chrysler, not a Mercedes, so the theoretical monetary damage isn't as bad!)

"Ya Ya" Daddy loves you so much that I had better stop saying it, because the tears of love are going to short-circuit the keyboard.

Sam Andrew Resnick, born March 1, 2001. It isn't a coincidence that you were born on our anniversary. You are equally half your mother (the better half) and half Daddy. You are without question the entire male package. Chicks already want you. Guys (my friends) want to hang with you, as your new nickname is "Stats." You're a dream. You're an unbelievable athlete. You're so handsome that it's intimidating to other guys. But without question the best part of you is how sensitive, caring, and deeply loyal you are. And I'm incredibly proud of how much you honor and love Mommy. I melt every time I see you come to her defense. It's adorable when Daddy looks at a hot chick (which he loves to do) and you start saying "she's bullshit," and that the only girl for me is Mommy. It's hysterical, but the subliminal message is priceless. I love you, son, and I thank God every day that I have the opportunity to teach you and allow you to learn from my mistakes. Don't be afraid to make your own; just for the love of God, please don't repeat mine.

Harley M. Resnick, without question my best confidant. I love you, buddy, more than I can ever tell you. I wouldn't even pet a dog until Mommy brought you into my life. I'm so very sorry that you will be so hurt and won't be able to communicate how sad you are when Daddy is gone. It breaks my heart. Thank you for allowing me to cry and tell you every secret I ever had (you could have told me the Lakers were never gonna cover). I love taking care of you. Please will yourself to live until I get home.

And finally, thank you, Meredith, for being the best mommy in the universe. The love of my life. The most innocent (not perfect) soul I have ever known. Your innocence is what made me love you (along with your tushy and a few other things). It was in a strange way what I yearned to have in my life. I worship the ground you walk on. I watch you sleep (okay, so a lot of people watch you sleep, since you do it twelve hours a day). I hope you understand that all the pain and stress will be worth it. I assume you do, since you're still here. I love how much you love me in so many ways. I love that we have taught each other how to love in so many ways. I love (is there a synonym for this word already?) how beautiful you are. I love when you touch me (I wish it was more often)—it is such a powerful grip. I love that you are with me (are you still there?) on this journey. I love that you have turned the most devastating event in our life into a positive. I love your strength. I love how excited you are for our addictionless future. I'm so sorry that you will be spending so many nights without me (you better be) watching you sleep. But I truly believe we've shared so much love that it will support you during the most trying time of your life. I'm sorry I won't be able to help you with the day-to-day responsibilities of a family. I can't change that. However, I can promise you that I will only improve myself while I am gone, so that you know you too made the right choice. I love you forever.

—Adam